DALIT LEADERSHIP IN INDIA

DALIT LEADERSHIP IN INDIA

Vivek Kumar

KALPAZ PUBLICATIONS
Delhi–110 052

DALIT LEADERSHIP IN INDIA
(Sociology)

Rs. 850

ISBN: 81-7835-087-4

Published in 2002 in India by
Kalpaz Publications
C–30, Satyawati Nagar
Delhi–110 052
E-mail: kalpaz@hotmail.com

Laser Typesetting by: Varsha Graphics, Delhi
Printed at: Mehra Offset Printers, New Delhi

Dedicated
To
Papa
'Hanuman Prasad'

Contents

List of Tables

Foreword

There is no denying the fact that certain misgivings have surfaced about Dalits or Dalit movements in almost all writings by both the professional social scientists and the literati or the self-styled intellectuals who have produced abundant literature on the subjects. One misgiving is about the term Dalit itself which has been and is being frequently used without caring for its conceptualization. The concept of Dalit has two connotations broad and narrow. In the broad sense, it is inclusive of all the ex-Untouchables or the Scheduled Castes and the Scheduled Tribes across the numerous castes and tribes included in the Schedule conferred by the Indian Constitution. In this sense, the concept is frequently used by the socially and politically conscious and articulate persons especially the youth of these castes and tribes. With such connotation, the concept is closer to both the concepts of class and ethnicity, although the latter differs from that of the Dalit in the sense of its origin from a common descent or descents, use of a particular language and being proud of that or degree of 'we-feeling'. Secondly, the term Dalit is used, in narrow sense, by socially and politically conscious youth of a particular caste or tribe for their own caste or tribe itself. Similarly, the concept of Dalit movement too has been used in two senses—broad and narrow—for all varieties of movements organised by the Dalits throughout the length and breadh of the country over a period. In narrow sense, it is used for a single movement of any sort organised by the Dalits of a particular village, or of a few neighbouring villages, town(s) or a region including even a few neighbouring regions.

A section of social scientists who have shown keen interests in studying Dalit movements in India since last few decades heavily draw inferences from movements organised by Jyotirao Phule and Periyar E.V. Ramaswamy Naicker in Maharashtra (earlier Bombay Presidency) and Tamil Nadu (earlier Madras Presidency) respectively. While doing this not only they ignore Sri Narayan Guru's movement better known as Sri Narayana Dharma Paripalana Yogam in Kerala but also erroneously conceive of Phule, Periyar and Ambedkar in a trio. Their such inferences are based more on ideological constructs rather than factual issues that they had addressed to or the segments of the population they had organized separately. More specifically, both Phule and Periyar had articulated the interests of non-Brahmins (not necessarily and compulsorily of the erstwhile Untouchables) or of the Shudras or Sat-Shudras (if one would accept this nomenclature) or the Other Backward Castes or Classes. In fact, the historical evidences of the Dalit movements organized earlier or even during their time suggest that in the movements of Phule or Periyar the vital issues pertaining to the Untouchables were either ignored or relegated. It is, however, well accepted that the main focus of Ambedkar's movement was to ameliorate the miseries of the Untouchables or the Scheduled Castes or the Dalits (both in narrow sense as well as in broad sense) as well as to prepare them to assert for their dignity and self-respect. It does not mean that he had completely ignored the interest of the Shudras or the Other Backward Castes or Classes. Thus, the trio of Phule, Periyar and Ambedkar is not fully grounded, though Ambedkar had acknowledged the reforms brought by Phule through the latter's Satya Sodhak Samaj Movement.

Prior to political Independence of the country, the Dalit leadership as such had been either contested or undermined. Babasaheb Ambedkar's leadership was, in no way, an exception. This has been well documented in the history of struggle for freedom of the country as well as of the Dalits. For instance, both Marxist and non-Marxist historians, have given credit to Mahatma Gandhi and to the Indian National Congress for uplift of the then Untouchables by completely blotting the intelligently articulated leadership of Ambedkar. In other words, the pre-Independent India had witnessed the processes of both inclusion or co-option and exclusion or undermining the independent Dalit leadership. Contrarily, the free India has produced, though abruptly, an independent Dalit leadership in certain regions but the process of co-option and elimination still continues which may be attributed to the pluralistic structure of the society and the electoral arithmetic of the democratic polity in India.

Dr. Vivek Kumar's book addresses more wittingly the above stated issues. His book talks about Dalit leadership vis-a-vis Dalit movements in historical as well as contextual perspectives in analysing nature and dynamics of Dalit leadership in three specific regions of the largest populated state, namely Uttar Pradesh, which also determines the leaps and bounds of the country's politics. In my reckoning, his analysis given in the book provides quasi-perfect parameters for analyzing the Dalit leadership as well as the Dalit movements found in different parts of the country. This is a significant addition to the recent literature written on the Dalit movements and the Dalits leadership, and it may be well-received by both the social scientists as well as general readers.

NANDU RAM
Director General
October 14, 2002.
Dr. Babasaheb Ambedkar National Institute of Social Sciences,
DONGERGOAN, MHOW, Indore (Dist) M.P.

Preface

The present study envisages to conceptualise the Dalit Leadership in the modern day national politics. It tries to trace its origin, growth and development, and examine its nature and dynamics, besides inquiring into its strategy or strategies adopted for mobilisation and empowerment of the Dalit masses. On the basis of existed temporal reality; we have divided the Dalit leadership into three broad streams.

First, the Dalit leadership, which existed before the advent of Ambedkar on the political horizon. The second stream or phase of Dalit leadership includes the leaders such as Ambedkar and a few of his contemporaries. Ambedkar's leadership ha, however, been viewed as the most significantt aspect of the Dalit assertion. Further, for our convenience, we have divided his leadership into three inter-related and inter-connected phases. The first phase began in the early 1920s and got over in early 1930s. During the period, he acted more like a social reformer in fighting against the rigidity of caste system and its rude practice of Untouchability. The second phase of his leadership started during mid of the 1930s and ended with his resigning from the Nehru Cabinet in 1951. During this period, he was fully recognised as the undisputed political leader of the Dalits. He succeeded in getting the Dalits recognised a unified separate political entity. During this period, he was fully recognised as the undisputed political leader of the Dalits. He succeeded in getting the Dalits recognised a unified separate political entity. During this period, Ambedkar also established political parties. He also became the Chairman of the Drafting Committee of the Constitution. This was a job he had taken up against his wishes but for the sake of the Dalit community. In the third and final phase (1952-56) of his leadership, Ambedkar acted like a religious reformer. He embraced Buddhism along with lakhs of his followers on 14th October 1956 in Nagpur. He, thus, gave to the Dalits a new religion and identity so that they could be free from the clutche and stigma of the Hindu social order.

The third and the last stream of the Dalit leadership on the temporal basis is the leadership after Ambedkar. This leadership can be seen in terms of electoral politics in the country after independence. A number of political parties came into being after the demise of Ambedkar and functioned independently. The RPI, Dalit Panthers and now Bahujan Samaj Party fall in this category. Yet, because of the democratic polity, many Dalit leasders are also found in other political parties dominated by the upper castes or classes. Thus, the contemporary Dalit leadership in the country as well as in the state of Uttar Pradesh (UP) is composite of both the independent and dependent Dalit political leaders.

After providing the aforesaid socio-historical profile of the Dalit leadership in the country as well as in UP, we have analysed nature of Dalit leadership in the present study on the basis of all these years. We have tried to bracket the whole traverse of changing stances of the Dalit leadership into two major groups. We have termed the first type of Dalit leadership as socio-religious pursued, first of all, change within the Dalit community asking the Dalits to partake with carrion eating, liquor drinking, pursuing traditional occupation, etc.

Contrary to this, the Dalit political leadership of the earlier period had many issues in the secular realms like the issues of right to vote, separate elaborates, political representation in the Parliament and Legislative Assembly, in the Cabinets and other statuary bodies. The Dalit leaders had also demanded reservation in the government services and preferential recruitment in the Army, deletion and addition of caste names in the Schedule, etc. They formed political parties and contested elections for achieving these rights. On the basis of the party membership and functions of the Dalit leaders, we have further divided Dalit leadership into two categories: one, 'dependent' Dalit political leadership and, two, 'independent' Dalit political leadership. The dependent Dalit political leadership has usually ever existed in the different political parties dominated by the upper castes and classes.

On the other hand, we have found in our study that the dependent Dalit political leadership had established, even in the past, its own organisations and political parties. The cases are of Ambedkar's Indian Labour Party, Scheduled Castes Federation and later the Republican Party of India conceived and blessed by him, the Dalit Panthers and now the Bahujan Samaj Party.

Anyway, such Dalit political leadership had played in the past and continues to play in the present time the vanguard role and set its own independent agenda often hovering around the Dalits. Usually, the Dalit leadership is guided by ideology and vision of Ambedkar. However, the Dalit leadership is guided by the ideology and vision of Ambedkar. However, the Dalit leaders of this category occassionally add some other programs and thereby expand their ideological base because of the existing socio-political reality of the particular geographical and social context. Their parlance is very critical of the Hindu social order and of the existing general political leadership. Not only that but their challenges to the *status-quoist* forces have raised new hype of consciousness among the Dalit masses. Also, they have successfully pressurised the dominant socio-political forces to accede to their demands and formulate new policies and programmes for amelioration of the Dalits. Such Dalit leadership has raised occasionally even the issue of separate-electorate for the Dalits. So also, the empowerment of Dalits through the political process independently forms the core of their policies and programmes. They wish to change the structural composition of the existing institutions of state enabling the Dalits to remain active players in functioning of these institutions.

As far as dynamics of the Dalit leadership is concerned, it has been analysed, in the present study, on the basis of shift in its instance from social reform to political power, lack of a unified socio-political ideology and identity, lack of permanent allies both in the social and political realms, impact of globalisation and privatisation on reservation, and the demand for inclusion of the cases of atrocities inflicted on Dalits in the purview of the human rights inviting the international support for their redressal. More precisely, we have analysed, in the study, the shift in the agenda of the Dalit leadership from social reform to acquiring political power. We have found that this act has been greatly influenced by the vision of Ambedkar.

The present study has also analysed ideology of the general leadership as well as that of the Dalit leadership. We have done ths, as ideology is an integral part of the political culture and process of the Indian society, or for that matter any society, and of politicisation of the people and their mobilisation by the political parties. We found that the Dalit political leadership, more or less, claim to believe in 'Ambedkarism' as the core of its ideology. But in our study, we have noted that the leadership occasionally adds some programmes and even slogans to its ideology depending upon the needs of the time and context.

We have also analysed dynamics of the Dalit leadership in terms of its failure in evolving a common social identity be adopted by the Dalits who continue to suffer, even today, from same stigma and exploitation throughout the country. In course of our analysis, we have noted their socio-religious, political and constitutional identities. We have also mentioned in our study that a very recent identity of the Dalits is that of the 'Bahujans' prorogated by leadership of the Bahujan Samaj Party (BSP). We have also observed that effectiveness of the Dalit movements launched in different parts of the country including Uttar Pradesh.

We have finally analysed dynamics of the Dalit leadership in terms of having its permanent allies both at the social and political arena. We have noticed in our study that the Dalit leadership has ever faced since its inception the problem of searching its allies and has generally acted alone. This factor has definitely affected negatively the Dalit leadership as far as its political battle is concerned. But in the present era of coalitions and alliances, the Dalit leadership especially of the BSP is trying to mobilise the most backward castes in Uttar Pardesh as their political allies.

Vivek Kumar

Acknowledgements

Years ago I started this research work. All these years paradoxes and contradictions were solved and construction and deconstruction of new ideas and thoughts took the shape of the present work. Many testing moments became the part of this research with the significant support of number of people. Each and everyone cannot be mentioned here. But some of them need special mention. Without acknowledging them, I think, this work would be incomplete.

First and fore most I am deeply indebted to my supervisor Prof. Nandu Ram who not only encouraged me to take this academic endeavor but also provided me moral and intellectual support. His methodological insights crystallized the vague notions of my research. He kept his patience to bear my mistakes and saw it that my work is completed in time. Even today his perfectionist attitude, in the realm of academic research haunts me and keeps me on the toes if I want to take a short cut in any academic exercise.

My teachers at the center especially Prof. T.K. Oommen, Prof. M.N. Panini, Prof. Dipankar Gupta, Prof. Anand Kumar and Dr Avijit Pathak provided me their valuable comments whenever I went to them to discuss my research work. I extend my sincere gratitude to them. Thanks are also dew to other teachers and collogue of the center for their moral and intellectual support.

All my batch mates had encouraged me during my M. Phil. and Ph.D. Days but now every one has left the campus. However, my new intellectual friends Shailesh Darokar, Lecturer in the Unit for Urban Studies at Tata Institute of Social Sciences Mumbai and Research Scholar Habibullah, have helped me during proof reading of the manuscript. Thanks are due to them for the same and also for their informal chats on the research topic. My thanks are also due to my childhood friends Sanjeev, Arvind, Ashutosh and S.S.Verma.

During the period of my Data collection some reputed Journalists of Uttar Pradesh helped me by providing lots of insigh' about the Dalit leadership. I extend my sincere regards to

Mr. Udai Sinha Resident Editor, The Pioneer, who contributed in more than one way for developing my understanding on the topic. Mr Kamal Jayant of Rashtriya Sahara, Mr. Kashi Yadav of Hindustan Times, Mr. Udai Yadav, Dainik Jagran, K.B. Singh of Pioneer Saptahik, and Pankaj Shrivastav of Amar Ujala gave me their valuable comments on the topic. I really thank them all. In Delhi Mr. Ashutosh of Aaj Tak, Chandrabhan prasad and Gaurav Dwevedi gave their valuable comments on Dalit leadership. Thanks are also due to them.

It is difficult to thank and repay back the debt of my Family members. Despite sufferings my parents never complained me for my not helping them at the domestic front. They absolved me from every duty which eldest son of a family should perform after his parents grow old. My mother though she herself never had any formal education, always motivated me to go for higher education. My father has been guiding force because of his exemplary courage with which he has faced the discrimination through out the life. His fighting spirit in turning the tide in his favor has given me this opportunity to pursue the highest level of education.

Thank are due to my brothers, Mr. Sudhir Kumar, Er. Gagan, my sisters Dr. Geeta Narain, Dr. Pushp Lata Chaudhry, Suman, Tripti, my sister in-law Neeta and my nieces Tanaya and Ashi for their moral support.

It is also impossible to record the sacrifice made by my wife Jaya and daughter Vijaya. Both of them have suffered the trauma, agony and loneliness and spared me from my duties of husband and father respectively. But they never complained to me about this criminal neglect on my part. I feel helpless and really don't know how will I compensate for this.

In the end I am solely responsible for all the mistakes in the book.

Vivek Kumar

Introduction

One of the major factors that determine the ultimate success or failure of a movement is the nature and dynamics of its leadership. The strategic moves made by the leaders decide the direction, scope and nature of the movement. History is testimony to the fact that most of the socio-political movements in India and elsewhere saw a strong leadership at the helms of their affairs. Their leadership provided a vision, direction and *modus operandi* to these movements. But time and again, it has been observed that in India a Dalit movement emerges, flourishes to a certain extent and stagnates after a point, although with some achievements. With the exception of Ambedkar's dynamic leadership, Dalit movements have been a tragic story of conflicts and contradictions among their leaders. This phenomenon of fragmented and divided leadership has retarded the development and amelioration of the Dalit community. The leadership of the Republican Party of India [RPI], Dalit Panthers, Backward and Minority Communities Employees Federation (BAMCEF) and recently of the Bahujan Samaj Party (BSP), to quote just a few, are the glaring examples of the fragmentation.

The Problem

The militant self- assertion of the Dalits today is a socio-political reality of Indian society. Unlike earlier the sections, whose interests Ambedkar primarily championed, have now attained the capability to influence the political and social agenda lying before the country. It is a well known fact that Dalits are involved in the process of deconstruction and reconstruction of the earlier and the existing social orders wherein the latter has heavily been derived from the former.

It is really a paradoxical social milieu of persisting inequality and contest for equality. Today, the Dalit liberation movement has expanded its scope and territory. The Dalit Movements against the atrocities inflicted on them, or for their liberation from the bondage, or their assertion for achieving social mobility and respectful social identity have derived their inspiration from

Ambedkar's ideology, philosophy and strategy of movements for liberation of the Dalits. But to reach to the present stage, Dalit leaders after Ambedkar had to follow a long path of protests and struggles, which still continues.

A large number of Dalit leaders sacrificed their lives and comforts in achieving the contemporary socio-political gains by Dalits. They perennially confronted with the 'cumulative dominance' of the upper strata in Indian society. They also helped the Dalit masses to overcome the cumulative deprivation heaped on them since ages by the same strata. If we look at the history of the Dalit movements organised in different parts of the country, it becomes clear that a number of socio-political organisations, struggles and various types of activities of the Dalits had emerged out of different socio-economic and political conditions in the past to ameliorate their wretched condition. However, these activities of Dalit leaders and their organisations are part of a general neglect in the academic realm. More specifically, nowhere these leaders and their activities find place in the annals of history and sociology. Therefore, the proposed study is a modest effort to understand and analyse the nature of the Dalit leadership and various activities of the Dalit leaders for socio- political amelioration of the Dalits in the past and in the present time.

The autonomy of Dalit leadership has always been perceived as synonymous to the leadership provided by Babasaheb Dr. B.R. Ambedkar. It is a well known fact that though Ambedkar was the first Dalit leader who had an All India following, the autonomous Dalit leadership of several varieties had existed much before he appeared on horizon of the Dalit liberation. More precisely, political mobilisation of the Dalits on the national scene can be traced to the early 1920s when the British Government initiated a series of legislative measures to provide social and political safeguards and representation of the various communities including the Dalits in the Centre and State Legislatures and other official besides. But this is again debatable as one can see the seeds of the Dalit leadership existed, much earlier to this in different parts of the country. Dalits had organised several demonstrations against the Indian National Congress in Poona and Madras way back in 1895 and had burnt its effigy (Ambedkar 1991:97). A systematic account of this may give us insight of a socio-historical profile of the Dalit leadership in the past. We may also equip ourselves with other facts like nature of major demands pursued by the then Dalit leadership, the major issues on which it confronted and the patterns or strategy(ies) it adopted for communicating to and mobilising the Dalit masses during that period. We may also take stock of achievements, failures and crises encountered by the Dalit leadership at that point of time.

The development that followed Ambedkar's leadership provides us with another vantage point to assess changes in the nature and crisis of Dalit leadership during that period. It cannot be denied that Ambedkar along with other Dalit leaders created a new ambience for liberation of the Dalits at an All India level. An in-depth analysis of the nature and role of the Dalit leadership of that period depicts the evolution and developments of Ambedkar's leadership into three inter-related yet inter-dependent phases. It is imperative to know these phases, if we want to understand the proper paradigm of his leadership. This is also important because each phase of his leadership saw a different forms or models of mobilisation and protest which was located in the contextual space and time. By knowing these phases, we may also easily understand when and why he changed his *modus operandi* for mobilising the Dalits. Thus, the first phase of his leadership started roughly since the middle of the second decade of the previous century. During this period, his major emphasis was on social reforms in the Hindu social order with reference to the Dalits particularly the Mahars in Maharashtra. He used at this stage a few religious symbols as the basic means for mobilising and energising the Dalit masses who were subjected to the various types of social and religious disabilities and were demoralised by their age-old oppression, suppression, isolation and exploitation. In this connection, he was very critical of the philanthropic roles played by the Hindu social reformers and lip services extended by the Indian National Congress to the upliftment of the Dalits (Ram 1995:61).

Ambedkar changed his stance in the second phase of his leadership. When he realised that the social reforms had failed to bring any positive and significant change in the socio-economic conditions of the Dalits, he impressed upon the then government to bring about the political reforms and to provide political safeguards to the untouchables or the Depressed Classes as they were known by that time. Ambedkar knew that the Dalits could bring about basic changes in their socio-economic conditions by occupying important positions in the state power structure. As they did not have any economic power to enthrone themselves to the political power or authority, their number was the only strength. Ambedkar was of the view that in the politics of numbers Dalits might clearly work out a strategy and occupy important positions of power in government, bureaucracy, etc.

Thus, realising the significance of awakening and consciousness among the Dalits, Ambedkar went in for seeking political safeguards for them as mentioned above. The great political successes of Ambedkar for the Dalits were achieved in the short period - from 1919 to 1932. By the end of this period, the Dalits had firmly been recognised as a group distinguishable from the caste Hindus and thus deserved special electoral arrangements. At the outset, Ambedkar asked for the representation of Dalits through their leaders elected by them only. He logically proved Dalits to be minority, separate from caste Hindus, on the basis of their socio-religious disabilities. Since the various minorities were already awarded separate electorate as early as in 1909, Ambedkar championed the issue of separate electorate for Dalits also. But he was compelled to accept the system of joint electorate by signing the Poona Pact in 1932.

Ambedkar, however, formed the Independent Labour Party (1936) and then the Scheduled Castes Federation (1946) to make Dalits socially and politically conscious of their rights. The main motto behind forming such political parties was to bring the Dalits, the then Depressed Classes (by that time the term Scheduled Castes was legally adopted) into the mainstream of the political life. At the fag end of his political career, he worked for the formation of the Republican Party of India (RPI) for forging /augmenting alliance of all the depressed sections namely SC/ST, OBC and Minorities of Indian society. Ambedkar's formation of a few political parties for bringing different sections of deprived has acted as the guiding principle for a few political parties dominated by the Dalits in contemporary period. Also, the change of his stance and tactics from social reforms to political safeguards for the Dalits is another very crucial issue to be examined in the present research. Today, it is a known fact that Dalits have become politically more conscious as a few Dalit political parties have sprung up which are involved in capturing the political power. Moreover, a number of Dalit leaders actively working in different political parties often claim to be the true representative of the Dalits. Whether their claim is legitimate is another issue to be examined in the present study.

Ambedkar's conversion to Buddhism is regarded as the third and final phase of his movement. This phase of his movement emanated from his disillusion about the social reform with more stress on spiritual or religious reform of the renaissance period of the nineteenth century, and also from social reform, with prime motive of the transfer of political power from the colonial regime, in the first decade of the twentieth century. He was also guided by his growing detachment from any possibility of changes or transformation in the orthodox Hindu society. He saw no future for his people in Hinduism. Hence, he opted for conversion to Buddhism. He was of the opinion that with the conversion there could be greater possibility of emergence of an alternative egalitarian social order for the Dalits. They would be at least away from the caste discrimination and stigmatised social identity in the Hindu social order which lacks all the three tenets of an open social order, i.e. equality, liberty and fraternity (Ambedkar 1987:96-117). That is why, conversion is presently considered by Dalits as a movement to achieve social equality, sense of self-respect and establishment of their social identity separate from that of Hindus. The phenomenon of conversion as a protest movement continues till date. It will be fruitful to analyse the use of 'conversion movements' as an effective tool by the Dalit leadership for amelioration of Dalits.

Today, the nature of Dalit leadership has changed completely as compared to that in the past. There have occurred both qualitative and quantitative changes in it with the gradual development of democratic polity, multi - party system and political reservation given to the Dalits at different levels in the contemporary Indian polity. More precisely, if we analyze closely the activities of the Dalit leadership, it was more social and reformative in nature in its formative years. It stressed the internal reforms within the community asking the masses for cleanliness, giving up carrion flesh eating, drinking alcohol, leaving heriditary caste occupations, etc. The leaders followed the policy of persuasion and petitions instead of direct confrontation. And only after the advent of Ambedkar as their leader, the policy and strategy of mass action started, and nature of the Dalit leadership changed gradually as stated above. As the time passed by, with its social demand, it added the political safeguards for the Dalits of different regions in the country. In the contemporary period, the Dalit leaders as well as leaders as a whole have left the social reforms in isolation. They are more oriented towards achieving political power and rights for themselves as well as for the Dalit masses. Hence, our concern in this study would be to inquire into the reasons for the major shift in the orientation in objectives of Dalit leadership at present in comparison to that in the past.

The present crisis of the Dalit leadership has a parallel in the history in terms of its extension of the past. In past the Dalit leadership mainly faced the crisis of unity of inter-caste allies, particularly alliance with OBCs and minorities in carrying out agitation or movements for capturing political power, and for bringing out social change and transformation in the society. In fact, the Dalit leadership has been lagging an ideology which can bind together first all the Dalits, and then the OBCs and minorities both at regional and national level and which, in turn, may provide it with political identity different from identity of the general leadership in the country.

The Dalit leadership is divided along the party lines and speaks the language of its respective party is another crises which the Dalit leadership has today. Occasionally, the Dalit leaders act like a pressure group with more peripheral and cosmetic-like demands such as that of renaming of streets, installing a statue or portray of Babasaheb Ambedkar, fulfilling of reservation quota, etc. But there is general neglect of leaders on more fundamental issues like demands for putting curbs on atrocities inflicted on the Dalits, for distribution of lands power to powerless, more educational facilities, financial help for developing entrepreneurial skills, etc. Why has the Dalit leadership failed on these aforesaid issues is also of the general interest examined in this study.

Retrospectively, the leadership of Ambedkar already set a stage from where the contemporary Dalit leadership should have moved in the positive direction in carrying out its movements for capturing political power and bringing out social change and transformation in the society. It was also envisaged that with the adoption and implementation of various constitutional safeguards and with pursuing the ideology and strategy of Ambedkar, the Dalits would progress rapidly. But with his untimely demise, there has been a dearth of effective and committed Dalit leadership. The contemporary Dalit leadership has failed to make any progress in fulfilling his incomplete mission. There has been no substantial improvement in the conditions of the Dalits (Joshi 1982, Mendelshon & Vicziany 1998, Ram 1995). The increasing cases of untouchability and atrocities inflicted on the Dalits (153167 cases of atrocities were committed during 1981-92), the growing ratio of their illiteracy, unemployment and poverty, low standards of their nutrition, housing, clothing, health care, etc can be taken as indicators to prove their deteriorating condition. Moreover, if we add the social discontentment suffered by the Dalits due to their status inconsistency, alienation because of gap between their awakened desires and their fulfilment, then their condition becomes more miserable.

In grasping the significance of crisis of Dalit leadership, we have to investigate it at other levels also. The failure of the Dalit leadership can be seen in terms of finding its genuine allies who could politically and socially help the Dalits in their struggles, as stated above. There have been minor efforts to unite SCs/STs, OBCs and minorities by the RPI, Dalit Panthers and recently BSP but, more or less, with limited success. Secondly, the issue of a separate socio-cultural and political (an independent political entity/pressure group) identity is still unresolved. This is evident from the fact that some sections of Dalits claim to be the original inhabitants of the country and, hence, separate from the Hindus whereas others accept themselves as part and parcel of Hinduism.

Further, Dalits are also not comfortable with the various nomenclatures like Harijans, Untouchables, Scheduled Castes, etc. which are given to them by others. Quite a few Dalits are not even happy with the identity of 'Dalit' coined by them. They are also unhappy with their new religious nomenclatures of neo-Buddhists, Neo-Muslims and Dalit Christians either. And nobody knows with what nomenclature would the leadership be able to organise all the Dalits under one banner in future. It is imperative to have one common identity if Dalit leadership wants to have politico-social unity. In more concrete sense, the lack of one common dominant ideology is another form of crises of the contemporary Dalit leadership. Though the Dalits at large face, more or less, common problems of stigma of untouchability, economic exploitation, social degradation and so forth, they are unable to develop the common ideology to face the challenges. Without one type of ideology and identity, the Dalit leaders are divided in a number of political parties as stated earlier. There is no proper consensus or coordination among them on a common agenda or strategy to deal with multiple problems of the Dalits in the country.

Lastly, it is observed that though the gender inequality among the Dalits is relatively less, the Dalit leadership has not been able to develop leadership among the Dalit women- folks. Women are seldom seen participating in the leadership affairs. Though they are doubly exploited, their exclusive demands have never found a place in the agenda of the Dalit leadership. It is true that a few Dalit women have started contesting elections and establishing their own organizations. But it is too early to say that any significant type of leadership has emerged among Dalit women.

The present study envisages to analyse the nature and dynamics of Dalit leadership in India. Alongwith it the study has located the same characteristics about it in Uttar Pradesh (UP), the most populous state of India. For this particular analysis of Uttar Pradesh we have gathered data from primary sources. This has been done precisely because though a plethora of studies have focussed on the Dalit protest movements of different varieties in India and the socio-economic and educational mobility of Dalits, we do not find many studies either on nature and significance of the Dalit leadership in general or on the Dalit struggles or movements for their liberation in particular in India or U.P. Also, there has not been any evaluation of contributions of Dalit leadership both in terms of its successes or failures. Whether there could be a concept of 'Dalit leadership' in the democratic set up in Indian polity is also a moot question discussed at length in the present study. Both the facts and analyses about the ideology, philosophy and strategies of functioning of the Dalit leaders in the state are totally ambiguous. The Dalit leadership though has a long history of struggle, achievements and failures in the country and state, its critical evaluation is absent. Even, the enigma of difference between Dalit leadership and general leadership, and the perception of the general masses about the former has rarely found place in the writings of the Dalit movements. In the light of the aforesaid issues about the Dalit leadership, a number of hypotheses have been formulated and verified in the present study.

Objectives of the Study

In the light of the above, the present study intends:

1. To explain the concept of Dalit leadership. This is important in view of the fact that with the limited representative democracy before independence Dalits were not even allowed to exercise their adult franchise. Then, it is interesting to find out if there could have been a concept of Dalit leadership at all at that time. It is also important to enquire into if it is feasible to have such concept especially with adoption of the democratic polity, with parliamentary democracy, universal franchise and the joint electorate system where Dalit political representatives are jointly elected by both Dalits and non-Dalits from the reserved constituencies. Though Dailt leaders are allowed to contest from the general constituencies as well, the conceptualisation of Dalit leadership also becomes difficult especially when the Dalit leaders elected from reserved constituencies ought to represent both the Dalits and non-Dalits of their respective constituencies though in principle they ought to represent and safeguard interests of the former.
2. To analyse nature and dynamics of the Dalit leadership in terms of articulating demands of and *modus operandi* adopted for mobilizing the Dalit masses. As stated earlier, in its formative years the Dalit leadership had raised the demands of social reforms within the Dalit communities. Later on, it had asked for their economic and political rights too. In the light of this, an attempt has been made in this study to analyse the reason for absence of mass action and active participation of Dalit leadership at least in the initial period which, in turn, was compensated by the strategy of presentation of prayers and petitions to press the demands of the Dalits. In the same sequence, attempts have also been made to find out reasons for both qualitative and quantitative change in terms of active resistance and mass action in the nature of the Dalit leadership with advent of Ambedkar on the horizon of the Dalit liberation movement.
3. To inquire into the question of political identity of the Dalit leadership and the consequent socio-cultural identity of the Dalit masses who have been involved, in one way or the other,

in the process of ascertaining a separate identity from the Hindu social order. As stated earlier, with their claim of being the original habitants of this land and later conquered by the Aryans, the Dalits had organised the various Adi-Hindu movements all over the country in the late nineteenth and early twentieth centuries (Omvedt : 1994). For instance, in Uttar Pradesh the Adi Hindu movement led by swami Achhutananda was quite prominent. Thus, by now Dalits had come to be known with different names such as untouchables, *Antyaja, Adi-Hindu*, Depressed Classes, *Harijans*, Scheduled Castes, and today Dalits. It is, therefore, interesting to find out how these different identities have affected the Dalit leadership in regard to its articulation of demands of the Dalits for their distinct socio-cultural and political identities.

4. To assess the possibility of adoption of an ideology on which both Dalit leadership and various organisations involved in carrying out Dalit movements may work together. Though majority of the Dalits has common problems of stigma of untouchability and atrocities inflicted on them, economic poverty, powerlessness and a common reference of thoughts and philosophy of Ambedkar, yet they have failed to embrace a common ideology. It is, therefore, necessary to examine why are they unable to accept a common ideology, which may bind them together both at the state, and national levels and may bridge their inter-and intra-caste differences?
5. To explore the possibility of having permanent allies of the Dalit leadership in the political and social realms is another objective of the study. It was envisaged by Ambedkar that the backwards (now OBCs) and minorities could be natural allies of the Dalits, as they also had suffered from inequality and exploitation of the upper strata (Ambedkar 1989:115-116). It was also found that Dalits have supported the Muslims on number of occassions when latter were in crices (Lynch: 1974, Jurjensmeyer: 1982, Mendelshon & Vicziany: 1998). But time and again, it has been witnessed that such an alliance has in actuality not worked or has not last long even if there has been some. The most recent and glaring example is the alliance between the Bahujan Samaj Party (BSP) and the Samajwadi Party (SP) in Uttar Pradesh in the year 1993 which could not last long and belied the aspirations of the Dalit and

OBC masses. Moreover, it has also been observed that the OBCs have perpetrated numerous types of atrocities on the Dalits in the rural areas. Under such circumstances, the proposed study tends to examine the possibility of any successful political alliance between the Dalits and others including the Congress Party, both at the state and national levels.

6. Finally, this study proposes to inquire into the causes of dearth of more effective and articulate Dalit leadership among Dalits including their women-folk though the latter enjoy more freedom in their socio- economic activities and social life as compared to women in general in the country.

Besides, the present study has also a set of specific objectives given below.

1. To analyse the reason why Dalits in a State like UP have not produced any dynamic leadership in spite of their being more politically conscious and successful in organising a number of movements like Adi Hindu movement, Jatav movement, Scheduled Caste Federation, RPI, etc. in the past. Such inquiry is also important as emergence of the Republican Party of India (RPI) and other Dalit organisations in the post-independent period could not produce any dynamic leadership among the Dalits in the state.
2. To examine the emergence of the Bahujan Samaj Party (BSP) and the renewed political consciousness among the Dalits in event of a euphoria created by its leadership for capturing power in the country, and then getting splintered and entering into alliance with the upper caste and class dominated political parties like Bhartiya Janata Party (BJP) and Congress (I) Party. Has this type Dalit assertion through a political party empowered them or not is also to be analysed.
3. Lastly, to inquire into why the existing Dalit leadership has failed to raise the basic issues of the Dalits such as atrocities, land reform, wage hikes, problem of bonded labour, housing, education, etc. which are presently more vital to the Dalits.

Review of Relevant Studies

A brief survey of the existed literature explains that there have not been many significant studies on the Dalit leadership in

India and particularly in Uttar Pradesh. However, different authors have evaluated the mobility pattern, various Dalit movements, and the structure and functioning of a few specific Dalit organisations. Therefore, we shall review critically only those studies, which are relevant to the objectives of and analysis done in the present study.

In his study of Jatavs (Chamars) of Agra city, Lynch (1974) has found that sanskrtisation, a process of cultural mobility among the lower castes, is not applicable to all the types of movements for social mobility in the post-independent India. He has shown how the Jatavs of Agra have rejected sanskritisation and the caste system, and opted for political participation and parliamentary democracy for their socio-economic mobility. He has also found the legal innovations adopted specially after Independence and the country's democratic Constitution, which permit modern democratic political activities, have opened new means for raising their social status. Lynch analyses the efforts of the Jatavs to rise in terms of political, economic and religious aspects of their social life. Further, he shows that the conflict is now within the political arena specially in terms of attempting to make citizenship and achievement as the recruiting principles to the structures of the existing opportunity and power, on the one hand, and to destroy the caste and ascribed rank as the recruitment principles to these structures on the other.

In terms of the temporal history of the Jatava movement of Agra Lynch's study covers the period of reform from 1900 to 1963. It traces the evolution of the movement in both the pre and post-independent periods. According to him, the Jatav movement started as a socio-religious reform movement and travelled through the formation of political parties like the Scheduled Castes Federation and the Republican Party India (Agra branch) and, finally, leading to conversion by the Jatavs to Buddhism along with Babasaheb Ambedkar in 1956. The author has very eloquently explained the factors helping the Jatavs to accept Babasaheb Ambedkar as their leader even though he was not from their caste and the region. It is interesting to note that during the struggle between Ambedkar and Gandhi over the issue of separate electorates for Dalits, the Jatavs along with the other Dalit groups, wired to London to insist that Ambedkar and not Gandhi was their leader. The politics of vote led the Jatavs to have alliance with minorities, some upper castes and upper caste-dominated political parties like the Jan Sangh and the Congress Party has also been highlighted by the author. A glaring feature of the Lynch's study about the Jatava movement is that it has highlighted its relationship with both national and international level. It is not a mean achievement for oppressed and subordinated Dalits of a local area to relate themselves at the National level cutting the regional barrier.

Further, Joshi (1982) has examined a question of who are the scheduled castes? Calling them as ex-untouchables instead of 'scheduled caste's she has evaluated their existing socio-economic status and concluded that their current position in education, occupation and land ownership is still far below to that of the national population. Explaining the causes of their illiteracy she states, "The causes are family poverty, lack of educational experience and their attendant hazards- pressure to take children out of school and into the labour market, the absence of important informal education from educated parents at home, the need for part-time employment that cuts into study time" (Joshi 1982: 12). Her data also show the continuing discrimination in recruitment of Dalits in government services resulting into the rampant unemployment among them. She argues that in both absolute and relative terms the Dalits have very restricted access to crucially important rural economic resource such as land. Several decades of land reform legislation have done little to correct basic inequalities of the Dalits. The general agricultural development programmes have also been substantially less beneficial to the average rural Dalit family than to others. Much of the prosperity of the 'green revolution' in terms of scientific farming has gone to those who already have relatively abundant investment capital and acreage (Joshi 1982: 20).

Accepting urbanization as the most important source of over-all socio- political change in the so-called 'developing nation' Joshi has further examined the socio-political changes occurred among the Dalits in four major urban centres of North India-Delhi, Kanpur, Aligarh and Agra. Urbanization has different effects on the socio-political change among the Dalits. Joshi opines, "Indeed, the cities served in the past as centres for the development of the formal philosophies and literature legitimising the widespread practice of untouchablility. Urban residential patterns persisting into the present have often graphically reflected hierarchic caste division. Benaras... Delhi, Agra, Aligarh - (all) preserve large areas of residential clustering of different castes" (Joshi 1982: 98). Dalits are still segregated in the occupational structure and are employed in the traditional caste jobs in the modern industries.

The study has also evaluated the influence of Dalit politics in the course of political events. It is a fact that a Dalit with a relatively meagre resource-base suffers from serious restraints or constraints in the electoral arena. Even if he/she is elected to Parliament or Legislative Assembly, his/her such constraints always come in the way of articulating the problems and aspirations of the Dalits. This, in turn, means unsatisfactory level of socio-economic change among the Dalits through the politics though a few authors have found in some other situations the positive impact of politics on social change among the lower caste people (see, Bailey 1959; Bhatt 1971 and 1974). She has concluded by saying that the dramatic socio-economic changes through political action that were once so confidently expected and are still so ardently sought, have failed to materialize. Further, she says that the reservation system has meant persistent pressure within the political changes taking place in the country. The Dalit legislators elected from the reserved constituencies have proved to be neither conservative nor as apathetic as so often claimed.

Regarding political empowerment of Dalits at the grass-root level, a study (Kumar 1989) of Scheduled- Caste Panchayat Pradhans in western Uttar Pradesh has analysed the impact of political socialisation on their political outlook, the pattern of their recruitment and their performance. Based on the analysis of the village panchayat elections of 1982 in Uttar Pradesh, the study suggests that the elections had brought a major change in the 'political socialization,' recruitment' and 'performance' of the Dalit leaders at the grass-root level of democracy in the rural setting. Quite a few pradhans (heads of the village councils) from the higher castes had held earlier the office of the panchayats. However, in one Block of the Ghaziabad district seven of the pradhans were elected from amongst the Dalits (Chamars), even without reservation, which was not a mean achievement.

Their performance was also said to be far satisfactory in comparison to the upper caste pradhans of these areas. Thus, the presence of the Dalit leaders in the Panchayati Raj Institutions has proved to be helpful to the Dalits in solving of their day-to-day problems. The Dalits have also learned the craft of using the rampant rural caste and economic factionalism and alliances with other middle castes to wield formal power. The most important observation made by the said study is that the younger generation of the Dalit community have acted as the catalyst in socialising their elders to enter in the political contest to gain the formal power. Besides, the views of Dr. Ambedkar remain their guiding force for self-assertion. It is worth mentioning here that this study dates before the 73rd constitutional amendment came into effect and the first elections to the Panchayats were held only in 1996 in the state.

Yet, another study (Singh & Sundaram 1987) has found the emerging elite among the Dalits in Uttar Pradesh, though they are not of very high ranks, i.e. highly placed political leaders or bureaucrats or businessmen. This was so as the study - sample had consisted of the school teachers and the lower level government officials the clerks. Thus, the study has remarked that the elite do not break ties with community after gaining jobs in the government offices and in schools. On the contrary, they encourage their caste-men, and a few of them were found organizing social and cultural activities for their community (Singh & Sundaram 1987:183). However, the study has noted that the provisions of concessions provided by the Indian Constitution to the Dalits have helped them gain mobility in different realms. Their advancement on the educational and occupational scales has somehow made them distinct from their unfortunate brethren. This feeling of distinctness appears to have manifested in regard to the adoption of life style and the emulation of behaviour patterns of the dominant caste group. But the simple adoption of life style of the dominant caste group and emulation of their behaviour patterns do not automatically insure the integration of the educated Dalits into the dominant group. Hence, the study has concluded by saying that "...Dalit elite also face alienation as far as their acceptance from upper castes are concerned" (Singh & Sundaram 1987: 178)

Outside Uttar Pradesh which in a way has remained late comer with regard to Dalit politics as is clear from the above discussion, Maharashtra and a few southern states had taken leading role in evolving and crystallising the Dalit leadership. Even in the contemporary period, the Dalits in these states have adopted politics vis-à-vis their organised movements as an effective means to challenge the traditional Hindu belief systems, customs and other socio-cultural practices. Zelliot (1986) for instance, has emphasized the use of political means by the Mahars of Maharashtra, most consistently and unitedly, in their attempt to better their socio-economic condition. She has analysed the process whereby they have rejected the traditional belief systems and adopted new ideologies. She has also examined the motivational and psychological dimensions of social change among the Mahars, and has chronicled the emergence and development of the Buddhist movement. Her study throws more light on the manner in which they have participated in the political process and, in turn, acquired political skills and responses favourable to their assimilation in the broader political culture of the nation.

In the same sequence, another study (Gokhale 1993) presents a social history of political movement of the Mahars in Maharastra. Gokhale argues that the emergence of the Dalits on the political scene in the state is one of the significant events in the history of the twentieth century India. In fact, she has discussed the history of the Mahar movement from the early days of self-reform through the successive stages of Ambedkar's Satyagrah (insistance on truth), his formation of political parties such as the Independent Labour Party (1936) and the Scheduled Castes Federation (1942), and after his death the Republican Party of India and the Dalit Panthers along with their gains and failures. She has also identified the causes of the Mahars' rejection of Hinduism and their conversion to Buddhism. Further, she has described the Dalilt literature movement for the revival of the Dalit culture and the Dalits' assertion for a separate social identity as a unique instance in the Indian cultural history. Gokhale, also gives a passing reference of relationship of Mahar movement in different parts of the country, special that in Uttar Pradesh. But at the same time, she has also pointed out limitations of the Mahar movement which could not develop a rural base and, hence, has failed in ameliorating the Dalit masses. She has presented the picture of fragmentation in the Dalit movement specially the tussle of ego among the RPI leaders in Maharashtra and Uttar Pradesh.

Besides, Murugkar (1991) has attempted to analyse exclusively the Dalit Panthers' movement which had emerged and become quite effective in Maharshtra during the period 1972-1979. Using the framework of the sociology of social movements, she has argued that the Dalit Panthers' movement initiated by a few angry and audacious Dalit youths is closely interlinked with the

Dalit literature movement and it is impossible to think of one without the other. Analysing the factors responsible for the emergence of the movement, its organisational set-up, leadership pattern, its ideology and programmes, and assessing its contributions to the betterment of the Dalit community in Maharashtra, the author has reflected that the Dalit Panthers' movement was born as a spontaneous reaction to the deteriorating socio-political conditions of Dalits during this period. Hence, it lacked a structural ideology. This factor, in her opinion, led later to confusion, resentment, wrong moves and splits in the movement. Ironically, by the time some sort of ideology was formulated in the form of a manifesto, the movement was on the brink of collapse. And in the lack of an ideology, adhocism was the characteristic feature of the action programmes adopted by the Panthers. The author has further depicted that the Dalit Panthers' movement had many parallels with the Black Panthers' movement of USA which had emerged in California with the formation of the 'Black Panthers' Party for 'self- defence' in 1966. But, it is ironical that the author has failed to take note of, Dalit Panthers movement at All India level.

Alongwith the aforesaid studies, few studies have also tried to analyse the Dalit movements, organised specially during the colonial period, at a relatively wider plank. Such studies have focussed on the Dalit movements organised in the wider regions, and have also curiously touched upon such movements organised in other parts of the country. For instance, Omvedt (1994) has focused on the Dalit movements in the colonial period. In the pre-independence period the anti-caste movements had emerged in most of the regions of the country and the Dalit movement was its important component. During this period, the anti-caste movements comprised strong non-Brahmin movements in Maharastra and Tamil Nadu. But as the Dalit movements were exclusively organised in Maharashtra, Punjab (the Ad-Dharm movement), Western U.P (the Adi-Hindu movement), the undivided Bengal (the Namshudra movement), Kerala (Kumaran Assan movement along with Narayan Guru's movement), Tamil Nadu (Adi-Dravida movement), Coastal Andhra (Adi-Andhra movement) and Hyderabad (Adi-Hindu movement). In addition, there were a few unorganised Dalit assertions in such areas as in Mysore and Bihar. Omvedt has classified the Dalit and non-Dalit movements into two broad streams. She has called the first type of movements as anti-systemic movements or 'value-oriented movements' opposed to the norm-oriented movements. According to her, this type of movements challenged and sought to transform the basic structure of the Indian social system -replacing caste system and the accompanying social oppression, economic exploitation and political domination by an equalitarian society. The movements of Gopal Baba Walankar in Maharashtra, Swami Achhutanand in U.P., Ayyankalli in Kerala, Bhagyareddi Verma in Andhra Pradesh and Mangoo Ram in Punjab and Ambedkar first in Maharashtra and later of All India level fall in this category. The second type of movements were reformist in nature. These were represented, within the Dalit movements, by those movements organised specially by the political leaders such as Jagiivan Ram of the Indian National Congress, and the Dalit leaders of the Hindu Mahasaba such as M.C. Rajah and G.A. Gavai and their respective organizations which wanted social reforms within the Hindu Social order rather than the Structural change of it. (Omvedt 1994:10)

Omvedt has further, stated that both the Marxist and pro-Congress nationalist leaders as well as scholars have undermined the importance of the Dalit movements and have treated these as sectarian or caste movements. In her opinion, Dalit movements have been seen as diversionary either from the economic class struggle because of their argument for the necessity of struggling against social oppression or from the needs of a national struggle because of their insistence on putting the needs of the most oppressed or exploited groups first and also treating the Indian elite and not the foreign power or colonial rule as their main enemy. Yet, the most significant aspect of her study is the description of the confrontation between Ambedkar and Gandhi on the issue of caste or caste system raised by the Dalit movements. Further, like any other study of the Dalit movements, this study also includes an in-depth analysis of the leadership of Dr. Ambedkar. The author opines that being its historic leader and the formulator of an enduring ideology of Dalit movement, Babasaheb Ambedkar was the dominating figure of the Dalit movement in the Marathi-speaking region. By the 1930s and 1940s, he came to dominate the all-India Dalit movements as well, though his organisations never attained a strong hegemony outside Maharashtra. Finally, she argues in this study how in spite of the organisational weakness of the Scheduled Castes Federation and its successor the Republican Party of India, it is still 'Ambedkarism' a theoretical framework which dominates the movements in different parts of the country today.

A few studies have also inquired into the roles of the Dalit political leadership. For instance, Sachchidanand (1977) in Bihar has found that the Harijan elites or the elected legislators play positive roles in bringing about social change among the Dalit masses. Similarly during the 1970s, based on his study of 30 Dalits including a few Dalit leaders elected to the Parliament (Aggarwal 1983) found them helpful to the Dalit masses. In his opinion, by getting elected to the legislature, they got some monetary strength to do something for the masses. He cited the example of Jagjivan Ram, the Dalit leader, whose presence in the government at the Centre had helped the Dalits in many ways. In the words of Jagjivan Ram, "Yes, my holding high positions in the government has very definitely helped the cause of the Harijans. I have been instrumental in getting the money for several institutions. I have helped many individuals in their careers. I have pushed many legislations relating to Scheduled Castes through Parliament. I have used my power to help the Harijans as much as possible... they now resist exploitation. It is partly due to political participation" (Aggarwal 1983 270-271). Aggarwal has further stated that practice of untouchability is still rampant in the society and is practised in one form or the other even against these leaders. Even after attaining highest status in political circles, prejudices and stereotypes of the high castes against these leaders have not been removed. He has opined that because of this fact even Jagjivan Ram was forced to say that, "untouchability is deep rooted in the minds of our people and I notice it frequently" (ibid).

But contrary to this, Parvathamma (1989) has found that the Dalit leaders are not only self-centred but also behaving with the Dalit masses almost in the same fashion in which the non-Scheduled Castes have traditionally been behaving with the Scheduled Castes. Hence, she has called them neo-Brahmins who exploit the poor Dalits and treat them as Untouchables. She has also called them classes vis-à-vis Dalit masses. But her argument suffers from the limitation as she has not gone into the genesis of the class or classes of Dalit politicians and also reasons for their such behaviour.

Further, in a more recent study Mendelsohn and Vicziany (1998) have tried to conceive the untouchables or Dalits as a social and political category. They have also examined the historical background that led to such a definition of the untouchables and their position in Indian society today. The authors have discussed the different social identities of Dalits and divided these two broad categories: one, political in character which includes the Adi identities, Harijans, Dalits, etc. And, two, the constitutional or bureaucratic identities like in the Depressed Castes, Exterior Castes and Scheduled Castes (Mendelsohn & Vicziany 1994: 3-4). Then, they have focussed on the rampant phenomenon of atrocities inflicted on the Dalits specially in the country-side and divided these into two categories: first, the traditional violence and, secondly, the ones which flow from the modern form of resistance of the Dalits or those relating to the caste Hindu responses to the changing situation of Untouchables or Dalits. They accept the second category of atrocities as the dominant one in the present time (ibid : 45). The authors' have also traced the history of various Dalit movements organised in different parts of the country, and their successes and failures (ibid : 77-117).

Besides analysing the role played by the policy of compensatory discrimination for the Dalits, Mendelsohn and Vicziany (1998) have also traced its history by stating that, "Seemingly the first case of preference in employment was taken as far back as 1902. Under the influence of non-Brahmin movement of Maharashtra, the Maharaja of Kolhapur issued an order that half of all government positions in his princely state were to be filled in from castes other than Brahmin (Omvedt 1976:127). Theoretically, this opened the public service of the state to the untouchables as well as to other backward castes...The major development of the period is attributable to Ambedkar, who was then serving as a member of Viceroy's Executive Council: in 1943 orders were adopted to reserve places in the central government service in exactly the same proportions (8 a per cent) as had already been adopted in Madras. This quota replaced a policy of general preferment which had been in place since 1934 but which had been officially pronounced in 1942 to be ineffective. In June 1946 the quota of position reserved for the Scheduled Castes was raised to 12½ per cent, roughly proportional to their population in undivided India...This figure was ultimately raised to 15 percent in 1970" (ibid:128-131). They have argued that the compensatory discrimination is much less impressive than it might superficially appear to be. Analysing the turning point in the Dalits politics, they have concluded that Dalits can no longer be taken for granted as a dumb vote bank. Moreover, it is abundantly clear that though the common political task of the Dalits is to add their collective power, yet here can be no single political strategy for Dalits throughout India.

It is, thus, clear from the brief review of the above studies that no study has exclusively and extensively focussed on the nature and dynamics of the contemporary Dalit leadership. Most of the studies are either related to the general condition of the Dalits or to the impact of the government policies on their socio-economic condition. A few have also evaluated the functions of the Dalit organizations, and the successes and failures of the Dalit movements in the past. Therefore, the present study is a modest attempt to analyse the roles played by the contemporary Dalit leadership in giving the shape and direction to the different types of Dalit movements and also the present day polity or the political system and processes. Accepting the leadership as the dominant factor for the success and failure of the contemporary Dalit movements, this study also tries to enquire into the causes of dearth of the committed Dalit leadership, the nature and types of its demands and the problems faced by it in achieving the desired goals for the Dalit masses.

Rationale of the Study

The entire movement for the country's freedom from the colonial rule and the parallel movements for social transformation had the futuristic orientation in the nascent body politics in which hopes and aspirations of the people in India had been aroused and promises made to lay down the foundation of a modern democratic and egalitarian society. But with the political independence of the country, each segment in the national body politics desired to ensure for itself a path of opportunity for its socio-economic development through a genuine share in the national resources including wealth and power. The parliamentary democracy and the Constitution of free India whose basic principles included democracy, freedom of individual and more importantly the universal franchise gave rights to the erstwhile deprived sections of population namely Dalits and Tribals to intervene in the state agenda obliquely. But the political participation during the last two and half decades has placed this historically disadvantaged and marginalized strata specially the Dalits at the centre stage of the political institutions and governance at all levels. Their desire for greater voice in formulation of public policy and participation in the political process which can help in implementing the Dalit agenda has multiplied. The significant change in Dalit politics in the different parts of India has brought them to the stage wherein they can no longer be taken for granted as a dumb vote - bank.

Keeping the above mentioned fact in mind, the present study is significant in terms of analysing various processes like the rapid politicisation of the Dalits, nature and dynamics of organization, of Dalit leadership, its articulated demands and its allies, mobilization pattern and so on so forth. The impact of these processes on consolidation of democracy and the integration of Dalit leadership in it becomes an important aspect of the present study specially in the light of the doubt raised by Babasaheb Ambedkar in the Constituent Assembly. After working on the draft Constitution for nearly three years, Babasaheb presented it in the Parliament on November 25, 1949 with the caution, "On the 26th of January 1950, we are going to enter into a life of contradictions. In politics we will have equality and in social and economic life we will have inequality. In politics we will be recognizing the principle of one man one vote, one vote one value. In our social and economic life, we shall, by reason of our social and economic structure, continue to deny the principle of one man one value. How long shall we continue to deny equality in our social and economic life ? If we continue to deny it for the long, we will do so only by putting our political democracy in peril. We must remove this contradiction at the earliest possible moment or else those who suffer from inequality will blow up the structure of political democracy which this Assembly has so laboriously built up" (Khairmode 1998:307). Whether this doubt still exists or has it been proved otherwise ? The analysis done in the present study may help us in formulating new policies and programmes for this deprived sections of the society in a more vigorous way and also at a faster pace. Moreover, the present analysis may also be of some use in gearing up the strategy (ies) of the Dalit leadership vis-à-vis Dalit politics for getting the new strategies to be more effective for the Dalits' proper and full integration in the mainstream society and polity.

The findings of this study may contribute, on one hand, to understand the furtherance of ideology and mission of Dr. Ambedkar for establishing a united Dalit front. which, in turn, may pressurize the state for evolving an egalitarian and democratic society based on equality, liberty and fraternity. And on the other hand, these findings may generate some new insights in the realm of understanding of nature and dynamics of the Dalit leadership, which time and again is involved in some type of protest or the other. In this protest, lot of human energy and public resources are wasted which could be channelled for the betterment of the society in general and Dalits in particular. Moreover, with such insight we may also be able to differentiate between Dalit leaders actually concerned with Dalit upliftment and those who are merely power-brokers and who want to use these protests for their own end. Finally, it may perhaps inspire the Dalit leadership to act as a bridge between the Dalit community as a whole and the state in the formulation and proper implementation of more effective policies for welfare and development of the former.

References

Aggarwal, P.C., 1983, *Halfway to Equality*, Manohar Publications, New Delhi.

Ambedkar, B.R., 1987, Philosophy of Hinduismin Dr, Babasaheb Ambedkar: *Writings and Speeches, Vol. 3,* Education Department, Government of Maharashtra, Bombay.

______,1989, Untouchables or the Children of India's Ghetto and Other essay, in Dr. Babasaheb Ambedkar: *Writings and Speeches Vol. 5,* Education Department, Government of Maharashtra, Bombay.

______, 1991, What Congress and Gandhi have done to the Untouchables, Mr. Gandhi and the Emancipation of Untouchables, in Dr. Babasaheb Ambedkar: *Writings and Speeches, Vol.9,* Education Department, Government of Maharashtra, Bombay.

Bailey, F.G., 1957, *Caste and the Economic Frontier,* Manchester University Press, Manchester

Bhatt, G.S., 1954 & 1971, "The Chamars of Lucknow", *Eastern Anthropologist, VIII,* Sep.

Gokhale, J., 1993, *From Concessions to Confrontation: The Politics of an Indian Untouchable Community,* Popular Prakashan, Bombay.

Joshi, Barbara. R., 1982, *Democracy in Search of Equality: Untouchable Politics and Indian Social Change,* Hindustan Publishing Corporation, Delhi.

Juergensmeyer, Mark, 1982, *Religion as Social Vision: The Movement against Untouchability in 20th Century Punjab*, University of California Press, Barkeley.

Kumar, Vijay, 1989, *Scheduled Caste Panchayat Pradhans: A Study of Western Uttar Pradesh*, Ajanta Publications, New Delhi.

Lynch, O.M., 1974, *The Politics of Untouchability: Social Mobility and Social Change in a City of India*, National Publishing House, New Delhi.

Mendelshon Oliver & Marika Vicziany, 1998, *The Untouchables: Subordination, Poverty and the State in Modern India*, Cambridge University Press, New Delhi.

Murugkar, Lata, 1991, *Dalit Panthers Movement in Maharashtra: A Sociological Appraisal*, Popular Prakashan, Bombay.

Omvedt, Gail, 1994, *Dalit and the Democratic Revolution: Dr. Ambedkar and the Dalit Movement in Colonial India*, Sage Publications, New Delhi.

Parvathamma, C., 1989, *Scheduled Castes at the Cross Roads*, Ashish Publishing House, New Delhi.

Ram, Nandu, 1995, *Beyond Ambedkar: Essays on Dalits in India*, Har-Anand Publications, New Delhi.

Sacchidananda, 1977, *The Harijan Elite*, Thompson Press, Faridabad.

S.S. Singh and S. Sundaram, 1978, *Emerging Harijan Elite: A Study of their Identity*, Uppal Publishing House, New Delhi.

Zelliot, E., 1986, Learning the Use of Political Means: The Mahars of Maharashtra in Rajni Kothari (ed.) *Caste in Indian Politics*, Orient Longman, New Delhi.

1

Research Design

As stated in the introductory chapter, the Dalits in the country as well as in a state like Uttar Pradesh (U.P.) have emerged as a political force to reckon with. But the precise nature and dynamics of Dalit leadership cannot be empirically examined at the macro level, be it the entire country or even in the largest state of the country like Uttar Pradesh. Since the present study is located in U.P., we have selected certain areas or regions for the purpose of data collection. But before we go into elucidating the reasons for selecting these areas and the methods through which the selection has been made and the data collected and analysed, it is pertinent here to explain a few terms and concepts which have been used time and again in the present study.

Conceptual Explanations

Leadership. A leader is that individual in the group who performs special tasks, makes suggestions, gives orders to others and shows them the Way. He/she also appears before others as an ideal and is respected by them. His/her suggestions and orders are unquestionably accepted and implemented by others. Further, leader is always present at the helm of the affairs in the society. He/she generally acts within the established norms and sometimes, if necessary, interprets them afresh by giving a new vitality. On the contrary, when an established order breaks or the norms get shambled, leader not only organises the forces of dissatisfaction but also gives them unity and direction for causing immediate rupture to the order or the norms. Some social scientists like Bogardus (1934), Schmidt (1933), etc. have called the relation between leaders and their followers the most important of all types of relationships in the society. It is more so because leadership in some degree and form is present whenever men assemble.

A few sociologists also have attempted to define leadership.

For instance, MacIver and Page have defined leadership as, "the capacity to persuade or to direct men (and women) that comes from personal qualities apart from office" (MacIver & Page1986:146). Analysing the concept of 'personal leadership' and 'charismatic leadership' as given by Weber, they further state, "personal leadership depends on the prowess, reputations, skill, oratory, or other attributes of the leaders" (ibid : 148). A personal leader may be on the side of the established order, or he/she may be opposed to it, seeking to create a new type of order. He/she may stand for a definite policy or set of principles or may be an opportunist. He/she may be blindly followed, or it may depend on his/her power to rally the people under his/her banner of some cause. Moreover, he/she may be little more than the delegate or simply the mouthpiece of some interest group.

Weber, on his part, has defined the charismatic leadership. He has used the Greek word, charisma meaning a special gift or power restricted to a select few. He has designated that quality on certain leaders whose authority is based on the popular conviction that they are divinely inspired and directed in their public undertakings (Weber 1958). Weber has also distinguished the power of the office holder, the 'rational' authority that permeates the large - scale bureaucracies of the modern world, from the charismatic leadership. He opines that charismatic leaders in times of psychic, physical, economic, ethical, religious, political distress, etc. have been neither office holders nor incumbents of an occupation in the present sense of the word, i.e. men who have acquired expert knowledge and who serve for remuneration (ibid). Further, the crisis of any sorts and the historical opportunity bring charismatic leadership to the fore. It is also argued that these leaders function in dual capacity with respect to the established norms and values of their societies. They may lead in the name of traditional values and customs, thereby serving to perpetuate and strengthen parts of the socio-cultural heritage. But they may also use their power of leadership to destroy or vastly alter the mores and institutional structure of their time.

The charismatic leadership, however, is temporary and remains valid till the time the leader is alive. At times if the qualities of the charismatic leader fail, it is likely that his leadership would disappear. Moreover, as power is located in the personal qualities of one individual, he becomes a threat to the routine of the established order. If the charismatic leader has to continue, the continuation of his leadership is to be regulated through evolving certain well accepted mechanism which, of course, is a difficult task. Therefore, the rational legal leadership is the answer for this uncertainty as it institutionalises not a person but an office with power. According to MacIver and Page, leadership is also very important feature of every association. In their own words, "An association is likely to be formed whenever people recognize a like, complementary, or common interest sufficiently enduring and sufficiently distinct to be capable of more effective promotion through collective action, provided their differences outside the field of this interest are not so strong as to prevent the partial agreement involved in its formation" (MacIver and Page op. cit: 437).

It is the leadership which tries to overcome the prejudices, inertias, and problems of ways and means within an association if it has to function smoothly. The task of the leadership in the early stage is to create or to intensify a consciousness among the people of the need for the new organization. In other words, its task is to generate awareness of the interest around which the organisation is formed, to instil confidence in the promoters and to harness the sense of need to the practical necessities of financial or other co-operation on the part of the members (ibid: 438). The task of leadership differs with the nature of interest around which an organization is formed. Moreover, the emergence and development of an appropriate leadership for a particular organization is a difficult task as it depends on the type of interests to be organized. Where economic interests are main consideration as in the business corporations or the labour unions, a strong competitive struggle for leadership is likely to take place. But where the common interests are object of an organization, other difficulties arise which may prove to be too strong for the sincere service of the leader to the common cause. On the basis of life histories of some political leaders and labour leaders, Mitchels (1911) and many other have concluded that these leaders tend to retain power for their own sake. Another obstacle to the effective leadership of an organization based an idealistic type of common interests is that control tends to fall into the hands of narrow-minded enthusiasts who, because of their zeal, are ready to undertake the onerous task of leadership while they are often least conscious of its problems.

In the political sphere, it is generally observed that the heavy responsibilities and often required personal sacrifices of leadership prove to be deterrent to some qualified and deserving candidates. This process leaves the field more free for those who seek power for self-aggrandisement or for personal gain (ibid: 440).

The Dalit Leadership

Before we analyse the concept of Dalit leadership, it is necessary to briefly look at the meaning of the term Dalit. The term Dalit has been used in this study exclusively for the ex-untouchable or the Scheduled Castes. According to Molesworth's Marathi English Dictionary of 1831, the term Dalit is a Marathi word which means 'ground' or 'broken' or 'reduced to pieces'. But the word was popularised by the Dalit Panthers' Movement which had emerged in the early 1970s in Bombay, Maharashtra. The Panthers tried to propound a class definition of the term Dalit which included "members of Scheduled Castes and Tribes, neo-Buddhists, the working people, the landless and poor peasants, economically and in the name of religion" (Murugkar 1991:237). But over the years, this term has been used by so-called untouchables for themselves as a symbol of assertion. Even in the academics, the word is used for them. In the words of Ram (1995:18), "But contrary to a heuristic understanding, the term Dalit is currently used for and by untouchable castes all over the country. Even social scientists have started referring to the Dalits and untouchables or the Scheduled Castes interchangeably". But it is interesting to mention here that all the Untouchables or the Scheduled castes do not use this term for them. It is only the educated and socially and politically conscious Scheduled Castes living specially in the urban areas who call themselves Dalits. They also try to popularise this term through their writings and speeches.

The Dalit leadership has been a continuous source of inspiration for the Dalit masses in fighting against the cumulative dominance of the upper castes. It is very closely linked with to their movement and its relationship with organizational development is indisputable. The conceptualisation of Dalit leadership emerges from the premise of the birth of a leader. We have defined a Dalit leader as one who has taken birth in the Dalit community and has continuously been taking part in their struggles. Therefore, we have excluded the leaders of the upper and backward castes who have worked for the upliftment of Dalits. This premise will also give the difference between the Dalit leadership and the general leadership. Putting somewhat in different context, Ram (1995) eloquently portrays the difference between the contextual location of great persons from general masses and from the communities having stigmatised of caste or ethnic identities. We have utilized his portrayal here to substantiate our point about the difference between the general and the Dalit leadership. He further opines, "It is evident from the life history of all great persons of the modern times that most of them were born in families with relatively better socio-economic background, high achieving parentage, and proper and sound educational training. They had also enjoyed the profound state-patronage and a high degree of uncritical appreciation from their followers if not initially then at least after achieving their imminence or greatness. Their imminence or greatness also relies on the tacit support from the *status quoism* ... Contrary to this, quite a few great persons have hailed from families with moderate or even below moderate socio-economic background and from castes or communities labelled with stigmatised caste or ethnic identities. These persons have reached to the highest level of achievement, translated scientifically their ideas into concrete action, and enjoyed the maximum prestige in the social esteem and the sincerest reverence of the people of different walks of life. Such persons are qualified to be unconditionally regarded great persons, though they may not enjoy supports from the elite or upper classes and from the *status quoist* forces. Nevertheless, greatness of such persons is indeed more genuine than that of great persons of the first type" (Ram 1995:47).

Therefore, on the basis of above defined qualities and socio-political background of the great men of the second type we can construct an ideal type' of Dalit leadership to use the phrase of Max Weber for the 'ideal type' personality (1958). The Dalit leadership can broadly be divided into two major categories: socio-religious and political. However, these two categories are not mutually exclusive and can overlap each other. Also, one type of leadership can give birth to another type though the latter type may not easily replace the former type.

The Socio-religious Dalit Leadership

The socio-religious Dalit leadership has a long history and

its emergence can be traced in the adherence to the teachings of the Dalit saints like Kabir, Raidas or Ravidas, Chokhamela and others of the Bhakti tradition. These saints raised fundamental issue of equality of humanity and preached the equal treatment to be accorded to every individual, as each one is the creation of the same God. They also focussed on the meaninglessness of the caste system. The devotional religion of the Bhakti, propounded by such saints or *gurus*, had enjoyed wide spread popularity in the north India between thirteenth and seventeenth centuries. At the end of the nineteenth century also, the Untouchable migrants in the urban areas in U.P. established the different Bhakti sects. Since the turn of that century onward, many Untouchables in the towns began to call themselves Bhagats, a term denoted by the followers of the Bhakti cults, though they were not ascetic (Gooptu1993: 278). In north India, the Arya Samaj also helped Dalits in the development of the socio-religious leadership among them. Many literate Dalits joined the Arya Samaj during 1910, as it was promising to facilitate the social uplift of the lower castes by setting up schools for them. It also gave them hope of eliminating caste divisions and allowed Untouchables to enter the Hindu caste hierarchy through purification or *shudhi* (ibid: 286). Dalits as members of the Samaj, after getting educated, became *Pracharaks* and started preaching Dalits in different localities which infused in them a sense of leadership. In south, the leaders of Sri Narayanguru Dharam Paripalan Yogam (SNDP) movement sowed the seeds of socio-religious Dalit leadership. Sri Narayanguru who organised his movement in 1896 was the most prominent religious leader in Kerala. However, in due course his movement became a caste movement of the Ezhavas, his followers (Mathew 1985: 23). The Dalits organized and mobilized themselves under the Gurus, the religious preachers, of various movements in the past, and their different beliefs or ideologies were termed as *panths* (sects) and all these movements were called sectarian movements.

These *panths* or sects had certain unique symbols which gave the Dalits a new life-style. The leaders of these *panths* tried to reform the Dalit society from within with the help of religious and cultural traits. They raised the issues like changing the food habits of the Dalits and also giving up traditional occupations which were polluting in nature. The *Bhandaras* (inter-dining) were organised among the followers of these sects which were aimed at dilution of inter-caste differences. *Bhajans* (religious prayers) were also chanted in the *Maths* or temples constructed after the names of these saints. Thus, creating the cultural symbols like *Bhajans, Bhandaras, Maths,* etc. was another means of mobilisation of the Dalits by these religious leaders. The main objective of all these activities was to establish and promote what may be called in Durkheimian terminology the 'mechanical' 'solidarity' among the Dalits who belonged to the same sects.

However, such socio-religious Dalit leadership was not interested in asserting the economic and political rights of the Dalits and as such did not contribute to the development of a distinct political identity among them. The socio-religious Dalit leadership was, therefore, gradually replaced by the political leadership. More so, this happened with the emergence of the modern polity and democratic mobilisation in the country during the last quarter of the nineteenth century. Though this type of leadership was successful in organizing the Dalits on many fronts, their leaders also largely failed to assert the economic and political rights of the Dalits during this period. It has rightly been suggested that, "The socio-religious Dalit leaders of the Bhakti movement argued against caste system, ideology, social evils and corrupted form of Hinduism. They could not be successful in transforming the society, mainly because the movement fostered equality only in the religious sphere and not in secular. The movement offered no new alternative programme of social and economic organization of Indian society. Its exponents appealed equality in emotional songs but they could not argue it out on rational principles. The movement never built up organisation which could carry out any positive social programme; even if they had one, at best they produced individual not collective opposition to the status quo (Gupta 1985:148).

The Dalit Political Leadership

This type of leadership emerged during the late nineteenth century, as mentioned above. The main reason for the emergence of this type of leadership was the socio-economic and political changes that had occurred in Indian society during this period specially after the British introduced far reaching changes in every walks of life. The introduction of separate electorate for different communities was one of the most important factors which gave the momentum for its development.

The Dalit political leadership can be divided into two types: the dependent and independent. The first type of leadership has never played a vanguard role in amelioration of the Dalits. The leaders of this type have ever remained subordinated to the dominant socio-political forces represented by the leaders drawn from the upper strata of the society. In fact, it is the latter who have played and continue to play even today apparently the leading roles for the betterment of the Dalits. The Dalit leaders align with them and try to bring some change in the socio-economic condition of the Dalits and also in the Hindu society, though within the parameters of the Hindu social order. For any political, economic and social demands for the Dalits, these leaders always depend on their political/organizational bosses. They have also very little say in framing of the ideology, and the policy and programmes of these political parties for the upliftment of the Dalits. In other words, this type of Dalit leaders speak the language of the respective political party of which they are members. The most glaring examples of this type of leaders can be given of Jagjivan Ram who had aligned with the Indian National Congress and with Mahatma Gandhi for the cause of the Dalits; and of G.A. Gavai who had aligned with the Hindu Mahasabha. In recent times, Ram Vilas Paswan, B.P. Maurya, Buta Singh and others represent the stream of the dependent political leadership among the Dalits.

Contrarily, the independent political leadership among the Dalits has always played the vanguard role in taking up the issues of the Dalits. Such Dalit leaders have never aligned with the dominant socio-political forces. Although the leaders of this type have aligned from time to time with the political forces of the same nature or of the similar ideology as well as policies and programmes, these leaders have always kept the reigns of their respective movements and organizations in their own hand and have remained their own political masters. Moreover, for political mobilisation of the Dalit masses these leaders set the agenda on their own with their self created symbols. Even the style of articulation and persuasion of demands of the Dalits by the leaders of this type differ from that of the socio-religious type of leadership. In fact, it believes in direct action and confrontation with the *status-quoit* forces. These leaders also believe that the rights given to the

Dalits are not a concession but their due share in the existing resources in the country.

The ultimate goal of this type of Dalit leadership has been to bring about social transformation rather than a cosmetic change within the society. The Dalit leaders of this type are convinced that the Dalits need the most this social transformation as they are the worst suffer of the existing system. Hence, only they can bring the social transformation. This is quite clear from Ambedkar's position in 1927 (Ambedkar 1994) and also of the contemporary Dalit leadership of this type. In the past specially in the last decades of the nineteenth and in beginning of the twentieth century, this type of leadership attacked the exploitative system through more secular means or strategies. Though the Dalit leaders of this era started with the social reforms within the Dalit society, they incorporated the economic and political demands of the Dalits as the Dalit leadership matured. The leadership of Gopal Baba Walankar, Babasaheb Ambedkar, the Republican Party of India and Dalit Panthers in Maharashtra and of Swami Achhutanand, the Republican Party of India (U.P. branch) and now the Bahujan Samaj Party fall under this category. But now-a-days, the independent Dalit political leadership has completely shifted its agenda from social reform to achieving political power.

Political Mobilization

As the politics is a mass based phenomenon, the articulation and support organization is to be done through the institutions and cultural idioms lived with by the masses. Since caste is the most pervasive institution of Indian society particularly of the Hindus who form the largest majority, they can easily be and have always been mobilized on the caste line. Although the constitutional system explicitly discourages the practice of caste, the party politics has been dominated by caste mobilisation of the various kinds. According to Rudolph and Rudolph (1987:24), there are three types of political mobilisation by which we can understand the role played by caste in the Indian politics. These are vertical, horizontal and differential mobilization. Explaining vertical mobilization, they state that this is a process in which traditional notables marshal political support. This is possible in Indian society (barring the minorities who ideologically deny the existence of caste among them) because it is organized and integrated along the caste line. In India, legitimacy of the traditional authority still survives. Due to their traditional authority, the notables are able to garner the support of their dependents or the socially inferior groups in the traditional manner wherein the local kings rather former kings or land lords used to protect and promote the interests of their subjects and, in return, gained loyalty and deference of the latter. Hence, vertical mobilisation still remains a viable strategy for the dominant castes and classes until the dependents, tenants and clients become sufficiently politicised to be mobilised through the ideological appeals to fulfil their class or community interests and sentiments. Rudolph and Rudolph further say that the traditional elite in India were characteristically the leaders of the locally dominant castes. They responded to the representative government and popular politics by mobilizing the socially inferior castes in the past and they continue to do so in certain ways even today (ibid: 25).

Further, horizontal mobilisation, in the opinion of Rudolph and Rudolph, "involves the marshalling of popular political support by class or community leaders and their specialized organization. Ignoring the leaders and members of natural associations or little platoons, they make direct appeals to class or communities. Horizontal mobilisation of solidarities among equal class or community introduces a new pattern of cleavage by challenging the vertical solidarities and structures of traditional societies"(ibid:25). The horizontal mobilisation also clearly illustrates how the cultural and structural transformation of a traditional institution contributes to the political modernization and democracy, including political participation and representation ot the people (ibid: 28).

In India, the core structure for the purpose of horizontal mobilisation has been a transformed version of caste, although class or socio-economic status too has played a part and is increasingly doing so. The caste associations termed by Rudolph and Rudolph as para-communities clearly bring out the factors responsible for horizontal mobilization. As far as leadership in these caste associations is concerned, it has also changed from the traditional hereditary leadership to that based on the achieved qualities. In the words of Rudolph and Rudolph, "Leadership in the caste associations is no longer in the hands of those qualified by heredity- the senior or more able members of the lineage, which traditionally supplied *jati* leadership. The availability of association leaders is conditioned by their ability to articulate and represent the purposes of the caste association, and for this purpose they must be literate in the ways of modern administration and the new democratic politics. Men whose educational and occupational backgrounds assure these skills helped from caste associations, and the more "democratic" of them occupy leadership positions. The new leaders stand in a more accountable and responsible relationship to their followers because their authority depends to a great extent on their capacity to represent and make good the association's purpose" (ibid:34).

Finally, the differential mobilisation involves marshalling of direct and indirect political support by political parties (and other integrative structures) from viable, but internally differentiated, communities through parallel appeals to ideology, sentiments and interests. The agent of mobilisation in this case is the political party rather than the local notable or community association, and its strategies of mobilisation also vary (ibid: 26). The factors of selection of a candidate differ in various situations. Parties may appeal to voters directly as individual or indirectly through the organized groups or parties to which they belong. The direct appeals to the individual voters may stress on ideology or issues, on the one hand, and on the community identification through caste on the other. These appeals may be contradictory or complementary. The size of the constituency and the number, homogeneity and cohesiveness of its community components decide the conflict and smoothness of both types of appeals. In constituencies in which one caste or community is numerically predominant or socially dominant, all parties, regardless of ideological, cultural or interest orientation are more likely to choose their candidates from such caste or community for contesting elections (ibid: 27). This has virtually been happening also along all these years in the electoral politics in India. Thus, the analysis of differential mobilisation suggests how caste plays an effective role in politics which depends on both external factors- its historical, social and political environment, and on internal factors- the caste's readiness and capacity for common consciousness, mobilisation and organization. The caste as an institution as well as a system has changed its character over time and so does the environment with which it interacts. The "entry" of any particular caste into the political arena and the strategies it pursues for fulfilling the interests of its members are affected by the circumstances it confronts in the environment, and also by its inner life and state of development (ibid: 28).

Kothari also has examined the impact of caste in the process of political mobilisation in India. He has identified three aspects which facilitate the process. The first is what may be called the secular aspect. This gives birth to factionalism and caste cleavages. A sub-feature of it is the alignments and realignments among the various strata and the incessant striving for ascendancy in caste councils and inter-caste councils in the villages. Also, the territorial distances no longer restrain the widening of the caste base, and there is an extension of the endogamous frontier (Kothari 1986: 8). Hence, the distinctive hierarchical relationships in the caste system and special type of mobility and differentiation have proved instrumental in facilitating political identities and secular associational urges among the people.

The second aspect of caste that is helpful in political mobilisation of masses is the integrative one provided by the *varna* frame. This means that by passing the *Jati* frame people grade themselves according to the four-fold division specially of the Hindu social system. The *varna* frame of reference represents a 'scale of value' which provides both a spur to integrative behavioural patterns and a symbol of competition that enables the aspiring and mobile groups to lay claim to high status (ibid: 11). This also means that the varnas do provide symbols of high status and enable the low-placed castes to widely affirm and lay their claim to high status. The third and final aspect of caste helpful in the process of mobilisation is the caste consciousness. Since the caste inherently exists in the minds of people, it politically mobilizes them in favour of the candidates belonging to their own caste. Kothari further argues that the process of mobilisation on the basis of caste occurs in a sequence of three stages. The first stage is characterized by the struggle among the castes for economic and political power. In his own words, "The struggle for power and for benefits (in the past) was at first limited to the entrenched castes in the social hierarchy... The domination of an entrenched caste thus produced a new response in the form of an ascendant caste, one that was not satisfied to simply function in the contest of inter-dependence and complementarity in the social sphere that characterized the social and economic system for so long. The caste structure thus got polarized. And gave rise to a bilateral structure of caste politics, very often between two castes or sub-castes" (ibid : 14).

This led to the second stage in which power striving and demands for benefits exceeded the availability of resources. In the beginning of this stage, the lower castes were left aloof and only upper castes dominated in the political arena. "All of this, however, was limited to the leading two or three castes-well-to-do, educated, and generally upper castes. The lower castes were still found to be in dependent relationship with the entrenched and the dominant castes" (ibid: 16). This has also led in the recent time to a process of competition between the entrenched castes and the more articulate sections of the society. The inter-caste competition between the entrenched caste and the ascendant caste is now supplemented by intra-caste competition and the process of political politicisation. Mobilisation of further support for each of the contending factions has given rise to a process of co-option from the other castes that till recently were kept out of the power system. It may, however, be said that during the second stage itself there started a process of mobilisation of the lower castes into politics for the purpose of adding to the factionalised support base of the rival leaders (ibid: 16). The final stage is that of weakening of the older institutions and induction of a new set of political values. The structure of particularistic loyalties gets overlaid by a more sophisticated system of social and political participation with the cross-cutting allegiances, a greater degree of awareness of individual's self-interest, and forms of involvement and alienation.

But it is interesting to mention here that in the more recent years all the above mentioned processes of political mobilisation have become topsy-turvy especially due to criminalisation of politics. There is now strong nexus between politics and crime in which not only politicians protect the criminals but even criminals support the politicians and they themselves become politicians as well. In many cases, people muster around the criminals turned politicians out of fear - psychosis and in several cases their fears are the genuine ones. Incidentally the number of such politicians has grown faster in the recent years. Hence, the well - argued processes of political mobilisation need to be looked at a fresh. Perhaps, there is need of adding one more dimension to the above mentioned processes of political mobilization, though it may not be easier to conceptualise such dimension at this stage.

Universe and the Sample

The present study does not intend to examine nature and dynamics of the Dalit leadership consisting of those who have taken lead in different fields like bureaucracy, Dalit literature, academics, etc. One may easily find a number of permutations and combinations in Dalit leadership increasing day by day in the contemporary Indian society in which more and more Dalit bureaucrats join politics after their retirement from the government jobs. Also, more and more educated and professional Dalits specially lawyers and doctors, like such people from the non-Dalits, participate actively in the political process and try to make in it a space for them selves for the future. There are only few Dalit leaders who have taken up politics as a vocation in the Weberarian sense (1958). Though it would be wrong to argue that there exists an exclusive category of Dalit political leadership, yet for the purpose of the present study we have concentrated on the Dalit political leadership consisting of those who have taken up politics or political activities either full-time or part-time vocation.

More precisely, in the second part of the book, the study has covered the Dalit political leadership found at different levels - block and district levels wherein a few blocks and districts have been selected from eastern, western and central regions of Uttar Pradesh. Then, the sample of the respondents for the purpose of data collection has been drawn both from the elected and non-elected Dalit leaders to make it more representative and comparable. A number of elected and nominated representatives like MPs, MLCs, MLAs, members of the block and village level statutory organizations and other Dalit leaders from certain districts from the three regions of the state have been selected for the purpose of this study. Initially, it was thought of interviewing 250 elected and non-elected leaders from all the three regions of the state for the purpose of data collection. But due to preoccupations of many of the Dalit leaders, only 185 such leaders could be contacted and the relevant data were extracted from them. The categories of Dalit leaders selected in the sample is given in the following table.

TABLE 2.1
Categories of Dalit Leaders Selected in the Sample

Sl. No.	*Category of Dalit Leaders*	*Number of Leaders*	*Percentage*
1.	Full-time Activists	19	10.27
2.	Former Members with Party Posts	27	14.59
3.	Members having District Level Party Posts	24	12.97
4.	Members Having State Level Party Posts	41	22.16
5.	Members of Village Panchayat	19	10.27
6.	Ex-Members of Legislative Assembly	20	10.81
7.	Members of Legislative Assembly	28	15.13
8.	Ex-Members of Lok Sabha	2	1.08
9.	Member of Lok Sabha	5	
10.	Member of Rajya Sabha	2	1.08
	Total	185	100.00

For the purpose of locale of the study, we have selected the state of Uttar Pradesh (U.P.), as stated earlier, which is not only the most populous state but also has the largest population of Dalits in the country. By extension, U.P. also has the largest number of Dalit and non-Dalit political representatives both at the state and central levels. Another reason for locating this study in U.P. is the long history of socio-political consciousness of the people of the state and their political contributions at the state and national levels both in the pre and post independent periods. Even the Dalit leadership in the state has remained quite active before and after independence. Today, it has become the centre of Dalit politics especially after emergence of the Bahaujan Samaj Party.

It is also worth mentioning here the reasons for selecting the three specific regions namely eastern, central and western U.P., as stated earlier, for the present study. The rational for selecting the eastern region is that, one, here population pressure on land is the highest in comparison to the other parts of the state. Secondly, the upper caste domination in this region is also very prominent as they possess maximum cultivable land, dominate in bureaucracy and of course in politics. Thirdly, the BSP has been able to garner substantial support from the Dalits this region. The western region is chosen because the first Dalit movement in the state namely the Jatav movement arose in this region during the 1940s. This movement first arose here as a social reform movement among the specially the Jatavs Dalits but changed to political one as the time passed by. They also had political parties like the Scheduled Castes Federation and the Republican Party of India, Agra branch. They had contested elections at various levels. But after the 1970s this movement phased out and the BSP still has not been successful in mobilizing Dalits of this region to a satisfactory level. Finally, the central region has been selected because Dalits here constitute the maximum (25%) percentage of the total Dalit population in the state. This region is also the seat of power as the capital of the state is located in this region.

Sources of Data

The present study is based on both the primary and secondary sources ot data. The primary data have been collected from the respondents with the help of an interview - schedule consisting of both structured and unstructured questions related to social composition, roles, nature and dynamics of the Dalit leadership in the state. The Dalit leaders drawn from all the regions have been interviewed, as far as possible, in their respective three regions. Yet, in many cases they were contacted and interviewed at the places like block and district headquarters, state and national capitals where they had gone for attending meetings or for some other works or for attending the Assembly or Parliament session. Similarly, the secondary sources of data consist of official records including reports of various commissions and committees on social composition and roles of the Dalit leaders. More specifically, the relevant informations have been collected from the various government departments and other organizations in the state.

Besides, a number of local, state and national level newspapers and magazines published both in Hindi and English, like Swatantra Bharat, Dainik Jagaran, Aaj, Amar Ujala, Navjivan, National Herald, The Pioneer, The Times of India, Hindustan Times, Frontline, India Today, etc. widely covering the news about various activities of the Dalit leadership have also been consulted. In addition, posters, pamphlets, booklets and memoranda prepared and published by the Dalit leaders, their magazines, periodicals, etc. have been used extensively for the purpose of extracting the relevant data. A number of small newspapers and magazines by the Dalit authors too have served the source of information. Finally, the relevant Dalit literature written by the Dalit scholars and ideologues have also been looked into for the purpose of providing analytical support for the data collected from both the primary and secondary sources.

References

Ambedkar, B.R., 1994, "Speech at Mahad (1927)" in *Status od Dalits*, Lal Bahadur Shastri Academy of Administration, Mussoorie.

Bogardus, E.S., 1934, *Leaders and Leadership*, Appleton, New York.

Gupta, S.K., 1985, *The Scheduled Castes in Modern Indian Politics: Their Emergence as a Political Power*, Munshiram Manoharlal, New Delhi.

Kothari, Rajni, (ed.) *1986, Caste in Indian Politics*, Orient Longman, New Delhi.

Mathew Joseph 1985 *Ideology Protest and Social Mobility: Case Study of Mahars and Pulays*, Inter-India Publications, New Delhi.

Michel, Robert (1911), 1959, *Political Parties: A Sociological study of the oligarchical tendencies of Modern Democracy*, Dover, New York.

Murugkar, Lata, 1991, *Dalit Panthers Movement in Maharashtra: A Sociological Appraisal*, Popular Prakashan, Bombay.

MacIver, R.M., and C.H. Page, 1986, *Society: an Introductory Analysis*, Macmillan India Limited, New Delhi.

Ram, Nandu, 1995, *Beyond Ambedkar: Essays on Dalits in India*, Har- Anand Publications, New Delhi.

Rudolph L.I., and S.H., Rudolph, 1987, *The Modernity of Tradition: Political Development in India*, Orient Longman, Delhi.

Schimidt, R., 1933, Leadership, Encyclopaedia of Social Sciences, Vol. IX, Macmillan, New York.

Weber, Max, 1958, *From Max Weber: Essays in Sociology* (Tr. and ed.) by Hans Gerth and C. Wright Mills, Oxford University Press, New York.

2

Socio-Historical Profile of Dalit Leadership in India and the Role of Ambedkar

Before locating the nature and dynamics of Dalit leadership in Uttar Pradesh as stated in the introductory, chapter at the outset we will look into the nature and dynamics of Dalit ledership from a historical perspective in this chapter. We have explored the historical material to probe into the fact, whether there was any type of Dalit leadership before the advent of Ambedkar. If it was there what was its style of functioning and what crises they forced in ameliorating the wretched conditions of the Dalits. In the second part of this chapter we have analysed the overpowering presence of Ambedkar's leadership for uplifting the Dalits at the grass-roots. We have analysed the nature of Ambedkar's leadership in terms of demands it has put to the British government and leaders of Indian National Congress and later on to the leaders of independent India.

An autonomous Dalit leadership in India has always been perceived as synonymous to the leadership of Babasahab Dr. B.R. Ambedekar. Though it is a well known fact that Ambedker was the first Dalit leader who had an all India following, the autonomous Dalit leadership of several varieties existed much before he came on the horizon of the Dalit liberation. Such leadership had existed in different parts of the country. For instances Dalits had organized demonstration in Poona and Madras against the functioning of the National Congress way back in 1895 and had even burnt its effigy (Ambedkar 1990:17). But they had carried out more organized movements for achieving their goals of equality, self-respect, self-right etc. in different parts of the country since the 1920's onwards. The political mobilization of the Dalits on the national scene can also be traced to the late 1920s when the British government initiated a series of Round Table Conferences to provide political safeguards and representation to various minority communities including the Depressed Classes (Dalit) as they were known by that time (Oommen 1990:23). Therefore, the 1920's can be taken as the culmination point for analyzing the nature, social composition and crisis the of the Dalit leadership in different parts of the country. Nodoubt there was very limited Dalit independent organizing before the 1920s; hence, limited autonomous degree of the Dalit leadership. The Dalit leadership had yet produced a number of leaders with a large following throughout India. For instance, among the early known Dalit leaders in Maharashtra were Kisan Faguji Bansode (1870-1947), Gopal Baba Walankar, V. Ravji Moonj pundit (1860-1924), Shivram Janba Kamble, Kalicharan Nandagawali (1886-1962), G.A Gawai (1888 -1974) and others (Omvedt 1994). Similarly, in South India M.C Rajah, the leader of the Adi-Dravida movement, was the chief spokesman of the Dalits and also their representative in the Madras legislative Council in 1926. The Adi-Dravida movement had been active in Madras since 1918. The other important leaders of the South were Bhagyareddy Verma, Murugesh Pillai, etc. Swami Achchutanand was working during the 1920s in the north India for the betterment of Dalits. The other key leaders during this period in north India especially in Punjab were Vasant Pai, Thakar Chand, Shudranand and Mangoo Ram (Juergensmeyer 1982:35).

Dalits began to form their independent political and social organizations also in the 1920s. The first independent Dalit political movement in India appeared to have been launched in 1910 when the All India Depressed Classes Federation was established in Maharashtra under the encouragement of the 'Bombay Presidency Social Reform Association'. Its initial purpose was to pressurize the Indian National Congress to include in its main planks the removal of untouchability. Consequently, the Indian National Congress had incorporated this in its agenda, adopted in its annual secession held at Calcutta in 1917. It is interesting to note that the Indian National Congress, after 32 years of its formation, had adopted the agenda of the removal of untouchability, which was in effect menifestations of its neglect about a grave problem effecting millions of human beings.

Afterwards, the political climate in the country **changed** substantially. The government of India Act, 1919 explicitly provided for communal representations in the Indian Parliament. This stimulated the formation of new Dalit organizations, which aimed not only to secure benefits for the Depressed Classes or the Dalits but also to organize them into coherent political blocks. Nodoubt there grew general concerns among the Untouchables or the Depressed Classes for forming their separate autonomous political organization (s) throughout India during the early 1920s. As the social, economic, political and geographical realities of the various regions in India were different, so were the dominant issues related to the emergence of autonomous Dalits leadership. Not only that but each region had different level of social-poliical consciousness about oppression and exploitation of the Unouchable castes resulted from their number of social movements organized in the past. Therefore, for a proper understanding of the nature and social composition of the Dalit leadership in the past it is necessary to analyz it region-wise.This is in consonance with the fact that , in absence of an all India Dalit leadership, the regional Dalit leadership had enjoyed relatively more imprtance during this period.

Dalit Leadership in South India

The decade of the 1920s saw the emergence of the Dalit leadership vis-a-vis movement as a conscious and organized force in the social and political life of the people in Northern (United Provinces and Punjab), Western (Bombay and Nagpur of Bombay Presidency), Central (Vidrbha) and Southern India (Hyderabad, Mysore and Kerala, of Madras Presidency). In South, the independent Dalit leadership emerged in the 1920s. Here, the agricultural commercialization laid the basis for a wide spread movement of the rural Dalits unlike their movements in the urban -industrial centers found in the Western and other parts of India (Omvedt 1994:114). The Dalit leadership emerged more distinctively in seven districts of the Coastal Andhra (Srikakulam,Visakhapatnam, East and West Godavri, Ongole, Guntur and Nellore) and four districts of Rayalseema (Kurnool, Chittor, Anantapur and Cuddapah) which were included in the Madras presidency during the colonial rule. Being influenced by the non- Brahman movement in the region, the Dalit movements concentrated on the agrarian issues like their rights over land, wages, etc. More precisely there emerged the non-Brahman movements (both of the Dalits nd the middle level castes) in 1917 in the Madras Presidency which challenged the dominance of the Brahman elites in Indian National Congress. It also rejected the Brahman dominance in the almost every walks of life and laid the basis for the Dalit leadership and its movements including a that for a non-Aryan or Dravidian idenetity.

The term 'Adi-Andra' rose in the past 1917 period when Dalits in the South influenced by the 'non- Aryan' theme of the Dravidian movement, were identifying themselves as Adi-Dravidians , Adi-andhras and Adi-Karnatakas- the original sons of the soil. Their such identities were accepted by the then government. For istance the census of 1931 enumercated the population of the Adi-Andhras at 6.5 lakhs as campared to little more than 8 lakhs Mallas and 6 lakhs Madigas, the major untouchable castes (Dalits) in Andhra Pradesh. The important leaders of the Adi movements were Sundru Venkaiah, Kusuma Venkatramaih, Mutakki Venkateswarlu, Devendrudu , Kamatam Shanmugan, etc. By organing meetings and conferences throughout the districts and the regions,the Dalit leadership had a broad rural base. The Adi-Andhra consciousness and the implied broad ideology of political autonomy were becoming significant social force in the costal Andhra even though much of the mass-based Telugu consciousness grew on the Hindu plank and acceptance of Hinduism.

Contrary to this, an active but fictionalized urban based Dalit leadership emerged during the 1920s in Hyderabad, the largest state of the British regime in India. Here the Dalit movement developed within an already dangerously polarized Hindu-Muslim communal tension. As stated by Omvedt, "In some way there was a closeness in Dalit and Muslims relations in the Hydrabad area itself. Yet, it was a closeness characterized by ambiguity" (Omvedt 1994:120). In this narrow and communalised framework, a small but vigorous Dalit (Malas) movement was oranized in 1910 in Hydrabad. Two imortant leaders who stood at the cente of it were Bhagyareddy Verma and Arigay Ramaswamy. It was Baghyareddy (1888-1939) who presided over not only the momentous conferences of the Molas at Vijaywada in 1913 when the 'PANCHAMA' identity was rejected but he also headed over number of other conferences thereafter. His organizing activity began in 1912 when he formed the Adi Hindu Jatiyonnati Sabha and and Many Sangam. These organizations were formed with the help of the Dalit employees of both government and Nizam of Hydrabad which also indicated the emergenc of a 'Dalit Middle class' (Omvedt 1994: 122). At the same time Arigay Ramswamy formed a social reform group in Secunderbad , and Maduri Audia. He had started another Manya Sangam with the objective of social reforms among the Dalit. Thus through these organizations the leaders stressed internal social reforms within the Dalit community. Attempt as were made to ban drinking of alcohol and eating meat at social functions, abolition of the custom of Devadasi etc. This group of leaders also found themselves in conflict with the 'caste chaudhris'(heads if the caste councils) as they had set up many alternative courts to handle the disputes within castes against customary arbitration's of the choudhrais.

The radicalization among Dalits throughout south India brought with it with the 'Adi Ideology' as stated above. Four Adi Hindu conferences were organized in Hyderabad itself between 1912 and 1924. Bhagyareddy tronsformed his Manya Sangam into the Adi-Hindu Social Service League, which became the main oganisation of the Dalits in Hyderabad. The term 'Adi Hindu was spreading among a sizeable number of north Indian Chamars during this time. This appeal to the Adi Hindu identity in the north was the result of Bhagyareddy's close connection with north India Adi Hindu movements. In fact, Bhaghyareddy himself had travelled and attended notably two conferences organized in 1927 and 1930 in north India which had described the Depressed Classes Adi-Hindus (ibid.:122).

However, the two opposing sections of Adi Hindus emerged in Hyderabad during this period. One group consisting of Tamil Untouchables represented the Adi Dravida and formed the 'The Adi Dravida Educational League'. The other group consisted of Telgu-speaking Untouchables who described themselves as Adi Hindu. The Adi Dravidas claimed to be the aborigines with their separate history, philosophy, civilization and culture, etc. which were distinct from those of the Hindus. On the basis of this they claimed their separate corporate group identity. The Telgu speaking Adi Hindus repudiated the above argument on the basis that the concept of God, the mode of worship, the system of rituals and code of customs, the manner of dress and the ways of life of the Untouchables or Depressed Classes were indentical to those of the caste Hindus. Therefore, they mintained that the Adi Hindus were like any other Hindus. This was, however not the case of the Adi-Hindus, for their co optern in the Hindu social system but it was their assertion for their acceptance at par with other Hindus with their distinct religious rituals and -cultural identities. Latter, the leadership got induged in intensive competitive struggles. During the 1920s, these straggles were primarily between Bhagyareddy and Arigay Ramaswamy. A similar trend contiued during the 1930's onwards. Consequently, the major issues initially addressed by the contemporary Dalit leadership started getting dimmed in the course of time.

The Dalit striving in south India was also witnessed in Kerala where Pulayas- the untouchables had organised, since the begining of this century their social-cultural revolts under the able leadership of Ayyankali and Vellikkara Choti. The aim of such revolts initially was not for economic gain but for entery into educational institutions and other public places (Mathew 1986:102). Consequently, the Pulayas won the freedom to walk along public roads and entry of their children to school by 1900. But that was not fully accepted by caste Hindus and others. Therefore, Ayyankkali and Vellikkara Choti had oranised again another movement in 1914 for school entry of Pulaya children with considerable amount of resistance by caste Hindus. Another leader Gopala Das fought against the custom of wearing bead necklaces by the Pulaya women. Thus ths socal revolts of the Pulayas brought a new awakenig to them which also coincided with a widespread political development in the State with the representation of the Dalit leaders in the Assembly and Legislative Council in 1911 and 1926 respectively. Consequently the voice of the Pulayas was heard first at the formal political fora in the state.

The Dalit organizations also came into existence in the earstwhile Mysore state were apparently Tamil supported, Adi Dravida Abhi-Vrudhi Sangh was led by Murgesh Pillai though it sought to include the Kannadigas too in its fold and programmes. The other organization called Adi Jambava Sangha was exclusively formed and supported by the Madigas -now a major Scheduled Caste in Andhra Pradesh. Being mainly a social organization its leader convend a 'Political conference' of the Panchamas in 1920,in which Ambedkar also was invited to participate but he could not attend this conference due to a state ban on his entry into the state. It is, however, nothing authentically known at this stage if the conference had adoped any political resolution. Other conferences were organised in the 1923 and 1925 under the presidentship of M.C. Rajah. These conferences passed resolutions on varous ossues concerning the Untouchables by using the Adi karnataka and Adi Dravida terminology. Their basic demand were admission of Dalit students in educational institutions, access to water tanks, temple entry, etc. Scince the 1920s onward Dalits were also asking the government for allotment of wastelends and other follo lands for cultivation. They asked for land to be alloted/leased/sold to them at the reduced/concessional price in the newly irrigated tracks of the Irwin canal. Besides, demands for relieving Dalits entirely from traditional caste duties were also made. It was also argued that if they were not relieved, government should directly pay to them for their duties out of the cess collected from the peasants.

But all these activities visa-a-vis movements continued to organized within the framework of the politics of pentions and patronage (Omvedt 1994:130). Another aspect of the movement especially in Mysore State was that Dalits hardly spoke in their own voice. For instance, when the issue of untochability was articulated as a 'social issue' since the end of 1920's it was first taken up by the Brahman dominated caste Hindu organizations like 'Mysore League Against 'Untouchability', 'Harjan Savak Sangh', etc. Here, it is not to deny the fact that the Dalits in rural areas in the Mysore State had the trementdous capacity of potential of struggle but ther were no leaders to organise it. The Kannada educated Dalits remained powerless and relatively voiceless in absence of a sound industrial base and political organization of their own.

The Dalits leadership up to the 1920 was thus multifaceted. It covered a wide range of issues relating to the life and socio-econmic status of the Dalits. It made the Dalits in the different parts of south India concious of their social existence, exploitation and social degradation. The Dalit leaders organised various movements through which they raised the issue of separate Dalits identity and Dalits' access to public places and resources. They also struggled for their representation in the different political bodies. Besides they also fought for economic rights including rights of land and the adequate wages to be paid to them. They succeeded in getting fulfilled some of their demands but failed on many counts. As a reult, they continued their movements in the subsequent decades.

Dalits Leadership in Western India

Unlike in south India, there was some limited independent Dalit organising in western India before the 1920s. Prior to the emergence of Dr. Ambedkar as saviour of the untouchables (Dalits), a few spokesmen had led the Mahar movement in the Bombay prsidency as mentioned earlier. For instace Gopal Baba Walangkar a retired army officer-led the Ratnagiri based group and sent a petition to the government as early as in 1890. This was the beginning of articulating the protest of Mahars against their socio-religious disabilities and powerlessnss. A Bombay newspaper 'Indu Prakash' reported, "the disadvantaged are raising their voices" and it quoted an evidence of the protest address of Walangkar to the leaders of the Hindu Society (Mathew 1986: 60). On his part, Walangkar highlighted the grievances of the Dalits by writing in 'Dinbandhu' and 'Sudharak'- Marathi newspapers in which he argued that casteism and untouchability had no religious base and were monsters created by the Hindus. To prove his thesis, he published a booklet titled, "Vital Vidwansak". In 1918 he formed the 'Anarya Doshpariharak Mandali' (non Aryan group for removal of wrongs) at Dapoli in the localities of Ratnagiri district where untouchable castes such as Chambhar and Mahar army pensioners lived.

Earlier, the Mahars, Mangs and Chambhars were recruited in the army of the East India Company but around 1890- 91 their recruitment ceased. Those already in service were also asked to leave. Enraged over this, Walangkar filed a petiton in July 1890 requesting re-acceptance of them in Army. The petition advocated for Mahars, Mangs and Chambhars who had already served both in the army and in domestic services. It was claimed that these 'Dalits were Kshatiyas', and were demoted by the Peshwas at the time of the Mahadurgadevi famine in 1676 for eating whatever they could find to save their lives (Zelliot 1986: 34). In this mission, Walangkar secured little support from his fellowers. Nevertheless, Walangkar sensitised the Dalits of Maharastra to fight against their economic, social and religious disabilities. Thus, with his efforts a new era had emerged in the Dalits' struggle for securing their rights and social jstice. He then may be termed as the first social thinker, the first revolutionary, and the first initiator of the Dalit movement in Maharastra (Jogdand 1991:46).

The pre-Ambedkar era saw the emegence of Shivram Janab Kamble, another Dalit leader in Maharashtra who had formed the Oppressed India Association in Nagpur. An eloquent in English language and Vocabulary Kamble sent in 1904 a memorandum to the governor of Bombay on behalf of 1500 Mahars of the Dellan and Konkan areas. Along with Gangaram Krishnajee, he also submitted in 1910 another petition supported by the relevant documents asking for employment of the Mahars at least in the lowest grades of the public services, i.e. in the ranks of police sepoys and soldiers in the armed forces. Being the first to hold a conference of the Dalits, Kamble organised later four conferences in Bombay during 1917-18 though a few of these were organised even under the leadership of some caste Hindus who were also concerned with the untouchables' (Dalits). Increased political importance in the overdue reforms. Besides, Kamble formed a Mahar caste association and published the 'Somvansh Mitra'a Marathi newspaper (Jogdand 1991:47). He was the leading figure in the 'Parvati Temple Satyagraha' organised by the Dalits and a few caste Hindus in 1929 (Jogdand 1991:46). He also fought against the customory practices of the Devidasi system prevalent among the Mahars and Mags. When Ambedkar appeared on the public scene in the 1920s, Kamble welcomed him as a leader of the Dalits. Both often met and discussed on the different issues. They had, however differences with regard to the 1937 election procedures which ultimately led Kamble's dissociation from Ambedkar. Yet, Kamble never undermined the efforts of Ambedkar for uplift of the untochables.

Besides Kamble, Kisan Fagoji Bansode was another Dalit leader from Nagpur who founded in 1903 the 'Sanmarg Bodhak Nirashrit Samaj' (Depressed Class Society showing right path). The Samaj existed for showing the principels of Right 'Panth' to Mahars. Besides founding many educational institutions including a school for girls in 1907, he started several news papers like the *Nirikshak Hindu Nagrik* (1910), *Vithal Vidhvansak* (1913), Mazur Patrika (1918) and Chokha Mela (1931). Bansode published from his own press several books on the Mahars, saint Chokhamela in 1941 besides setting up a library in Mohapa. He not only held conferences for the Dalits but went from house to house preaching self-respect among them. His Samaj argued with Mahars, Manga and Chambhars for not to becoming Christians for the removal of their ignorance, not eating what was not not to be eaten, for not drinking liquor, but taking to education, organising and create a feeling among Hindus that the Dalits should be raised up (Jogdand 1991:47). He further formed the 'Antaj Samaj' (Last Born Society) in 1919 and the 'Mahar Sudharak Mandal' in 1920. He also wrote 'Tamasha' (folk dramas) in order to educate and liberate his people form the yoke of Hindu customs and blind faiths. Bansode had close ties with Ambedkar till the latter's announcement of religious coversion in 1935. He went almost all the way with Ambedkar in social and political matters but retained belief that the progress of the Dalits could be made within Hinduism.

Even in the Pre-Ambedkar era there were two more Dalit spokesmen of a slightly younger generation—Ganesh Akkaji Gavai (1888-1974) and Kalicharan Nandagwali (1886-1962), who had done commendable works for the cause of Dalits in Amraoti district. Gavai began his activities by founding in his home village a 'Mahar library' and the 'Mahar Sudharak Mandal Mahar Reform Society. Kalicharan was convener of the Bhartiya Bahishkrit Parishad (Indian Council of excommunicated) which held its meeting at Nagpur in 1920. Under the chairmanship of Sahuji Maharaj of Kolhapur. He also highlighted the problems of the Dalis to the South brough Committee in 1919 and the Simon Commission in 1928. The Dalits stopped supporting him because of his inclination towards the Indian National Congress. On the other hand, Nandagwali less educated but wealthy malguzar was credited with founding the first girls' school. He along with Gavai became one of the First Dalit members of the Legislative Council of Bombay Presidency.

However, both Gavai and Bansode took pro-hindu position and were pulled into the orbit of the nationalists (Omvedt 1994:109). More specifically, Gavai was influenced by Vithal Ramji Shinde—a nationalist Maratha leader. Both Gavai and Bansode met "Shinde in 1910, joined his Prarthana Samaj and orgainised the Depessed Classes Association in 1915 though Gavai had also associated himself with Shinde's Depressed Classes Mission. He was involved in organing several Dalit confernces in Maharastra during the 1920's and also participated in the Adi Hindu conference of in north India. Gavai eventually supported a proposal of the Hindu Mahasabha for bringing about a compromise between Gandhi and Ambedkar in 1932 over the issue of sepate electorate for Dalits. Yet, having lost his influence over Dalits he ultimately joined the Hindu Mahasabha in 1933 and harshly criticized Ambedkar's call for religious conversion in 1935. In any case, the Gavai-Bansode group could not maintained its anti-Ambedkar and pro-Congress base among the Dalits in Maharastra in spite of its ganied prominence of the Dalit spokesmen, social reformers and members of the Legislative Council and of many Government committees.

Amidest a unique confluence of social and political leaders of the Dalit communities in Maharastra, there were some other social reformers like Keshavraoji Khandare, Vithoba Raoji Moon Santpande, Rewaram Kawade, Babu Hardas, etc, in the Vidharbha region. Being founder president of the Mahar Sabha formed in 1912, Vithoba Raoji built a separate bathing place around 1914 for the Mahars at Ramtek near Nagpur. And with the formation of the Sabha, the social movements of the Dalits from different parts of Maharstra were linked with that of the movement of the Dalits of Vidarbha. The Hindu social reformer took a note of the work of Vithoba and his colleagues in 1913. He fought against injustices and published booklets in order to mobilize the people of the Dalit community. Thus, the Dalit leadership up to the 1920's in Western India was committed to both social reforms and political representation of the Dalits. Though its loyalties were divided, it was concerned primarily with the cause of Dalits. It had succeeded in mobilising the Dalits and making them conscious about injustice, explanation and social degradation inflicted on them. It had also prepared them, to some extent, to organise and agitate for justice and for their rights to be accorded to them.

Dalit Leadership in North India

The contemporary movements of Dalits in north were limited in comparison to those in south and western India. Though limited historical account of these movements is available, three prominent movements which threw some kind of independent Dalit leadership were the Jatavas movement of Agra, the Adi Hindu movement organised of Uttar Pradesh, viz. Kanpur, Allahabad, Varanasi, etc. and the Ad Dharam Movement of Punjab. Initially being religious in nature, all these movements had later raised important socio- political issues related to the Dalits. According to Goptu (1993) Foundation of the independent Dalit leadership in Uttar Pradesh were first laid primarily by two inter-related factors. First, the relaxation of caste subordination in occupational relations as Dalit migrants from the country side were incorporated in the urban workforce, though the labour market here was highly segmented along the caste lines. Secondly, the emergence of new theories about the native and origin of the Caste System according to which caste was perceived as man made and was beneficial to those at the top in the caste-hierarchy. In other words, caste was not accepted universally functional but exploitative in nature either.

The process of migration and urbanisation started after uprising of 1857 and its subsequent suppression when the British military and civil administration was consolidated in the towns and contonment (Gooptoo 1993: 279). There was expansansion of urban-territory as well as sanitory infrastructure and Municipal services workers as a result of this reorganisation. The whole development created a demand for scavengers, sweeper, leather workers, washerman etc. who traditionally performed the menial work. Hence they migrated to find the jobs in cantonments and civil lines. For instance, writes Gooptoo (1993) in Kanpur Mochis— traditionally leather workers were also employed by the newly developing leather factories and tameries set up by the government and the British Industries. This urban occupation helped Dalits to break their caste subordination but in other social ranks their segregation and exclusion continued which gave birth a basis for assertion among Dalits. This has been diliveated by Gooptu, who argues, "In the late nineteenth and early twentieth centuries, therefore, the untouchable migrants to the towns were exposed to two contrary trends. On the one hand, caste domination ceased, to a large extent, to be a feature of occupational relations . . . on the other hand, continued caste-distinctions in employment or educational opportunities and settlement patterns, as well as their general poverty thwarted economic or social improvement among untouchables . . . The two simultaneous processes appear to have created an urgency among the urban untouchables to assert themselves and to undermine caste barriers, for it was amongst them in the early twentieth century in the towns in the Bhakti cults gained large following. That the idom of their self-assertion took the form of bhaki is not surprising, for bhakti emapsulated a message of the social equality of castes" (Gooptoo 1993: 282).

Against this background of persisting inequality and emerging equality, a millitant self-assertion of Dalits percipitated. This Dalit assertion had dual agenda on the one hand, it questioned the discriminatin and disabilities heaped on the Dalits even in the urban set up because of caste distinction and, on the other, it constructed an ideological theory of racial origin of the Dalits, to which we will come a bit tour when we discuss the dynamics of Dalit leadership in North India in the book.

The persuation of this theory took the form of the Adi-Hindu movement and the two most important leaders of this movement were swain Acctutanand (1879-1933) of Lucknow and Baba Ram

Charan Das of Kanpur. Acchutanand's real name was Hira lal, and he was taught by the missionaries and had gained extentise knowledge of religious texts. Supported by several Dalit leaders, he had published a small newspaper in Hindi entitled 'Adi Hindu. More Significantly, he had testified and submitted a memorandum to the Simon Commission in 1928 asking for separate status and rights, and representation to be given to the Dalits. According to Lynch, Swami also preached in Agra but because of his radical doctrines was driven out by the leaders of the Jatav-Kshtriya movement (Lynch 1974:76).

Anyway, the Adi Hindu movement of Uttar Pradesh was in contact with the Ad Dharm movement of Punjab which had arisen on the soil of Aryans and produced a number of leaders. In the early 1920's a handful of educated young Dalit activists who had been meeting in Jullundar began serious discussion about developing a circle of communication and gaining political strength. The three key leaders were Vasant Rai, Thakar Chand and Swami Shudranand who were educated in the schools sponsored by the Arya Samaj. "The Samaj provided an organizational model for a new social group to emulate, and for the Ad Dharam leaders it was initially something even more. It was the material context in which their movement was conceived, and from which it grew"(Shah 1990:109-110).

Before founding the Ad Dharam, Sant Ram B.A., a Dalit member of the Arya Samaj from Hoshiarpur had begun a new movement for Dalit equality within the Arya Samaj. Sant Ram's organization the 'Jat Pat Todak Mandal (Society for the Abolition of Castes) established in 1922 was involved in a major conflict with the Arya Samaj organization and eventually got separated from it in1924. The Central theme of the 'Jat Pat Todak Mandal' was that of intercaste marriages. The same organization had planned to have Dr. Ambedkar's presidential address in 1936, which was eventually cancelled due to ideological differences between him and the organization.

The Mandal, however, encouraged the Dalits of Punjab to create an organization of their own. As a result, the AD Dharam emerged in 1926 as an organised movement of Dalits in Punjab with Mangoo Ram as President of the Executive Committee. He was a folk hero and had lived with activists of the Gadar Party - a militant movement of the nationalist youths in California (USA). The main plea of the AD Dharam movement was that the untouchables (Dalits) constituted a quam, a distinct religious community similar to those of the Muslim, Hindu and Sikh communities, and their quam existed in India from time immemorial, i.e. before the Hindus (Aryans) arrived. At the later stage, the leaders of the Ad Dharam felt the lure of two models of social organizations and political influence. One of these was the example set by Muslim nationalists who had demanded a sepatate territory of their own land the other was provided by political parties and a netwok of the religious-communal supports for the electoral candidates. "Members of Dalit community in the Punjab adopted the first model along the lines of the Muslim separatism and came up with the notion of Achutistan, a geographically distinct "Land of the untouchables" (Juergensmeyer 1982:145). However, the idea was never woked out in any systematic way nor was there even a suggestion as to which area of India might be incorporated into such a nation.

Through the second model of the legislative representation the Ad Dharam supported the independent candidates in 1936 elections and, to the surprise of its leaders, they swept all but one of the seats. A consistent pattern of friendship developed between Muslims and the Ad Dharam in the electoral politics. Both the unionist Muslim landlords and the members of the Ad Dharam opposed the upper caste Hindus, Sikhs, and the Indian National Congress. Yet, Mangoo Ram and other leaders thought that the best way to bring benefits to the Dalits was to remain inside the governmnet rather than to protest from outside. Therefor, one of the first actions of Mangoo Ram as an M.L.A. was to demand greater Dalit - representation in the government jobs.

But with the political power coming in the hands of the Ad Dharam leaders, the faction became visible. The family rivalries and personal disputes created rift among the leaders. The lure of office, with all the power status that it seemed to imply, magnified the personal ambitions of those who had till then remained contented with the political arena provided by the Ad Dharam and aggravated their rivalries. This ultimately caused downfall of the movement, which was subsumed by Ambedkar's All India Scheduled Castes Federationin 1946.

In sum, the Dalit leadership in North India was confined primarily to two major issues: a separate Dalit identity emphasising the aboriginal status of the Dalits and their demand for political representation including that in administeration. The first type of demand in a sense lead to reconstruction of history of the Dalits. The Adi Hindu ideology provided a historical explanation for the poverty and deprivation of the Dalits, and presented a vision of their past power and rights. Another fall out the first demand was the demand for a separate homeland, which they did not pursue later. The Dalit leadership in the north also addressed the question of unity among the existing Dalit for us. Efforts were also made to avolve an all India Dalit Organization and establish contacts with the Dalits of other parts of the country. But that also could not materialise due to ideological as well as material differences among the leaders.

The Dalit Leadership in Eastern India

Ironically, Bengal – the land of Indian renuaisance produced a very faint voice of the Dalit leadership unlike that from other regions in the country as mentioned above. Influenced by the European socio-political philosophy of liberalism, utilitarianism and positivism, many social reforms took place in Bengal. The broad aims of these social reforms or reform movements carried during the second half of the 19th and early decedes of the 20th centuries were caste reform or caste abolition, equal rights for women, campaign against child marriage and ban on widow re-marriage, crusade against social and legal ineqalities, etc. Apart from individual efforts, the organised attempts were made by the Brahmo Samaj, the Social Reform Conference and the Ramakrishna Mission to eliminate the existing disabilities from the society. But the major issues relating to life and existence of the untouchable castes of the Bengali society were hardly addressed by these reform movements nor these movements made any significant impact on the socio-political status of the people of these castes.

Basically, the Dalits in Bengal were highly fragmented and divided into numerous castes, sub- castes and interest groups. But they gradually started orgnising themselves. Out of many Dalit groups in Bengal, the Namshudras were the largest and politically most organised group. They numbered over two millions in Bengal and Assam in 1905 and constituted about ninety percent of the entire lower caste Hindu agricultural population of East Bengal. It is said that due to their degraded position in the past many Namshudras converted to Islam way back in the 16th century as a mark of their protest against the tyranny of the Hindu religion. It is difficult to say anything at this stage who were the leaders who led this conversion. Yet, at a later age, with the emergence of consciousness of their exploitation and degraded status in caste system, the remaining Namshudras who continued to be Hindus organised themselves. The Namasudras of Bakarganj district convened a meeting on 2nd October 1906 which was presided over by Babu Rajendra Nath Mandal—a Dalit and a resolution was passed in which they supported the Secretary of State in India for the Partition of Bengal in 1905. They also passed a resolution asking for communal representation to the Dalits, like that to Muslims, in the Legistative Council and Assemblies. It was also expressed that Muslims and Dalits had very cordial relations, which should continue. Above all, the meeting passed unanimously a resolution stating that, "it is simply owing to the dislike and hatred of the Brahmins, the Vaidyas/ Vaishyas and the Kayasthas that this vast Namasudra community had remained backward; this community has therefore not the least sympathy with them and their agitation, and will henceforth work hand in hand with their Mohemadan brethern" (Fuchs: 1981).

Yet, another group of Namshudra leaders had connections with the Ad Dharam movement of Punjab. In fact, a branch of the Ad Dharam was actively working in Calcutta. Members of the movement were basically manual labourers working in the metropolis of Calcutta who used to send monetary help to the Ad Dharam in Punjab. Later on, being influenced by Ambedkar's movement, the Namsudras organised themselves under the Scheduled Caste Federation during the second-third decades of the present century. Under this organization, they again demanded their political and social rights. Moreover, they maintained links with Ambedkar by extending their support to him during his presentation of the case of the Scheduled Castes in the Round Table Conferences and later nominating him from Bengal to the Constituent Assembly to draft and pilot the Constitution of free India.

Though a number of Dalit movements were organised by the Dalit leaders in the eastern part of the country these were to some extent, parochial in their orientation in spite of similarities of problem faced by Dalits in other regions. This is more evident from the fact that except the Namsudra movement which had necessary links with and supports from the Ad Dharma movement of Punjab and Ambedkar's movement of Maharashtra which of course was expanding, by that time, its horizon at the all India level, other Dalit movements of this region lacked all India appeal and, hence, could not nuster supports of the Dalits at large. Moreover, these did not produce vibrant Dalit personalities and leaders besides one or two who could lead the Dalits cause to its logical end. As has been rightly suggested by a Japnees sociologists Usuda (1997: 224), "In Bengal self-emancipating endeavours among untouchables' as a part of the Scheduled Castes movements were ardent enough to expect satisfactory results. The status of their movements within the all-India framework, however, remained marginal on account of their strategy which would not set the removal of untouchability as their central lask. Ironically enough, one of the reasons that Mandal (J.N. Mandal) could not be Ambedkar is attribute to this fact".

Conclusions

The dalit leadership of several varieties had emerged in different regions in the country by the 1920s though it was not entirely, independent in its ideology, setting agenda, and pursuing its activities. The leadership had crutches of other social and political groups like the liberal caste Hindus, Arya Samajists, Indian National congress, Missionaries etc. It is quite evident that there was very little unity, contact and communication among the activities of the dalit leadership located in four different regions in the country. Some of the important reasons for such state of affairs were geographical distance, vernacular language, contextual and specific problems of the regions, etc. which retarted the intensity of interaction and unity among the dalit movements organised during this period. It can, however, be said that even though there was not many interactions among these movements the nature of their demands were more or less similar. Hence, there functional unity if not organic. In fact, these movements more reformist in nature in which they called upon the dalit communities for internal refors like giving up habits of meat eating, drinking alcohol, etc. They also emphasised the need for the dalits to change the age-old caste customs, occupation and sufferings from the inferiority complex. They also demanded for the Dalits rights to use the public places and facilities like roads, wells, schools, etc.

The dalit leadership until the 1920's had followed the policy of persuasion and petition. Except a few demonstration organised against the indifference of the Indian National Congress towards the cause of the Dalits, the Dalit leaders could not organise any strong and effective demonstrations, agitations, strikes, etc. except in the earstwhile East Bengal and may be in few other places but these are not widely known in the history of Dalit movements in India. The Dalit leadership also wore a posture of exclusivism or separatism from the hinu philosophy and social system. Skuch posture and the resultant articulation was almost universal to all the dalit leaders and reformers all over the country. They Proclaimed their aboriginal status and thereby being original inhabitants of India. But Ambedkar who at a later stage deserved their such claims and traced the origin of the untouchables, today's Dalits, as broken men. Nevertheless, the Dalit leaders of that era also opined that social disabilities were imposed upon the Dalit by the caste Hindus who were outsiders to this land. A demand of the separate land the 'ACHHUTISTAN' also emerged during this period but soon faded out.

Though the dalit leadership of this period was more social in nature in terms of addressing the social problems of the Dalits and demanding for their resolution, in course of time the leaders added many political demands too. Consequently, the leadership, which had started the various types of movements for the socio-religious reforms, incorporated the politiacal safegaurds for the dalits in its agenda. Economic rights for the dalits also drew attention of the leaders in due course of time. Hence, the dalit leadership became divese in nature for addressing the multiple issues pertaining to the Dalits over the years.

Also going by the inetensity and frequency of the demonstrations, agitations and in a world movements organised by dalit leaders. The Dalit leadership in western and southern India was more active and vibrant than that in northern and eastern parts. In fact, the dalit leadeship could not emerge as an active force in eastern India except for the Namshudra movement in undivieded Bengal, as stated earlier. Another intresting point to mention is that neither the Dalit movements of various *shadis* nor the Dalit leadership as such during this period had encouraged Dalit women's participation movements and various political activities. Though the gender inequality was minimal among Dalits in comparision to non-Dalits specially the upper castes, the Dalit leadership never tried to adopt and develop leadership among thier women folk.

The Dalit leadership on its part could not bridge the inter-caste differences and rivalries within the Dalit community itself. It could not solve the problem of the fragmented (sub-castes) identities of and choose a single common nomenclature for the Dalits. Also some of the leaders and groups wished to identify themselves with the caste Hindus while other insisted to come out of the Hindu social order. Consequent upon that they referred the Dalit community with different names at different places. For instance some organised under the name of Adi-Hindus, and others under the Adi-Dravida, Adi-Andhra, Adi-Karnataka and so on so forth. Their official nomenclature was Depressed Classes which was changed to Scheduled Caste by the year 1935. This identity of Scheduled Caste also created lot of confusion for the leaders too.

Besides, the Dalit leaders all over the country could not find their natural allies in their struggle against the dominant social order. This was due to the fact that the interests of the Dalits were totally different and even opposed to the interests of non-Dalits. The lack of solidarity among the Shudras (OBCs) and the Dalits was a very sorry state of affair. It is noteworthy here that though Mahatma Jotiba Phule, Chattrapati Sahu, E.V. Ramaswamy Naicker 'Periyar' and a few other – all of them being Shudra – had initiated the amelioration of the Dalits. Had this unity been achieved, the socio-political fabrics of the Hindu Social Order would have easily been changed in course of time.

Dalit Leadership in India and the Role of Ambedkar

It is difficult to conceptualise the Dalit Leadership without acknowledging the most significant role played by Babasaheb Dr. B. R. Ambedkar for the upliftment of the Dalits in India. With him emerged completely new type of socio-political consciousness among the Dalits and equipped with this consciousness there also sprang an autonomous Dalit leadership. According to Zelliot, Ambedkar's programmes were intended to integrate the untouchables (Dalits) from a state of 'dehumanization' and slavery into one of equality through the use of modern methods based on education and the exercise of legal and political rights (Zelliot 1992:158).

We have mentioned in the previous chapter that there were several Dalit leaders who had organised a number of Dalit movements in different parts of the country before Ambedkar emerged on the political scene. Most of these leaders had their allegiance to the Indian National Congress and they tried to achieve upliftment of the Dalits within the Hindu-fold. Only a few Dalit leaders had their independent organizations and asserted themselves for achieving a separate social identity for Dalits. This in turn marred the militancy of the Dalits and discouraged their strife for achieving their group autonomy. Accordingly, the earlier Dalit leaders were blamed by growing numbers of the lower castes as having compromised with the status quo. Before Ambedkar there were no lower caste leaders of national stature who could speak the language of the educated elite without being too closely identified with them? In fact Ambedkar was the first major leader of the Dalits who rose to the height of logical articulation and materialization of their socio-political aspirations and interests.

It is not very difficult to find at what stage the idea of protest takes shape in the mind of an individual. It is yet relatively easy to say when that idea of protest gets crystallized in some form of social action (Gore 1993:74). From this standpoint, the year 1919 seems important in tracing the historical beginning of the Ambedkar's movement, because he appeared on the political scene for the first time in the year 1919, when he was called to testify to the Southborough Committee (Zelliot 1986:40). Ambedkar's first public political plea for Dalits in 1919 resulted in failure. The Southborough Committee ignored him and a number of others who urged for the direct representation of the depressed classes to the Bombay Legislative Assembly but the Committee made provision for one member to be nominated to the same. But Ambedkar did not stop at this point. In 1920 he established a Marathi fortnightly, 'Mooknayak' (Hero of the Dumb) which was dedicated to making the Dalits aware of their conditions. Through its editorials he addressed himself to two *important* strands of thought. One of these reflected his reactions to the dominant nationalist movement as led by the Indian National Congress. He addressed the questions of whether and how the Dalits should relate themselves to the Nationalist movement and how they could successfully articulate their own specific goals without appearing to obstruct the larger National goal. The second issue was the relationship of the Dalits' own movements for securing their rights to the reformist movements carried on caste-Hindu social reformers on behalf of the Dalits.

In clarifying his own stand on the national movement for transfer of political power and the upper caste-led reformist movements, he argued, as Gore writes "in such a stratified society self- government was not enough. There must be an equal emphasis on good government-a good government dedicated to opening up the channels of development to all sections of society"(Gore 1993: 75). Ambedkar raised this question because the Indian National Congress, which initially had achievement of good government as its main objective, under the influence of the extremists' leaders of Congress, had changed its goal to attainment of self-government. He opined in the Mooknayak, "while one cannot object to the principle involved, we would not be able to support this change in objective unless we know whose self-government this is going to be and what will be its practical goals - for practice is more important than principle" (ibid.:75). He further writes in another issue of the Mooknayak, 'freedom' or 'self-government' must mean freedom and security for the individual, the recognition of his right to property, equality before the law, freedom to act in consonance with one's conscience, the right to be represented in the legislature and the right of opportunity for employment in public or government agencies" (ibid.:76). He wanted to be assured that the untouchables (Dalit) would also have a share in such self-government as without it the 'self-government' would mean a government to rule over the already depressed people. Ambedkar argued that the untouchables (Dalits) should receive not just a proportionate but a weighted representation in the legislatures. The more backward a group, the higher should be its representation. Without opposing the struggle for political freedom, Ambedkar made it clear that the agitation for 'self-government' could not appeal to the Dalits unless it gave them an adequate share of political power in the legislatures and that too through their own representatives. Moreover, Ambedkar criticized the upper caste leaders for keeping the government ignorant of the true conditions of Dalits. He also wrote that the upper castes were opposed to the Dalits for demanding share in the political power through their independently chosen representatives.

Later at an All India Conference of untouchables (Dalits) held in May 1920 at Nagpur, Ambedkar criticized the representation submitted by V. R. Shinde to the Southborough Committee and made an important policy speech. As a result, the conference passed a resolution requesting the government to reject Shinde's suggestion of nominated member and to let the Dalits select heir own representatives. Gore writes about this resolution, "This demand for a separate electorate was the most important political demand of the Ambedkar movement. It followed logically from the ideological position taken by Ambedkar in the first instance, viz., that the interests of the untouchables were not the same as the interests of caste Hindus and that they could not be subsumed in the latter" (ibid.:79). Thus, with these three events of submitting a testimony to the Southborough Committee, publishing the 'MOOKNAYAK' and appearing at two major conference of Dalits during 1920, Ambedkar made his claim to be an alternate but independent leader of the Dalits. His main objective was to prepare the Dalits for having their own identity and not being used any more by caste Hindus in the Indian society.

Three Phases of Ambedkar's Leadership

Ambedkar's leadership spread into three inter-related phases. These phases were complementary and supplementary to his efforts for achieving equality, liberty and justice for the Dalits. Each phase enriched his experience in fighting against the existing inequalities of the Hindu social order. The periodisation of his leadership is also necessary to understand the rational of his changing socio-political stances in his long struggle. The first phase began in early 1920 and continued till 1930. Mathew dates the Ambedkar's first phase of leadership from 1918 while Jogdand fixes 1924 (Mathew 1986:60 & Jogdand 1991:52). During this period he acted more like a social reformer in fighting against the rigid caste system and its rude practice of untouchability. The second phase started in 1930 and ended with his resigning from the Nehru Cabinet in 1951. Being fully recognized as the undisputed political leader of the Dalits he emphasised the need of acquiring political power for raising their socio-economic status. Towards the close of the second phase he established a number of educational institution as well. Finally in the third phase of his leadership (1952-56) he embraced Buddhism along with his followers. He emerged during this period a religious reformer for Dalit and led a revolt against Hinduism.

Social Reforms

Throughout his life Ambedkar favoured social and religious reforms instead of harping directly on political reforms. Hence in the early 1920s he participated in a few attempts of the Dalits for their 'sanskritization' in which they imitated some rituals of the caste Hindus. For instance he supported a number of Mahar satyagrhas for their entry into several Hindu temples which we will discuss later. But soon he realized the futility of such efforts for Dalits because their efforts of sanskritization failed to accord them a higher status in the caste hierarchy. Therefore, before taking on to mass action to gain socio-religious and political rights for the Dalits, Ambedkar formed a society the Bahishkrit Hitkarini Sabha, society to serve the interests of outcastes on July 20, 1924 which could place their social and political problems before the government. The prime motto of this organization was 'Educate, Organize and Agitate'. In a note seeking enrolment of members, Ambedkar clarified the objectives off the organization. "In order to bring about the uplift of outcastes it is first necessary to awaken them. Any community before it can progress must develop a consciousness. As someone has put it while the poor are certainly handicapped by their poverty, the real obstacle in their path is their inertia and their indifference! To overcome this inertia and indifference it is necessary that they should become charged with resentment of the injustice of their own condition. Without it, they cannot get rid of the factors that obstruct their progress" (Gore 1993: 84).

Ambedkar went for a mass action programme in 1927 and in the same year he was nominated by the Governor to the Bombay legislature. The event that catapulted Ambedkar to the front-rank of Dalit leadership was the Mahad satyagrah campaign. This was the first act of public protest by Ambedkar. The Satyagrah consisted simply of the assertion of the right of Dalit to drink water from 'Chowdar' an open public tank in the Tehsil town of Mahad in Konkan. A group of several thousands Dalits moved en mass to the tank and drank water. Later in 1927 Ambedkar called another conference at Mahad to reiterate the Dalit rights to use the public water supply. In his presidential speech he said that the movement was not only to gain access to the water or the temple or to remove the barriers to commonality. But its aim was to break down the Varna system, which supported inequality in society. One can observe here a definite broadening of goal of achieving equality and eradication the contradictions of the Varna system. The Immediate programme of drinking water from the Mahad tank was only symbolic protest (Gore 1993:86).

Another very unique event that took place during the Mahad Satyagrah was burning of the 'MANUSMRITI' the sacred law book of the Hindus. Moreover, the resolution proposing the burning of the Manusmriti was moved by Gangadhar Neelkanth Sahasrabuddhe, Brahman associate of Ambedkar. Justifying his action of burning the 'Manusmriti', Ambedkar said in the 3 Feb. 1928 issue of his Bahishkrit Bharat, that his reading of the Manusmiti "had convinced him that it was abusive and insulting in its treatment of the Shudras and it did not even remotely support the idea of social equality. To burn a thing was to register protest against the idea it represented. By so doing one expected to shame the person concerned into modifying his behaviour. He further said that it would be futile to expect that anyone who revered the Manusmriti could be genuinely interested in the welfare of the untouchables" (Gore 1993:106). Gore (1993) argues that Ambedkar compared the burning of the Manusmriti to the burning of foreign clothes recommended by Gandhi. Further, he argues that though Ambedkar justified the burning of the Manusmriti, he still regarded himself as a Sanatan Hindu. Ambedkar revealed, "though I do not accept the authority of the Vedas, I consider myself to be a Sanatan Hindu" (Ibid: 106).

Ambedkar organised the largest and longest Satyagraha on 2nd March, 1930 at Nasik for the Dalits, entry to the 'Kala Ram' temple. Around 15,000 Mahars and Chambhars had assembled at Nasik. But the temple had to be closed for about a year to keep them away from entering it. The Parvati Satyagraha in Poona also met the same fate. Thus, Ambedkar's effort of social reforms could not bring any positive result in changing the Hindu social order which he argued was based on graded inequality.

Yet, he took up the challenge as he was convinced by his knowledge about the social and political reforms carried all over the world. He argued that "history bears out the proposition that political revolutions have always; been preceded by social and religious revolutions. The religious reformation started by Luther was the precursor of the political emancipation of the European People. In England Puritanism led to the establishment of political liberty. Puritanism founded the New World. It was Puritanism, which won the war of American independence, and Puritanism was a religious movement. The same is true of the Muslim Empire. Before the Arabs became a political power they had undergone a thorough religious revolution started by the Prophet Mohammad. Even Indian history supports the same conclusion. The political revolution led by Chandragupta was preceded by the religious and social revolutions of Buddha. The political revolution led by Shivaji was preceded by the religious and social reform brought about by the saints of Maharastra. The political revolution of the Sikhs was preceded by the religious and social revolution led by Guru Nanak. It is unnecessary to add more illustrations. These will suffice to show that the emancipation of the mind and the soul is a necessary preliminary for the political expansion of the people" (Ambedkar 1980:34-44). That is why he used to criticise the Indian National Congress for giving precedence to political reforms over social and religious reforms. Moreover, Ambedkar was much critical of the types of reforms, which the Congress was promoting, and the genuineness of its concern about the amelioration of the conditions of the Dalits.

Taking note of the kind of social reform which reformers were agitating for, Ambedkar opined that it was necessary to make a distinction between social reform in the sense of reform of the Hindu family and social reform in the sense of the reorganization and reconstruction of the Hindu society. The former had emphasized widow remarriage, prohibition of child marriage etc., while the latter related to abolition of the caste system. The Indian National Congress and the contemporary reformers were concerned mainly with reform of the high caste Hindu family. That is why the social reforms did not provide any help to Dalits. This fact has been highlighted by Barbara Joshi, She argues, "Early Indian social ferment sprang from high caste Indians who focused first on changes relevant to those of their own status. For instance, the early heated debates by reformers about Sati and window remarriage were largely irrelevant for the lowest castes, whose traditional cultures usually permitted and sometimes encouraged widow remarriage. Widespread ignorance of low caste living conditions plus instructive defense of elite preeminence...The high degree of sub-culture variation and a very low level of communication and empathy among castes plagued Indian Social reform" (Joshi 1982:38).

Regarding the genuineness of the Congress for the amelioration of the conditions of the Dalits, Ambedkar was very suspicious. His suspicion was based on the historical resolution passed by the Congress at its annual meetings; it's various programmes and views of its leaders. The Congress passed after 32 years of its existence in 1917 a resolution for the amelioration of the conditions of the Dalits. Ambedkar blamed that the Congress did this with an ulterior motive of getting some concessions announced on 20th August 1917 by Mr. Montague, the then Secretary for India. Prior to that Ambedkar had a bitter experience of B. G. Tilak leading the anti-social reform section of the Congress workers and threatening to burn the '**Pandal**' if the Congress allowed the use of it for the Social Reform Conference.

Taking note of Annie Besant, the President of the 1917 annual session of the Indian National Congress. Ambedkar said, "I don't know that she was ever a friend of the untouchables. So far as I know she felt great antipathy towards the untouchables" (Ambedkar 1991:3). To prove his point he quoted from Annie Besant's article in which she had expressed her opinion on the question whether the children of the Dalits should be admitted to the common school where the upper caste children also studied. She wrote, "Here, as everywhere, education is the lever by which we may hope to raise them, the untouchables, but a difficulty arises at the outset...The children of the depressed classes need, first of all, to be taught cleanliness outside decency of behavior, and the earliest rudiments of education, religion and morality. Their bodies, at present are ill-odorous and foul with the liquor and strong smelling food out of which for generations they have been built up; it will need some generations of purer food and living to make their bodies fit to sit in the close neighborhood of a school - room with children who have received bodies from an ancestry trained in habits of exquisite personal cleanliness, and fed on pure food-stuffs. We have to raise the Depressed Classes to a similar level of Physical purity, not to drag down the clean to the level of dirty, and until this is done, close association is undesirable" (Ambedkar 1991:5). Focusing on the reforms envisaged by the socialists for the amelioration of the Dalits he argued that, the socialists of India following their fellow in Europe are seeking to apply the economic interpretation of history to the facts of India. They preach that political and social reforms are but gigantic illusions and that economic reform by equalization of property must have produce over every other kind of reform. He rejected the realization of socialism in the Indian society without uniting the Proletariat of India with social reforms. Unless and until the felling of equality and fraternity is not there the Proletariat cannot bring about the revolution. Currently, "Can it be said that the proletariat of India, poor as it is, recognise no distinctions except that of the rich and the poor? Can it be said that the poor in India recognize no such distinctions of caste or creed, high or low? If the fact is that they do, what unity of front can be expected from such a proletariat in its action against the rich? How can there be a revolution if the proletariat cannot present a united front? Suppose for the sake of argument that by some freak of fortune a revolution does take place and the Socialists come in power, will they not have to deal with the problems created by the particular social order prevalent in India? I can't see how a Socialist State in India can function for a second without having to grapple with the problems created by the prejudices which make Indian people observe the distinctions of high and low, clean and unclean" (Ambedkar 1991:190).

This entire event compelled Ambedkar to take up social

reform as his Primary goal for the amelioration of the conditions of the Dalits. He also confessed that social reform was very necessary for Dalits because it was through this that they could be united and made conscious. Equipped with a clear-cut ideology and sorting out who were friends and who were enemies, Ambedkar prepared himself and his followers for the second phase.

Strife for Political Power

In the second phase of his leadership, Ambedkar emphasized on acquiring political power for his people. Why did Ambedkar resort to the political weapon to get over the age-old disabilities, degradation and backwardness of the Dalits? This may be because "religious movements have failed to bring about any improvement in the social status of Dalits in a substantial measure, it was thought that this (Hindu social order) should be attacked from more secular grounds like economic betterment, education and political representation of the downtrodden in the body politic" (Parvathamma 1989:132). Ambedkar wrote, "when the untouchables lost all hope for their salvation through social reform, they were forced to seek political means for protecting themselves" (Ambedkar 1990:190). Moreover, Ambedkar proved that the problems of Dalits were essentially political. Contrary to the Congress treatment of Dalits problems as social, Ambedkar opined, "it is wrong to say that the problem of the untouchables is a social problem. For, it is quite unlike the problems of dowry, widow remarriage, age of consent, etc., which are illustrations of what are properly called social problems. Essentially, it is a problem of quite a different nature in as much as it is a problem of securing, to a minority, liberty and equality of opportunity at the hands of a hostile majority which believes in the denial of liberty and equal opportunity of the majority and conspires to enforce its policy on the minority. Viewed in this light the problem of the untouchables is fundamentally a political problem" (ibid: 190-191).

Ambedkar's plan to lift the status of Dalits through political means became very clear from his submitting a memorandum to the Simon Commission, testifying before Southborough Committee, his participation in the three Round Table Conferences and forming political parties. As a result of the political plea made by him to the Southborough Franchise Committee legislatures as stated earlier D. D. Gopala and Ambedkar himself were nominated to the Bombay legislative Council (Ambedkar was nominated in 1926). This was basically a result of the 'Muddian Committee report'. Further Ambedkar along with eighteen depressed classes (Dalits) associations testified willingly to the Simon Commission in 1928 and asked for separate electorates for Dalits. (The Congress boycotted the Commission). Ambedkar told the Commission that "The untouchables were relieved of anxiety because the Simon Commission did not include an Indian, since such a nominee could not be truly representative of all groups" (Zelliot 1992:101). However, he did not renew, till 1931-32, his 1919 demand for separate electorates for the Dalits, instead he asked for adult franchise and reserved seats, up to 22 in all, in a Bombay Assembly of 140 (15 according to their numbers plus seven weightage to insure their rights). Ambedkar also requested guarantees of the Depressed Classes, as did an appeal from the Central Provinces Depressed Classes Association. This group requested: (1) an increase in the government power of veto for protection of the minority, (2) separate representation not only in legislature, but all public bodies including universities in proportion to their numerical strength, (3) posts in government service for Depressed Class members, with minimum qualification required, (4) representation in the Cabinet dependent only upon Depressed Classes votes, (5) special grants for education, and (6) no application of a bill affecting the Depressed Classes if three-fourths of the community opposed it (ibid.:102). Though Ambedkar couldn't achieve anything by his representation to the Simon Commission, these demands proved to be a testimony to the confidence, which Ambedkar had revived, in the modern political institutions by which he sought to uplift the Dalits.

Later, Ambedkar was nominated to the 1930 Round Table Conference held in London to discuss India's future constitution. This was an acknowledgement of the leadership he had gained among the Dalits. Zelliot writes that by this time his fame had extended to every corner of Maharastra and beyond. For Ambedkar, his own and of Dewan Bahadur R. Srinivasan's nominations to the Round Table Conference meant, that " the untouchables were regarded not merely as a separate element from the Hindus but also of such importance as to have the right to be consulted in the framing of a constitution for India" (Ambedkar 1990: 40-41). This was a great achievement so far as Dalits were concerned. Though their efforts through social reform movements could not give them a separate identity this political movement accorded the same in no time. This can also be seen as a victory for

Ambedkar's political vision to shift from the social reform to acquire a separate political identity for Dalits. He opined that, "it is only in a swaraj (self) constitution that one has any chance of getting the political power in one's own hand without which one cannot bring salvation to one's people" (Zelliot1992: 162).

At the First Session of the Round Table Conference held in November 1930, Ambedkar put the list of the safeguards to be providing to the untouchables (Dalits) for their protection against the tyranny and oppression of the Hindus. The list included subjects like 'equal citizenship', fundamental rights, free enjoyments of equal rights, punishment for boycotting of Dalits, their protection against discrimination, adequate representation in the Legislatures and Cabinet adequate representation in the services, special departmental care, etc. The list of demands proves his knowledge of law and also his ability to use the Round Table Conference as a forum for asking for political safeguards for Dalits so that social justice can be assured to them.

Gandhi opposed the demand of Ambedkar of separate electorate for Dalits at the second session of the Round Table Conference convened in 1931. Speaking on behalf of the Congress he said, "the Congress has reconciled itself to special treatment of the Hindu - Muslim - Sikh tangle. There are sound historical reasons for it but the Congress will not extend that doctrine in any shape or form to the untouchables. Therefore, I would most strongly resist any further special representation" (Ambedkar 1990: 57). Gandhi further said that the separate electorate "Will create a division in Hinduism which I cannot possibly look forward to with any satisfaction whatsoever. I do not mind untouchables, if they so desire being converted to Islam or Christianity. I should tolerate that, but I cannot possibly tolerate what is in store for Hinduism if there are two divisions set forth in the villages" (Ambedkar 1990: 69). Replying to this version of the Congress and Gandhi, Ambedkar opined after some period, "The reasoning of the Congress appears to be correct. But it is only a superficial view of the matter. These elections take place once in a five years. It may be asked how can social solidarity between the Hindus and the untouchables be advanced by one day devoted to joint voting if for the rest of the five years they are leading severely separate lives. Similarly, it may well be asked how can one day devoted to separate voting in the course of five years make greater separation than what already exists or contrariwise how can one day in five year devoted to separate voting prevent those who wish to work for union form carrying out their purposes. To make it concrete how can separate electorate for the untouchables prevent intermarriage or inter-dining being introduced between them and Hindus? It is therefore futile to say that the political recognition of the untouchables as a separate element and granting them constitutional safeguards will perpetuate separation between them and the Hindus if the Hindus desire to put an end to it" (Ambedkar 1990: 191).

Ambedkar succeeded in getting the separate electorate accepted for the Dalits like for the rest of the minorities. It was an important achievement for him. British Government announced its decision known as the Communal Award on August 14, 1932. The Communal Award gave 78 seats to Dalits. Besides, Dalits had two more advantages. Viz., (i) A fixed quota of seats for the Dalit representatives to be elected buy separate electorates and (ii) The provision of the Double Vote, one to be used through separate electorates and the other through the general electorates. According to Ambedkar the separate electorate system gave a special status to the Dalits. "The second Vote given by the Communal Award was a priceless privilege. Its value as a political weapon was beyond reckoning. The voting strength of the untouchable in each constituency is one to ten. With this voting strength free to be used in the election of caste Hindu candidates, the untouchables would have been in a position to determine, if not to dictate, the issue of the General Election. No caste Hindu candidate could have dared to neglect their interest if he was made dependent upon the votes of the untouchables" (Ambedkar 1990: 90). But before any thing could be achieved in concrete terms; Gandhi opposed the Communal Award and went on a fast unto death. Ambedkar issued to the press statement on Gandhi's fast exposing his tactics, "suffice it is to say that although Mr. Gandhi declared a fast unto death, he did not want to die. He wanted very much to live" (Ambedkar 1990: 88). The fast created a problem of how to save Gandhi's life. All eyes turned on Ambedkar for the same. Because the Prime Minister had made it clear that the British Cabinet would not withdraw or alter the Communal Award of its own. In response to the urgent plea of the Congress party leaders and others, Ambedkar agreed with lot of pain to forego the privileges of the Communal Award and signed a Pact which later became famous as the Poona Pact. In the words of Ambedkar, "As to myself it is no exaggeration to say that no man was placed in a greater and graver dilemma than I was then. It was a baffling situation. I had to make a choice between two different alternatives. There was before me the duty, which I owed as a part of common humanity, to save Gandhi from sure death. There was before me the problem of saving for the untouchables the political rights, which the Prime Minister had given them. I responded to the call of humanity and saved the life of Mr. Gandhi by agreeing to alter the Communal Award in manner satisfactory to Mr. Gandhi" (Ambedkar 1990: 88).

The Poona Pact had produced different reactions. Ambedkar himself felt that Dalits were at a loss. Because he thought that the joint electorate was not useful to the Dalits as far as their effective and real representation was concerned, he opined that in the Joint electorate only that Dalit would be elected who was a nominee of the Hindus and, hence, a tool in their hands. He also argued on the basis of the composition of the constituencies in which the Dalit voters were out numbered in the ratio of 1 to 24 or in some cases 1 to 49. Further, according to Parvathamm, "Ambedkar was forced to sign the 'Poona Pact' and retrace his steps. Gandhi shot two birds with one bullet. He proclaimed that Dalits are Hindus. As Hindus they cannot have communal representation. But as socially, economically, politically and educationally degraded Hindus, he was willing to concede some special provisions for their upliftment. Ambedkar thus lost the cause of the SCs as a separate entity. Having retraced his steps once - rightly or wrongly - he was just not able to claim for SC separatism, though he kept on 'fumbling along these lines for the rest of his life" (Parvathamma 1989: 218).

Anyway, Ambedkar had to satisfy himself with the social and political reservations, which he got through the Poona Pact. But he did not restrict himself to these gains only. Having won the privilege for the Dalits to elect their own representatives for the first time in history of Indian political scene Ambedkar went on to form a separate political party for Dalits. He had realised during his struggle that if the interests of the untouchables had to be protected in the era of electoral politics which was about to being, the Dalits needed to be organised as apolitical party hence he established Indian Labour Party. Convinced about the less effectiveness of the Dalits, own party, he sought the support of the industrial and agricultural labourers who had common interests with the Dalits. Ambedkar's new party won as many as 11 of the 15 reserved seats in the 1937 elections to the Bombay Legislature. This was a great achievement for Ambedkar, as his party became a political force within no time. The Indian Labour Party was not very successful though it had won some rights for Dalits. It failed in t he areas concerned with labour and agricultural policies. It also failed to secure a base among caste Hindus.

In 1942, Ambedkar reformulated his political plans. He formed a new party with the name the 'Scheduled Castes Federation'. This time he limited its organization to the Dalits only in the hope of uniting all the Dalits in anew battle for political power. But in the 1945 elections to the provincial legislature the Scheduled Castes Federation was declared an organization with local influence in Bombay and the Central Provinces by the Cripps Mission. This was a set back to Ambedkar, as the Congress gained an upper hand. In 1956 Ambedkar made another attempt to transform the Scheduled Castes Federation into a party which would speak for all the 'dispossessed' - the Scheduled Castes, Scheduled Tribes, other Backward Classes and the minorities. This attempt again was for taking Dalits out of untouchability into a larger political group. But Ambedkar passed away before the party could start functioning.

Ambedkar not only worked independently for political and social rights for Dalits. In 1942 he joined the Viceroy's Executive Council as the in-charge of labour affairs. There also he asked for the safeguards and protective discrimination for the Dalits in services and scholarships in education. It is thus evident that Ambedkar always tried to avail every possible opportunity for gaining rights for Dalits whenever and from wherever they came. After independence Ambedker joined hands with that vision with the Congress government at the Center as the Law minister. He was also made the Chairman of the Drafting Committee to draft the constitution. His presence in the Constituent Assembly facilitated the making of suitable provisions in the Constitution in favour of the Dalits. Since he never compromised on the basic issues related to the Dalits, he resigned from the Cabinet in 1951, when he found that the government was not interested in uplifting the Dalits.

Final Phase of Leadership

Being out of the Cabinet, Ambedkar faced two election defeats and increased illness in the final years of his life. But the last two public acts of his life namely his conversion to Budhism and the foundation of the Republican Party should not be accepted as symptoms of his failures or renewed expression of separatism,

Zelliot tellingly portrays, "The conversion to Buddhism in October 1956, which came just before his death was the result of a personal conviction as well as a conscious effort to lay down a way his people could follow after his death" (Zelliot 1992:136). Further, Vishwanathan argues differently, "Drawing on Ambedkar's writings on culture and religion, I shall argue that, despite his disappointment with the aborted demand for separate electorates, his conversion was less a rejection of political solutions than rewriting of religious and cultural change into a form of political intervention. Such intervention was important not simply in demographic terms (that is, creating a numerically significant sonstituency distinct from Hinduism), but more so in terms of creating a new mythology around which the political identity of dalits could be mobilized. This mythology offered an alternative to mobilization around a structure of electoral reform that was flawed from the start because of its derivation from brahmanical and colonialist ideologies " (Viswanathan 1998: 212-213). This conversion which is considered as a religious movement has been regarded as the final phase of his movement. Basically, he declared his intention to relinquish Hinduism at the Yeola Conference in 1935. It was because of his growing detachment with efforts to change the orthodox Hindu opinion and with Hindu reformist elements. He saw no future for his people in Hinduism. "His major critique against Hinduism was that it supported institutionalised inequality in society -inequality based on the birth in a caste. He said that the Hindus had no social conscience. What they had was only a tradition, a ritual for social life and an abstract philosophy whose noble doctrine declaring man to have the essence of the divine in him, bore no relationship to the prescription for daily life" (Gore 1993: 50). Criticizing Hindu society he himself opined, "the first and the foremost thing that must be recognized is that Hindu society is a myth. Hindu society as such does not exist. It is only a collection of castes. Each caste is conscious of its existence. A caste has no feeling that it is affiliated to other castes except when there is a Hindu-Muslim riot. On all other occasions each caste endeavors to segregate itself and to distinguish itself from other castes. Each caste not only dined among itself and marries among itself but each caste prescribes its own distinctive dress. What other explanation can there be of the innumerable styles of dress worn by the men and women of India which so amuse the tourists. Indeed, the ideal Hindu must be like a rat living in his own hole refusing to have any contact with others" (Ambedkar 1979:50). That is why he turned to Buddhims.

To him Buddhism differed from Hinduism. He observed, "Hinduism believes in god. Buddhism has no god. Hinduism believes in soul. According to Buddhism there is no soul. Hinduism believes in Chaturvarnya and the caste system. Buddhism had no place for caste system and Chaturvarnya" (Keer 1962:492). He thus embraced Buddhism because Buddhism spoke of this worldliness, social equality between human beings, and self-respect to the individual. It emphasised compassion as a central moral and spiritual principle. In sum it had all the three elements of liberty, equality and fraternity which a democratic system should have. Hence, it was more useful for the Dalits. In his own words, "I Prefer Buddhism because it gives three principles in combination which no other religion does. Buddhism teaches Prajana (understanding as against superstition and supernaturalism), Karuna (love), and Samta (equality). This is what man wants for a good and happy life. Neither god nor soul can save society (Keer 1962: 490). When Ambedkar was asked why he was embracing Buddhism he had stated angrily, "Why cannot you ask this question to yourself and your forefathers as to why I am getting out of the Hindu fold and embracing Buddhism? He asked why they want his men to remain Harijan to enjoy only such 'benefits' as those of reservations. He asked them whether the Brahmins were Prepared to be untouchables to enjoy these privileges ... He also declared that he had once told to Mahatma that though he differed from him on the issues of untouchability, when the time come 'I will choose only the least harmful way for the country. And that is the greatest benefit I am conferring on the country by embracing Buddhism; for Buddhism is part and parcel of Bhartiya culture. I have taken care that my conversion will not harm the tradition of the culture and history of this land" (Keer 196: 498).

Another reason for embracing Buddhism by Ambedkar could be that he wanted to propagate the Buddhist faith in India. Dhananjay Keer has portrayed this fact; "Ambedkar also declared that he would propagate Buddhism in India when equipped with proper means for the task. As maker of the constitution, he had already achieved several things to that end. He described the provision for the study of Pali made in the constitution, the inscription of Buddhist aphorism on the frontage of the imposing Rashtrapati Bhavan in New Delhi, and the acceptance of the Ashok

Chakra by Bharat as her Symbol, as his personal achievements. The Government has declared Buddha Jayanti a holiday mainly through his efforts" (Keer 1962: 481-483). His last effort to popularise the Buddhist faith in India was a book ' Buddha and His Dhamma'. He tried to explain the tents of Buddhism, in this book, in most simple language for the common masses. We may conclude, that all this exercise for the propagation of Buddhism was undertaken by Ambedkar to provide Dalits a new identity and way of life, so that they can lead a dignified life.

Ambedkar and the Contemporary Dalit Leadership

Though there were Dalit leaders and Dalit Leadership at the time of Ambedkar but these was overshadowed by the dynamic and colossus personality of Ambedkar. Some of these leaders were with the Congress Hindu Mahasabha and some were working independently. Ambedkar became the sole representative of Dalits. Not only this, he became the focal center of the other political organizations too. His growing popularity can be testified by the episode relating to the Poona Pact. "Ambedkar's chief rival for Depressed Class Leadership, Rao Bahadur M. C. Rajah of Madras, was also involved in political action. Rajah, the first nominated member from the Depressed Classes on the Central Legislative Assembly, also instituted Depressed Class Conferences, testified to the Simon Commission, and had some following among the Mahars of Vidarbha as well as in the South of India. He and Dr. B. S. Moonje of the Hindu Mahasabha brought forward a compromise plan allowing reserved seats in general constituency for the Depressed Classes in 1932 before the Poona Pact was signed, but although M. C. Rajah was present at the Poona Pact negotiations, he was eclipsed in importance by Ambedkar" (Zelliot 1992 : 105).

M.C. Rajah (1883-1947) Dalit leader from south was born at St. Thomas mount, Madras. He belonged to the Pariah Caste. Educated in a Missionary school and Christian College he became a schoolteacher in 1906. In 1917 he was nominated to elementary education committee and in 1924 to the Madras University senate. He started Dravidian school at Nungambakkam in 1936. He was of the view that education should infuse in the students the sprit of social uplift. He became secretary of the state Adi-Dravid Mahayan Sabha in 1916. Through this organization he worked for the upliftment of the Dalit masses. Considering Britain as the liberator of the lower classes in India Rajah popularised the view of free and compulsory education to the Dalits. In 1928 he was also elected as the President of ALL India Depressed Classes Association. Nominated to the Madras legislative council in 1920 and in 1927 as the member of Indian legislative Assembly, he continued as a member of Indian legislative Assembly till 1937.

One of the most significant achievements of M.C. Rajah was regarding the change of nomenclature given to Dalits during his period. In the year 1922 as a member of Madras Legislative council M.C. Rajah had moved a resolution for the deletion of the terms Panchama' and 'Paraya' which were used to designate the Dalit at that time. His demand was accepted as Government of Madras issued an order forbidding the use of terms Panchama and Pariah in the region. When the demand of separate electorate for the Dalits was put forward by Dr. Ambedkar and R. Srinivasan at the Round Table conference (RTC) in London in 1930, Rajah supported the said demand. He criticized Mahatma Gandhi and Indian National Congress for not supporting the demand and there by the Dalit cause. However, he entered into a pact for joint electorate and reserved seats, with Dr. Monje, the leader of the Hindu Mahasabha. Slowly he was sidelined and faded with Ambedkar's success in mobilization of the Dalits.

The other leader acknowledged by Ambedkar himself in the Dalit movement was Dewan Bahadur R. Srinivasn (1859-1948) a member of the Dalit community from Madras. He was born on 7th July 1859 in Chengalpet district in Tamil Nadu. His father Rattamalai was a poor Adi-Dravida former. He became a Government servant on Mill Station of Nilgiri District where he met Colonel Olcott and Madam Blatvastky. In order to organise Dalits; he founded Adi-Dravida Mahajan Sabha in the year 1891. Through his organisation he convened first conference of Dalits in December 1893. He carried out many struggles against untouchability, caste system and religious myths. He also started a magazine named Parayan in 1893 to concentize masses about the exploitation of the Dalits. Srinivasan was nominated to the Madras Legislative council as a representative of depressed classes in the year 1923 and remained in legislature till 1935. Later on he was nominated as a representative of the depressed classes in India to the Round Table Conference held during 1930-32 in London along with Babasaheb Dr. Ambedkar.

Like Ambedkar, Srinivasan also believed that the tyranny of untouchability can be removed it the Dalits are granted political power. He opined that separate electorate is only a temporary measure for the Dalits to improve their conditions. In fact he wanted reservations of seats on a population basis. However, Srinivasan did not support the declaration of conversion by Babasaheb Ambedkar in 1935. Later, he remained aloof from the Dalit political movement.

Shyam Sunder was another Dalit Leader who was also a scholar, thinker and writer. The credit for transposing many of Ambedkar's revolutionary thoughts into an action packed programme goes to Shyam Sunder. He had formed Bhim Sena; a militant force of dedicated Dalit youths, which created tremendous impact particularly in the three states of Karnataka, Andhra Pradesh and Maharastra (Jogdand, 1991:62). In fact the Bhim Sena, derived its name from Ambedkar's name, Bhim Rao. He called the Bhim Sena a self-defence force based on truth and justice. But he also could not make his independent identity and remained in the shadow of Ambedkar.

Besides these, B.S. Venkat Rao was a prominent Dalit leader from Hyderabad State Depressed Classes Association, established in 1938. In 1939 this organization agitated for separate electorate along with the reservations of seats for Dalits in the state. The organization also asked for educational concessions. Besides, there were other Dalit leaders also like G.A. Gavai and Jagjivan Ram but they were associated with the Congress. Hence, they had no independent status but Jagjivan Ram needs a special mention here.

Jagjivan Ram (1908-1986) was born on April 5th 1908 at Chanddwa, Ara district in Bihar. He was born to a literate farmer Shri Shobi ram who had 20 Acres of land. His mother's name was Basanti Devi. Having done his schooling in village he went to Banners Hindu University (BHU) for higher education. He passed his graduation in 1931 from Calcutta University. In his school days he also suffered the same type of discriminations as were suffered by Ambedkar. Jagjivan Ram was conscious of the plight of the Dalits from his school days that is why he established Ravidas Mahasabha to unite Dalits in 1928 when he was in Calcutta. In 1930 he joined congress and remained in it till 1977. It is said that said that he wad influenced by two personalities, Madan Mohan Malviya and M.k. Gandhi. Malvia had advised him in his childhood to shift to Kashi Vidhyapeeth for his higher studies. On the other hand Gandhi's call to Hindus to give up the practice of Untouchability during the Civil Disobedience Movement of 1930. Added together these two personalities unconsciously dragged him in the fold of Hinduism and made him pro Congress. It also distanced him away from Ambedkar's movement and time and again they found themselves standing against each other. It is said that Congress deliberately groomed him to oppose Ambedkar and attract Dalits to its fold. He was one of the signatories of the Poona Pact in 1932 and opposed the proposal of separate electorate of Ambedkar.

Dr. Rajendra Prasad initiated Jagjivan Ram in his own organisation Anti Untouchability Society working for the Dalit upliftment in Bihar. Later on he introduced him to Mahatma Gandhi who entrusted him with the responsibilities of Harijan Sevak Sangh in Bihar. In the year 1934 in the annual conference of Ravidas Mahasabha at Calcutta it was decided to establish the Depressed Classes League following which a conference was organised in 1935 at Kanpur. The conference formally declared the formal establishment of the Depressed Classes League with Rasik Lal Biswas as its President and Jagjivan Ram and P. N. Rajbhoj as Secretaries. Jagjivan Ram during 1935 also participated in the Hindu Mahasabha conference held at Lucknow. The main aim of the conference was to plan a policy to stop Dalits from converting to other religions. Infact Jagivan Ram had moved a resolution to throw open the temples, watering places, schools, etc. for the Dalits which was opposed by Shri Shankaracharya of Puri, but later on the resolution was passed. Madan Mohan Malviya praised Jagjivan Ram in hiss Presidential address for his services to Hinduism by keeping Dalits within the fold of Hindu Society.

Another trait of Jagjivan Ram's leadership was that unlike Ambedkar he wanted the upliftment of the Dalits within the fold of the Hindu Society. He opposed the conversions of the Dalits to other religions. When Ambedkar had given a call that "he will not die as a Hindu" it was he who persuaded Dalits to postpone the mass conversion programme indefinitely in the conference of the Dalits held at Lucknow in the year 1936. Jagjivan Ram was elected to the Bihar Provincial Assembly on Congress platform for the first time in the year 1937. He became one of the strong pillars of the Congress during the Quit India Movement in 1942 and had to undergo imprisonment for a period of 14 months. When the interim Government was formed on August 12, 1946 under the Priministership of Nehru, Jagjivan Ram was inducted as Labour Minister. He also became the member of the Constituent Assembly. In the post-Constitution era he became the Minister for Communication in which Ambedkar was the law Minister. From the above description of activities, offices held by him, it can be argued that Jagjivan Ram aligned with the dominant socio-political forces of his time to achieve some rights and privileges for the Dalits. Moreover, he was the sole representative of the Dalits in the eastern part of the country as Ambedkar's movement was largely restricted to western and to some extent northern parts of the country.

A highly educated man with his degrees, B. A., M. A., Ph. D., M. Sc., D. Sc., Barrister-at-Law, Ambedkar was a political person, practical and pragmatic. Hence, he could respond to most of the needs of Dalits. He tried to avail each and every opportunity for their upliftment. He attacked the stinking Hindu Society for the amelioration of the wretched conditions of the Dalits from social, religious, political, economic fronts with mass actions as well as his own intellectual writings. Throughout his socio-political movements Ambedkar did not succumb to the racial demands like "Lord of the Land", the "pre -Aryan Inhabitants of India", etc. of the early Dalit leadership. Since he regarded the Indian culture and the people homogenous, he did not ask for the racial identity of the Dalits.

Ambedkar wanted to make his people socially and politically conscious, which could not happen earlier. He made the Dalits aware of the indignities heaped on them and sought to arouse their pride as human beings. For that he started initially many satyagrahas which included the demands of Civil rights. These were the use of public places, like roads, tanks, etc. he organised Satyagraha for temple entry also as stated earlier. But he was very clear in his perception of the ultimate goal. In fact, it was an indirect action to gain political and educational power for the Dalits. In the words of Ambedkar, "I did not launch the temple entry movement because I wanted the Depressed Classes to become worshippers of idols which they were prevented from worshipping or because I believed that temple entry would make them equal members in and an integral part of Hindu society. So far as this aspect of the case is concerned, I would advise the Depressed Classes to insist upon a complete overhauling of Hindu society and Hindu theology before they consent to become an integral part of Hindu society. I started temple entry Satyagraha only because I felt that was the best way of energizing the Depressed Classes and making them conscious of their position. As I believe I have achieved that, therefore, I have no more use for temple entry. I want the Depressed Classes to concentrate their energy and resources on politics and education" (Zelliot 1992:131).

Abandoning the Satyagraha, Ambedkar took the cause of the Dalits via more secular institutions like politics and education. This was yet another innovation made by him for the Dalits. The earlier Dalit leadership had very little knowledge of using this weapon for the rights of the Dalits. Ambedkar used his American experience and knowledge for demanding the fundamental rights of the Dalits. And the best part of all this was that Ambedkar did this without the sponsorship of caste Hindus. He was always in the forefront. His presentations and negotiations with the British were incredible. His arguments to the Southborough Committee, Simon Commission and at the Round Table Conferences were based on a deep analysis of the Hindu social order, which he believed was based on graded inequality. He also criticized caste Hindus for not telling the real conditions of Dalits to the British. That is why, he always felt that the Dalits should be represented by themselves and not by caste Hindus. Maybe he believed more in the dictum that, 'only wearer of the shoe knows where it pinches'. He believed that caste Hindus could only sympathise with the cause of the Dalits but they would not empathise with them. Hence, they could not represent them properly. That is why, he once said, "the efforts of others are like a nurse and I am their mother".

Criticising Gandhi for not cooperating in the abolition of untouchability, he opined that Gandhi himself was perpetuating the caste and Varna system. Ambedkar argued that if Hindu social order was to reorganize and revitalise, then its caste system must go. He was of the view that sanctity of the sacred scriptures should be challenged because the social order draws its strength from these scriptures. But Gandhi was never in his favour. Rather, he relied on a change of heart and drew his morality from these sacred scriptures. That is why, Ambedkar accused Gandhi of being lost in his double role of the Mahatma and a Politician. He propounded, "As a Mahatma he may be trying to spritualise politics. Whether he has succeeded in it or not politics has certainly commercialised him. A politician must know that society cannot bear the whole truth and that he must not speak the whole truth; if he is speaking the whole truth it is bad for politics. The reason why the Mahatma is always supporting caste and Varna is because he is afraid that if he opposed them he will lose his place in politics.

Whatever the source of his confusion, the Mahatma must be told that he is deceiving himself and also deceiving the people by preaching under the name of Varna" (Gore 1993:147-148).

As mentioned earlier, he also criticized the Congress for not taking up the cause of the Dalits. Ambedkar time and again on account of exposed its 'genuine' concern whether it was passing a resolution about the Dalits after 32 years of its formation or it was bungling in the use of public money earmarked for the upliftement of the Dalits. For instance, one crore and thirty lakhs of rupees were collected in the Tilak Swaraj Fund in 1921 for undertaking the constructive programmes at the Bardoli session of the Congress in 1922. Out of this only seven thousands of rupees were spent for the abolition of untouchability. Such was the hypocrisy of the Congress.

Ambedkar exposed the hypocrisy of these leaders and organizations. Ambedkar emphasised on education. He started a number of fortnightly like the 'MOOK NAYAK, (Leader of the Dumb), 'BAHISKRIT BHARAT, (Ex-Communicated Indians), PRABUDHA BHARAT, (The Enlightened Indian) and JANATA. Through these he wanted to awaken the downtrodden masses from their age-old lethargy and inaction and unite them. He asked the government to grant concessions, scholarships and other facilities to Dalit students. He himself founded the People's Education Society in Bombay in 1945, which set up a number of colleges and schools to provide basic and non-discriminatory education to Dalits.

One significant feature of Ambedkar's leadership was that it was militant in nature. He reminded his followers that they had once belonged to the warrior caste and argued them to remain militant. He said, "Goats, not lions, are sacrifice". This militancy and bitterness was justified by the objective reality of the lonely position of the Dalits. Gore has stated that it may be also because of the hurt and the disillusionment caused by the realisation that even a highly educated individual like Ambedkar with a coveted foreign degree, did not have the right to live a life of self-respect in India's caste-ridden society as he was born a Dalit (ibid: 79). Further, Dhananjay, keer, the biographer of Ambedkar gives another reason for this militancy. According to him, it was due to Ambedkar's feeling towards the Congress which was willing to make all kinds of concessions to accommodate the Muslim interests, as could be seen from the Congress League Pact but it was not sensitive to the problems of the Dalits (Keer 1962:40). Whatever be the reasons for the militancy of his leadership, it was channeled for achieving the rights of Dalits.

As for as identity for the Dalits was concerned, the nature of Ambedkar's leadership became that of protest. With protest he wanted to change the identity of the Dalits, which used to be that of the meek and servile, uncomplaining and ever obedient, Dalits whom swept the village streets and worked in the farms of caste Hindus. Before embracing Buddhism Ambedkar had sought to establish the identity of the Dalits, through his explorations in history. In his book, Ambedkar put forth the hypothesis that the Dalits were historically "broken men", i.e., primitive tribes. They were defeated and hence, broken into segments. He rejected the theory of racial differences as the basis of untouchability. He believed that the broken men of ancient India were followers of Buddhism and had not cared to return to Brahmanism when the latter triumphed over the formers. Ambedkar postulated that the Dalits were made to live outside the village not because they were 'untouchables' because they had always lived outside the villages. They came to be regarded as 'untouchables' later because of their religious differences and the imposition of new Brahminism. So, when Ambedkar embraced Buddhism along with millions of his followers, it did not surprise many. But he definitely did this to take them away from untouchability and pull them into a larger religious group.

Nature and Crisis of the Dalit Leadership During Ambedkar Era

As far as the nature of the Dalit leadership during Ambedkar era is concerned it was more assertive than the pre-Ambedkar era. Dalits under the leadership of there own caste leaders have started learning the use of political means for achieving their rights and privileges. Dalits also learned the art of direct action i.e. agitation, sit-ups, strikes, etc., which were very scantly used by them in the early part of their oganising. The style of leadership of asking the rights for the Dalits through Petitions and Prayers also changed. With more and more Dalit political representative in the legislature, Dalits became more and more politically conscious. Newsletters, Pamphlets, Weeklies, became prominent medium of communication among the Dalits of different regions; this also indicated the increasing literacy among them. The unfortunate aspect of this era was the division of the Dalit leadership into two main streams, i.e., 'dependent' and 'independent'. The former aligned with dominant socio-political forces of their time like Indian National Congress, Hindu Mahasabha, etc., and the latter led an autonomous struggle of the Dalits without any support of the said forces.

As far as the crisis of the Dalit leadership of this period is concerned, it did not in the beginning have a viable unity and network at the All India level. More like the earlier leadership, it was also fragmented. The movement of Ambedkar was confined mainly to Maharashtra and the adjoining areas, though Dalits in country found in him a spokesman of their own. Though Ambedkar did try to unite them through social and political mobilizations but he could not succeed in bringing out a unifying formula for Dalits. The partonising skills of the Congress were stronger than Ambedkar's resources for the mobilization of the Dalits. Hence, the Congress attracted many Dalit leaders who could have given their valuable support to Ambedkar to make his movement stronger.

Ambedkar tried to unite the Dalits under a common banner when he formed the Independent Labour Party in 1936. He did it only when he saw that for electoral purposes it was necessary that the mobilization of Dalits and others could be on different lines. He thought that industrial workers would be the best allies of the Dalits. As the interests of Dalits coincided with those of the labourers, they could be brought together. And this paid also to a great extent. But in 1942 Ambedkar reformulated his political plans with a vision of uniting all the Dalits (untouchables). In the arena of power politics, he established a political party called Scheduled Castes Federation as mentioned above. It was exclusively restricted to the Dalits. This attempt to unite the Dalits on political lines failed miserably as Scheduled Castes Federation was routed in the 1946 elections. One of the many reasons for this failure was that the Dalits were still not conscious of the power of their votes. They had no education about the use of this power. Moreover, mobilization of the Dalits was restricted to western and some southern parts of the country. Ambedkar has been criticised by some of his closest biographers for the neglect of organisation building, which was also responsible for not socializing the Dalits in the political realm. Keer opines, "Ambedkar did not try to organise his political party on modern lines... There were no regular annual conferences or general meetings. When he wanted his people to assemble under his banner, he simply gave a clarion call and the organization sprang up like a crop in the rainy season.

In the summer there would be nothing in the field, the banner resting in his study corner and the people at home" (Keer 1962: 447). The Scheduled Caste Federation as a political organisation led to another problem. The Dalit movement led by Ambedkar became a very narrow based movement.

An another crisis of the leadership of Ambedkar and his era was that it could not solve the riddle of who were the possible allies of Dalits. The problem of earlier Dalit Leadership erupted again and could not find any solution. As far as Ambedkar is concerned this may be so, because he could not trust any body. And he had genuine reasons for that. He had argued that in the Hindu social order nobody could be the ally of the Dalits and uplift them except the Dalits themselves. Even his temporary trust in the British was not free from problems and it was a pragmatic move. Ambedkar could not resolve in his lifetime this riddle of allies. However, one gets some clue of resolution in his remark that, "we cannot fight all our enemies at once". And on the basis of this statement Omvedt has drawn an inference, "This meant making difficult choices about the 'lesser evil', for instance as between Muslims, the Congress, British imperialism etc. At other times it meant seeing forces or political parties as positive allies (the communists, non-Brahman parties, the Muslims). In terms of the traditional traditional caste structure even once Dalits had defined themselves as separate and taken an 'untouchable' 'touchable' distinction as providing the first of the Caste structure in a sharper sense were all 'touchables' equally enemies or should one make distinctions taking 'Brahmans' as the 'main enemy' while 'non-Brahmans' or 'Shudras' were potential allies" (Omvedt 1994:135). This question of the possible allies of the Dalits still haunt the contemporary Dalit leadership.

The crises of a separate identity for the Dalits remained unresolved through this era. Over the years the Dalits have had different social, religious and legal identities. Neither Ambedkar nor the other leaders did largely succeed in giving any separate identity to all the Dalits. His conversion to Buddhism did give a different identity to them but those who could not convert remained in the pale of the Hindu society. They are still part of the graded inequality though they have got legal identity of the Scheduled Caste. Even Dalit converts to Buddhism, Islam, Christianity etc. On the one hand do not identify themselves with Dalits at large, and on the other they still suffer from the stigma of untouchability and low status. Hence, Dalits still do not have one single identity, to fight untidily under the one umbrella of single name, though they have a single problem of untouchability.

Despite the shortcomings, which were very few, of Ambedkar's Leadership, his struggle helped the Dalits in getting that social and political rights which were enough for the Dalits to march ahead. A concrete foundation was prepared for the transition to a higher level of socio-cultural and democratic movement of the Dalits, for the Dalits and by the Dalits. In other words Ambedkar had provided such a dimension to the struggle of the Dalits, which had reached a point of no return. There was no question of going back to the past. But he was not very optimistic about the Dalit movement and the Leadership and he had solid reasons for that. In the last days of his life he told, "I also wanted someone from among the Depressed Classes to come forward in my life time and take the heavy responsibility of running the movement after me. There, however, seems no one who would rise to the occasion. My lieutenants, in whom I had full faith and confidence to run the movements, are fighting among themselves for leadership and power, unmindful of the heavy responsibility that is going to fall upon them", (Kadam 1993:241) but even then he tried to guide his followers and cautioned them as to how to channalize their action in future. He expressed that, "whatever I have been able to achieve for them (Dalits), I have done it single handed, passing through crushing miseries and endless troubles, in the midst of abuses hurled at me from all sides, more so from the Hindu Press. Fighting with my opponents, all my life, as also with a handful of may own people who deceived me for their selfish ends. But I will continue to serve the country and my downtrodden people till my end. With great difficulty, I have brought the caravan where it is seen today. Let the caravan march on and further on, despite the hurdles, pitfalls and difficulties that may come its way. They must rise to the occasion, if they want to live an hounourable and respectable life. If my people, my lienteuants are not able to take the caravan ahead, they should leave it where it is seen today, but must not, under any circumstances allow the caravan to go back" (ibid: 241).

References

Ambedkar, B. R, 1979, *Dr. Babasaheb Ambedkar Writing and Speeches Vol. 1.*, Education Department, Government of Maharashtra, Bombay.

Ambedkar, B. R., 1990 "What Congress and Gandhi have done to the Untouchables", in *Dr. Babasaheb Ambedkar Writings and Speeches Vol. 9*, Education Department, Government of Maharashtra.

Fuchs, Stephen, 1981, *At the Bottom of the Indian Society*, Munshiram Manoharlal Publishers, Delhi.

Gooptu, Nandni, 1993, *Caste And Labour: Untouchable Social Movements in Urban Uttar Pradesh* in The Early Twentieth Century in Peter Robb (ed.), Dalit *Movements and the meanings of Labour in India*, Oxford University Press, Delhi.

Gore M.S., 1993, *The Social Context of an ideology, Ambedkar's Political and Social Thought*, Sage Publications, New Delhi.

Joshi, R. Barbara, 1982, *Democracy in Search of Equality*, Hindustan publishing Corporation, Delhi.

Jogdand, P. G., 1991, *Dalit Movement in Maharastra*, Kanak Publications, New Delhi.

Juergensmeyer, Mark, 1982, *Religion as Social Vision: The Movement against Untouchability in 20th Century Punjab*, University of California Press, Barkeley.

Kadam, K. N. (ed.), 1993, *Dr. B. R. Ambedkar the Emancipator of the Oppressed*, Popular Prakashan, Bombay.

Keer, Dhananjay, 1994, *Dr. Ambedkar Life and Mission*, Popular Prakashan, Bombay.

Lynch, O. M., 1974, The Politics of Untouchability: Social Mobility and Social Change in a City of India, National Publishing House, New Delhi.

Mathew, Joseph, 1986, *Ideology Protest and Social Mobility*, Inter-India Publications, New Delhi.

Omvedt, Gail, 1994, *Dalit and the Democratic revolution, Dr. Ambedkar and the Dalit Movement in Colonial India*, Sage, Publications, New Delhi.

Omvedt, Gail, 1994, *Dalit and the Democratic revolution, Dr. Ambedkar and the Dalit Movement in Colonial India*, Sage, Publications, New Delhi.

Oommen, T. K., 1990, *Protest and Change: Studies in Social Movements*, Sage Publications, New Delhi.

Parvathamma, C., 1989, *Scheduled Castes at the Cross Roads*, Ashish Publishing House, New Delhi.

Usuda, MaSayuki, 1997, Pushed towards the partition: Jogendranath Mandal and the Constrained Namsudra Movement in, H. Kotani (ed.) Caste System, Untouchability and the Depressed, Manohar, New Delhi.

Viswanathan, Gauri,1998, *Outside the Fold : Conversion, Modernity, and Belief*, Oxford University Press, New Delhi.

Zelloit, Eleanor, 1986, Learning the use of Political Means: The Mahars of Maharshtra, in Rajni Kothari (ed.) *Caste in Indian Poitics*, Orient Longman, New Delhi.

3

The Research Setting

Having probed the Socio-historical profile of the Dalit leadership in different parts of the country alongwith the pivitol role played by Babasaheb Dr. Bhim Rao Ambedkar, now we will try to locate it in the state of Uttar Pradesh. As stated earlier, that we will have an in depth analysis of the Dalit leadership in Uttar Prasesh the universe of the present study. After giving brief socio-historical profile of the state, we shall also elucidate in this chapter the socio-personal background of our respondents drawn from the eastern, western, and central regions of Uttar Pradesh.

Socio-Historical Profile

In, ancient times, Uttar Pradesh was known as Madhyadesh but during the British period it was named as United Provinces of Agra and Oudh. Yet, after independence, the state was renamed as Uttar Pradesh (U.P.). Being on the route of invaders from north-west and forming part of the rich fertile plain of the Indo-Gangetic belt, its history has seen many ups and downs. Its vast and fertile Gangetic plains attracted invaders from the West and Central Asia. Besides, the history of Uttar Pradesh became in many ways the history of India. For instance, in the 6th century B.C the little republics in the name of 16 *Mahajanpadas* were prominent for their perpetual war and annexation of one over the other, and at least 8 of them were located in the state. The Nandas ruled from 343 B.C to 321 B.C. The rules of the Mauryan empire, the Sakas, Kushans, Guptas, Lodhis, Mughals, the Nawabs and finally of the British had made the whole history of Uttar Pradesh a blend of different races and cultures. Even the Mutiny of 1857 remained largely confined to the plains of Uttar Pradesh (Chandra 1989:32).

Since the early 1920s, U.P became the political center of the Nationalist Movement and Allahabad was the headquarter of the All India Congress Committee (AICC). Interestingly, it was also the center of the Muslim separatism. Most of the important leaders of the Indian National Congress and of the Muslim League were drawn from this state (Hasan 1998: 5). Hence, it is amply proved that Uttar Pradesh has been at the centre stage of Indian society and polity since centuries and it still remains the same. "It has been and still is the stage for the construction of new social and political designs in Indian democracy. Unlike the non-Hindi-speaking states which are distinctly regional and linguistic in ethno-cultural terms, U.P. self-consciously rejected a distinct regional identity because it was supposed to be the core of Indian civilization" (ibid : 6).

Among the Indian states, Uttar Pradesh ranks first in terms of population (139 million) and fourth in terms of the geographical area (294 thousand sq. kms) it occupies. Its population density is 473 persons per sq.km with 385 persons and 5553 persons in rural and urban areas respectively. About 80.2 per cent of the state population is rural and 19.8 per cent is urban. As of now, the state is divided into 83 districts, 308 Tehsils, 901 Development Blocks, 8814 Nyaya Panchayats and 123,950 villages. Out of these villages, 112,539 are densely populated, 11,102 are thinly populated and 309 are forest villages. In addition, there are 753 urban units also. The percentage of total work-force in the state is 32.2 which means 67.8 per cent population of the state is dependent. Also, out of the total work-force 72.2 per cent are engaged in the agricultural sector (U.P., Annual 1996-97).

As per the 1991 Census, the literacy rate of people in the state is 41.60 percent which is one of the lowest in the country and is obviously below the national average of 52.21 per cent. Further, the rural literacy rate is 33.66 per cent and that of urban is 61.0 per cent. As far as literacy rate of males and females is concerned, it is 55.73 and 25.31 per cent respectively but both are much lower than that of the national level. The state is well equipped with the educational centres. There are 26 universities, 9 Medical colleges, 12 Engineering colleges, 59 Degree colleges which also run post-graduate courses, 89 Polytechnic and 13 Women polytechnics. But on the other hand, "The outlay on education is extremely small compared to the needs of the State. Nearly 14,000 villages are without a Primary School, whereas 15,000 primary schools and 3000 middle schools have no buildings" (Hasan 1998:45).

Agriculture occupies a dominant place in the economy of Uttar Pradesh. The preponderance of the agricultural sector is evident from the size of population it supports, the volume of employment it offers and the proportion of income it contributes to the total income of the state. It also provides the largest share of 72.2 per cent agriculture workers out of the total workers and contributes around 41.5 per cent of total income of the state (1995-96). It is said that the "Concentration of population in the agricultural sector can be attributed to the backwardness of the non-agricultural sector of the state which has been able to provide jobs hardly for 25 percent of the working force" (Dwivedi 1973:9). On the basis of average agricultural production during 1994-95, the contribution of Uttar Pradesh to the nation was one of the maximum, as in rice it was 12.8 per cent and in pulses 19.1 per cent. In fact, in both the cases, U.P. was second only to West Bengal and Madhya Pradesh respectively. In the production of wheat (35.0 percent) and sugarcane (44.5 percent), it was highest in the country.

TABLE 3.1

Occupational Distribution of Working Population in the State

Sl. No	*Category of Occupation*	*Percentage*
1.	Agriculture (Farmer + Agriculture labour)	72.2
2.	Live Stock, fishing, forestry, hunting, horticulture and allied works	00.7
3.	Mining	00.1
4.	Renovation, Servicing and construction	07.7
5.	Construction	01.2
6.	Trade and commerce	06.2
7.	Transport and Communication	01.9
8.	Others	10.0
	Total main workers	100.00

Source: Dept. of Planning, Govt. of U.P. (1996-97).

The condition of industrial sector is not very encouraging as stated the daily factory employment of 5.1 per 1000 persons was the lowest in the country as against 18.2 in Gujarat, 19.3 in Maharashtra and 14.6 in Karnataka in 1991. The contribution of manufacturing sector to the total income of the state is also low as it is just 19.9 per cent. The unemployment problem both in agricultural and industrial sectors including even the tertiary sector is acute as one million unemployed are added every year. The percentage of capital development expenditure of Rs.406 in 1987-88 in the state was extremely small. The consecutive annual budgets have neglected the industrial sector. It is said that, "the government employs 80 per cent of the work force in the organized sector. Opportunities for employment are confined to agriculture and government service. Power, transport, irrigation and industry which generate employment are underdeveloped. Despite economic diversification, employment in the manufacturing sector has not increased substantially" (Hasan 1998: 46). Available data also indicate that the income or economic inequalities still exist in the state. The percentage of population below the poverty line was 60 in 1967-68. It decreased to 48.7 per cent in 1977-78 and further decreased to 35 per cent in 1988 as compared to 29 per cent for the country as a whole. Thus, the decrease in the percentage of population below the poverty line in U.P was marginal as compared to 11 per cent in the country (ibid:46).

As of now, the state's bureaucratic set-up in U.P. is the largest in India. The state employed about 15 lakh people in the government, semi-government and local bodies in 1986. There has been an increase of 25 per cent in it since 1982. The T.N. Dhar Committee (1998) has observed that the UP secretariat is overcrowded and there has to be rationalization of the posting of the employees. There are many officers from outside the secretariat cadre who have come and occupied various positions therein. According to the 1992 civil list, there were 580 Indian Administrative Service (IAS) officers in the state. Besides the direct recruitment in the cadre there are bureaucrats who join the IAS through promotion from Provincial Civil Services (PCS) cadre. Similarly, there is internal struggle between IAS and PCS officers and also between IAS and IPS officers. Such a large number of officers in the state has also made the administration inefficient, instead of increasing its efficiency. The hierarchies of official cadres have increased, paperwork has doubled, and more and more complaints of various nature come to the secretariat. This means, the district administration cutting the edge of bureaucracy has failed to satisfy and solve the grievances of the general masses. Dharam Singh Rawat, a retired IAS officer and now a Social Activist in Lucknow lamented that, "The bureaucrats think themselves as masters of the people and not the servant and, hence, they have gone out of bound and it is very difficult to meet them". Zoya

Hassan (1998: 50) writes, "The problems of governance were not resolved by a colossal bureaucracy. The only purpose it served was employment generation for the vast army of unemployed in a state where avenues for non-governmental employment were extremely restricted".

Social Structure in the State

Caste is the major component of social structure in India specially of the Hindu social system. It is also a fact that caste system in the north Indian plains, where the Aryans and their Sanskritic culture had made the deepest impact, differs in a fundamental way from that in the south. In the south, Brahmins though small in numbers are the only representative of the twice-born castes. There are no counter-parts of the north Indian Rajputs and Vaishyas in the south. As a result, Brahmins in the south have tended to be more separated from the rest of the Shudra population. But on the contrary, a relatively large proportion of population in Uttar Pradesh is composed of the twice-born castes. Hence, Brahminism in north has been relatively less tyrannical. There is a greater continuity in the ritual ranks of the various castes in Uttar Pradesh which, in turn, has led to a general sharing of social status and political power. Along with the Brahmins, the other twice-born castes also have access to modern profession and power structure. This has remained one of the most dominant reasons that the state had not witnessed any massive mobilisation of the lower caste Shudras or of the advanced Untouchable castes that had occurred in southern states and in Maharashtra in the past. The anti-Brahmanism characterized by steep and discontinuous traditional hierarchies, seems to have flourished in these states and this, in turn, have had fostered the political mobilisation of castes still lower in the ritual-hierarchy. These states with a relatively higher proportion of twice-born castes, as mentioned above, and having more gradual and contiguous social handicaps seem to be less susceptible to horizontal mobilizations from below comprising of ritually deprived castes seeking opportunities, status and political power (Rudolph and Rudolph 1987:76-79).

Anyway, the caste composition, according to the Rapid Census of 1994 in the state of U.P., showed the Brahmins comprising of 10 per cent, Rajputs 7 per cent, Baniyas and Kayasthas 4 per cent. Intermediate Castes like Jats, Bhumihar and Tyagis 2 per cent,

OBCs 37 per cent and Scheduled Castes 22 per cent. Except in the hills where Thakurs equivalent to Rajputs of the plains constitute more than fifty per cent of the population, there is no single caste with more than a quarter of a district's population. Only in the following five districts does a single caste approximate to nearly twenty per cent of total population of each district.

TABLE 3.2
District-wise Percentage of Population of Castes

Sl. No.	*Name of the district in the district*	*Caste*	*% of total population*
1.	Mainpuri	Ahir	22.0
2.	Azamgarh	Chamar	20.0
3.	Ghazipur	Ahir	19.0
4.	Mathura	Jat	19.0
5.	Saharanpur	Chamar	21.0

Source: Rapid Census of 1994 – U.P

Another feature of the caste distribution in Uttar Pradesh is that the castes like Brahmins, Rajputs, Ahirs, Chamars and Kurmis tend to be evenly spread throughout the state. However, Jats, Tyagis and Gujars in the West, Kachhis in South-Central, Kewats and Koris in a few North-Eastern districts, and Bhumihars in Varanasi, Ghazipur and Azamgarh districts have regional concentration. Uttar Pradesh, is thus, a multi-caste state with some sort of balance in terms of size of population, and economic and political dominance of several castes, except Scheduled Castes, in different regions. This goes in a way contrary to the general belief about regional dominance of certain castes such as Maratha in Maharashtra, and Kamma and Reddy in Andhra Pradesh, Jat in Haryana, etc. (see Ahmad and Saxena 1998:173-174). It is, however, a fact that the most influential other Backward Castes or Classes in U.P. (OBCs) are Yadav, Kurmi and Ahir. The Yadavs are an important force everywhere, except in Western region and in the hill districts in the state. According to a recent survey, they are over 10 per cent of the population in Shahjahanpur, Mohanlalganj, Pratapgarh, Faizabad, Phulpur, Jaunpur, Saidpur, Mirzapur, Azamgarh, Deoria, Gorakhpur, Balia, Ghazipur, Varanasi, Etawah, Kannauj, Farrukhabad, Mainpuri, Jalesar and Etah districts. Likewise, Kurmis and Ahirs are numerically dominant in Pilibhit,

Kheri, Sitapur, Barabanki, Kaiserganj, Bahraich, Varanasi, Phulpur and Chail (Rapid Census 1994). These are 'clean' Shudra castes, with their highest concentration in the eastern districts of the state, who traditionally worked as cultivators, cowherds, artisans and servants, field labourers, etc. In the eastern and central districts, the Brahmin, Thakur and Bhumihar Zamindars controlled, since the time of Akbar, the major share of land with others drawn from high status Muslim groups. But in western U.P their control was weakened, since the middle of the nineteenth century, by the challenge of Jats and Gujars who along with Bania money lenders made major inroads into landed property (Hasan 1998 : 124).

The dominant position of the Rajputs in terms of their control over land in eastern U.P. is determined by their pre-colonial history of rule and dominations. Some ethno-geographers (see, Singh 1968:203-20) have suggested the existence of a territorial basis for rule of the Rajput clan over the cys-Himalayan belt of Tarai tract of eastern U.P. particularly the districts of Basti and Gorakhpur. The Gazetteers (1907:83-96, 1929:109-114) of these two districts had recorded the wave after wave of arrivals of the Rajputs, from the western part of India, as the result of the Muslim invasions there from 13th to 17th century. The Rajputs conquered the indigenous population and captured their land. Singh (1982:71) argues, "All basic and primary rights in property emerge from the conquest of weak by the powerful. Subsidiary rights branch off at the consent of the conquerors. Power begets its own legitimacies and the cruelties of a conqueror are transformed into ballad of his valour - sung and recited by the vanquished subjects from generation to generation in praise and veneration of the victor...Proselitysation of tribal and semi-tribal local population by the accompanying Brahman into the Hindu structure went side by side with the uses of Rajput sword for subjugating the population. Sacred and secular power thus welded the rule of a class over a territory". The Rajputs were not satisfied with this only but they wanted to expand their economy and also to sustain themselves. Hence, "Rajputs deployed the subject population to clear the land for cultivation. Patches after patches of forest must have been cut down to make the farming field. Those who cleared the land, according to the tradition, started cultivating for and on behalf of the Rajput coloniser" (ibid:71) Thus, there existed the dominance of Thakurs or Rajputs in eastern Uttar Pradesh in land tenure settlement. Hasan (1998:125) also states that,

TABLE 3.3
Castes/Community-wise Households and Size of Landholding

Castes	Landless		0-1.00 acres		1.1-2.50 acres		2.51-5.00		5.00-10.00 acres		More than 1.00 acres		Total for Uttar Pradesh	
	House Hold	Area	House Hold	Area	House Hold	Area	House Hold	Area	House Hold	Area	House Hold	Area	House Hold	Area
(1)	(2)	(3)	(4)	(5)	(6)	(7)	(8)	(9)	(10)	(11)	(12)	(13)	(14)	(15)
Higher Castes	3.86 (2.30)	0.00 (0.00)	11.95 (7.59)	1.30 (9.96)	11.76 (10.18)	3.65 (13.02)	26.29 (27.39)	13.32 (28.79)	25.37 (41.44)	25.39 (42.25)	20.77 (52.07)	56.34 (57.36)	100.00 (15.63)	100.00 (40.71)
Intermediate Castes	26.69 (31.56)	0.00 (0.00)	25.30 (32.13)	6.49 (33.80)	18.58 (32.11)	13.10 (31.89)	15.00 (31.23)	20.61 (30.34)	9.01 (29.43)	25.80 (29.23)	5.52 (27.65)	34.00 (23.58)	100.00 (31.33)	100.00 (27.72)
Scheduled Castes	32.68 (56.52)	0.00 (0.00)	29.89 (55.14)	11.41 (50.78)	20.01 (20.24)	22.29 (47.84)	11.21 33.91	26.08 (32.82)	4.94 (23.42)	23.65 (22.90)	1.27 (9.22)	15.87 (9.41)	100.00 (45.50)	100.00 (23.71)
Scheduled Tribes	–	–	–	–	–	–	–	–	–	–	–	–	–	–
Muslims Sikhs	33.46 (9.53)	0.00 (0.00)	16.92 (5.14)	3.70 (5.46)	18.08 (7.47)	10.50 (7.47)	15.00 (7.47)	19.23 (8.03)	7.31 (5.71)	17.49 (5.62)	9.23 (11.06)	49.08 (9.65)	100.00 (7.49)	100.00 (7.86)
Total for U.P.	(26.31) (100.00)	0.00 (100.00)	24.67 (100.00)	5.33 (100.00)	18.13 (100.00)	13.39 (100.00)	15.04 (100.00)	(18.83) (100.00)	9.60 (100.00)	24.47 (100.00)	6.25 (100.00)	39.98 (100.00)	100.00 (100.00)	100.00 (100.00)

Source: Shrimali, 1981.

"At the time of independence, despite rapid turnover and fragmentation of holdings in the densely populated eastern districts 8 per cent of agricultural households owned virtually all the cultivated land. In the state as a whole, Thakurs and Brahmins owned 57 per cent of the land. The intermediate castes owned another 32 per cent, the Muslims 11 per cent and the Scheduled Castes a little more than 1 per cent. In contrast to eastern region, the hold of the Thakurs was relatively weak in Rohilkhand and the upper Doab". East of Lucknow, the Thakurs were again powerful landlords who, after their expulsion from their old territories in the north due to Muslim invasion, moved eastward and conquered the land from the Bhars, Doms and other early landowners (Connell, 1971). Table 3.3 shows the percentage distributions of households and area or land owned by size, class of ownership and caste groups:

In western Uttar Pradesh, caste groups like Jat, Gujar and Tyagi gained the control over land at the expense of Thakurs and Muslims as stated earlier. The money-lenders and bankers belonging to Bania, Brahmin, Kayastha, and Khatri castes also owned land. This happened precisely for three reasons. One, the collapse of the central Mughal authority led to the expansion of land control by castes like Jat, Gujar and Tyagi. Second, the revenue demand fixed under the Regulation IX of 1833 was high which resulted in many sales. Third, the money lending and the official class or those associated with official works were mostly Banias, Brahmins, Khatris and Kayasthas who kept on acquiring Zamindari rights through falsification of records, public auction, debt mortgage, etc (Ahmad and Saxena 1998: 176). Another reason cited by Hasan (1998:125) for this loss of land by Thakurs and other upper castes in the western region was "the emergence and spread of the market (which) facilitated the creation of new propertied class".

Certain interesting features emerge about land control conferring the privileged positions to certain castes in Uttar Pradesh, as is evident from the above. First, the Rajputs possessed more land under the proprietary right than under the cultivating right. Similarly, Banias, Kayasthas and Muslims owned more land than they actually cultivated. On the contrary, the share of Brahmins was higher in many districts in the cultivated land as compared to their share in ownership. That is, the Brahmins first gained security of tenure and finally ownership of land in 1952 due to Zamindari abolition. It may be emphasized that the Indian National Congress helped the Brahmins to secure more rights and privileges in the state as they were in dominant position in the Government. Secondly, the intermediate or Backward Castes and the Dalits farmed half of the cultivated land. With their hard labour, they were considered as superior agriculturists and could pay better land rents as their production was higher. That means, these castes fed the rest of the people in the state without having their actual rights over land. The Brahmins and Thakurs or Rajputs were aversed to cultivating land on their own because of the notion of the ritual purity and pollution, though they owned more land as mentioned above. Hence, their fields either remained neglected or were cultivated by others on lease or rent basis. The settlement officer of Sultanpur district had observed, "It is peculiarly unfortunate that fifty-two percent of the holding areas should be in hands of Brahmins and Thakurs, neither of whom are agriculturists by tradition" (Ahmad and Saxena 1998:178). Similar was the comment on the state of affairs about land in the district of Bahraich. It has been stated that, "Brahmins are generally inferior and careless cultivators; they do not handle a plough and have to depend upon hired labour. Thakurs and Kayasthas are also indifferent husbands men". Gilbert Eteinne, during his field visit in 1978, noted the same thing in Varanasi district where a Kayastha family having four hectares of land with 25 able-bodied men had hired one labour for the fieldwork (ibid).

It may, thus, easily be inferred from the above as to why Uttar Pradesh has lagged behind in the rural economic development. It may also be mentioned here that there is more pressure on land especially in the eastern region of the state, and the large majority of the backward and Dalit castes do not own land at all but only depend on the mercy of their landlords or the big land- owners. But things are changing and most of the landless labourers are shifting towards non-agricultural employment. Contrary to this, in western Uttar Pradesh the taboo that the people of the upper castes cannot plough the land was followed less rigidly because of difficulty in obtaining farm labour. Even Brahmins took up the cultivation of their own holdings. A significant class of rich and middle peasantry emerged here with the expansion of irrigation facilities and rise of prices of the agricultural produce especially in the early part of the twentieth century (Hasan1998:125).

In sum, land has remained the primary economic source

in the state and the struggle for rights either over the land or the land produce has formed the backdrop of much of the social history specially of the eastern region (Pandey 1983:68-9). During the colonial rule and even after that, the upper castes particularly Brahmins and Kayasthas were the first to achieve modern education, and they along with Banias comprised the bulk of bureaucrats and professionals like lawyers, doctors, teachers, etc. both in cities and towns (Hasan 1998:127). In turn, this consolidated the social and economic position of these castes along with their already superior ritual status in the society. Many of the nationalist leaders who took western education and became politically powerful in the state and a few at the central level came from the Brahmin caste. The intermediate castes or the Other Backward Castes or Classes and the Dalits were relegated to the periphery in all the realms of special life. They could not break for long the monopoly and hegemony of the upper castes, which was well-rooted in their ritual and secular legitimacy. Therefore, it can be said that caste, class and political power in Uttar Pradesh were closely intermeshed at the time of independence of the country (ibid). This also led the Dalits to be cumulatively dominated by the upper castes; and they could never assert in the past as they are doing now.

Dalits in Uttar Pradesh

The Dalits constitutionally known as Scheduled Castes constitute about 16.48 per cent of the national population, according to 1991 Census. Their total population in the country (excluding J & K) is 138.22 millions. There are no Scheduled Castes in Nagaland, Andman Nicobar Islands and Lakshdeep. The highest proportion (28.3%) of the Scheduled caste population is in Punjab and (0.10%) lowest in Mizoram. Numerically, they are the largest castes in Uttar Pradesh followed by West Bengal and Bihar. According to 1991 Census, the Scheduled Castes constituted 21.1 per cent of the total population in the state, which is one fifth of the total population of the country. The region and district-wise percentage distribution of the Dalit (Scheduled Caste) populations in Uttar Pradesh is given in Tables 3.4 and 3.5.

TABLE 3.4
Percentage Distribution of Scheduled Caste Population in Uttar Pradesh

Region	*Population (%)*
Uttarakhand	17.5
Rohilkhand	15.3
Upper Doab	19.3
Avadh	25.9
Lower Doab	20.7
Bundelkhand	25.4
Poorvanchal	20.4
State	21.1

Source: Census of India 1991, Series 25, Uttar Pradesh, Provisional Population.

TABLE 3.5
The District-wise Population Percentage of the Scheduled Castes in Utter Pradesh

S. No.	*District*	*Percentage of Population*
1.	Uttar Kashi	22.78
2.	Chamoli	17.49
3.	Tehri Garhwal	14.20
4.	Dehra Dun	13.40
5.	Garhwal	13.52
6.	Pithoragarh	20.45
7.	Almora	20.02
8.	Naini Tal	15.80
9.	Bijnor	20.67
10.	Moradabad	16.14
11.	Rampur	12.99
12.	Saharanpur	22.50
13.	Hardwar	21.58
14.	Muzaffarnagar	14.04
15.	Meerut	16.64
16.	Ghaziabad	17.89
17.	Bulandsahar	21.20
18.	Aligarh	23.01
19.	Mathura	20.23
20.	Agra	23.20
21.	Ferozabad	19.28
22.	Etah	17.32
23.	Mainpuri	19.29
24.	Budaun	17.34

(Contd.)

(Contd.)

25.	Bareilly	12.66
26.	Pilibhit	16.01
27.	Shahjahanpur	18.02
28.	Kheri	26.90
29.	Sitapur	32.22
30.	Hardoi	31.55
31.	Unnao	30.54
32.	Lucknow	21.88
33.	Rai Bareli	29.86
34.	Furrukhabad	17.59
35.	Etawah	25.03
36.	Kanpur-Dehat	25.17
37.	Kanpur Nagar	13.54
38.	Jalaun	27.35
39.	Jhansi	28.80
40	Lalitpur	25.12
41.	Hamirpur	24.89
42.	Banda	23.25
43.	Fatehpur	24.72
44.	Pratapgarh	21.49
45.	Allahabad	24.46
46.	Bahraich	16.46
47.	Gonda	15.57
48.	Barabanki	27.02
49.	Faizabad	23.15
50.	Sultanpur	22.36
51	Siddharthnagar	16.69
52.	Maharajganj	19.40
53.	Basti	21.17
54.	Gorakhpur	22.04
55.	Deoria	15.55
56.	Mau	22.06
57.	Azamgarh	25.61
58.	Jaunpur	21.78
59.	Ballia	14.69
60.	Ghazipur	20.57
61.	Varanasi	18.14
62	Mirzapur.	25.95
63.	Sonebhadra	42.50

Source: U.P. Annual 1996-97.

Further, taking the rural-urban distribution of population of the Scheduled Castes in the state, we find 11.79 per cent of them living in the urban and 88.21 per cent in the rural areas. Hence, urbanization among the Scheduled Caste people in the state is very low. Also, according to the 1991 Census, the percentage of literacy among Scheduled Castes in the country is 37.41 (23.76 per cent among females and 49.91 per cent among males respectively). It is a matter of grave concern that even after 50 years of independence, the literacy rate among Dalits in Uttar Pradesh is only 26.85 per cent which is one of the lowest literacy rates among Dalits in the country as is evident from the fact that in Kerala the literacy rate among Dalits is 79.91 per cent which stands at the top of the list followed by Gujarat (61.06 per cent), Tripura (56.66 per cent) and Maharashtra (56.4 per cent). The female literacy rate among Dalits in U.P. is also very low with 10.68 per cent (27.35 per cent in urban and 8.47 per cent in rural areas respectively). There are 34 districts in U.P., which have literacy rates of Dalits below 30 per cent, and 54 districts which have Dalit female literacy rates below 20 per cent. The literacy rates in various districts of the state have been given in the Table 3.6.

To raise the literacy rates among the Scheduled Castes several steps have been taken by the state government in the recent years. For instance, the State Government provides annual grants to 580 Primary schools run by the voluntary organizations and having more than 50 per cent students belonging to the Scheduled Castes/ Tribes. To ensure educational development of children of the safai-karamcharis (sweepers/scavengers), Mahatma Jyotiba Phule Government Ashram type School has recently been set up in Lucknow, the state capital. The school is imparting free education to approximately 1000 pupils ranging from class I to class-XII. A decision has also been taken to open such Ashram schools in the districts of Agra, Kanpur and Moradabad. Besides, a member of Navodaya Vidyalayas set up in the state also provide free education to the Scheduled Caste pupils.

TABLE 3.6

District-wise Literacy Rates of the Scheduled Castes in Uttar Pradesh

S. No.	*District*	*Literacy Rate (%)*
1.	Uttar Kashi	31.44
2.	Chamoli	35.40
3.	Tehri Garhwal	32.48
4.	Dehradun	49.37
5.	Garhwal	51.86
6.	Pithoragarh	45.54
7.	Almora	41.81

(Contd.)

(Contd.)

8.	Nainital	45.66
9.	Bijnor	30.71
10.	Moradabad	23.52
11.	Rampur	19.02
12.	Saharanpur	32.19
13.	Hardwar	56.27
14.	Muzaffarnagar	34.04
15.	Meerut	39.36
16.	Ghaziabad	42.46
17.	Bulandshahar	33.23
18.	Aligarh	28.66
19.	Mathura	31.27
20.	Agra	32.39
21.	Ferozabad	36.66
22.	Etah	28.16
23.	Mainpuri	37.78
24.	Budaun	17.71
25.	Bareilly	24.03
26.	Pilibhit	22.82
27.	Shahjahanpur	20.47
28.	Kheri	17.93
29.	Sitapur	19.41
30.	Hardoi	24.05
31.	Unnao	24.18
32.	Lucknow	30.59
33.	Rai Bareli	20.25
34.	Furruknabad	31.33
35.	Etawah	40.85
36.	Kanpur-Dehat	33.89
37.	Kanpur Nagar	49.83
38.	Jalaun	39.53
39.	Jhansi	38.16
40.	Lalitpur	16.43
41.	Hamirpur	25.85
42.	Banda	19.20
43.	Fatehpur	27.11
44.	Pratapgarh	22.23
45.	Allahabad	21.66
46.	Bahraich	14.51
47.	Gonda	14.22
48.	Barabanki	15.57
49.	Faizabad	23.58
50.	Sultanpur	19.54
51.	Siddharthnagar	16.43
52.	Maharajganj	18.59
53.	Basti	22.58
54.	Gorakhpur	27.81

(Contd.)

55.	Deoria	23.75
56.	Mau	30.43
57.	Azamgarh	25.78
58.	Jaunpur	26.73
59.	Ballia	31.12
60.	Ghazipur	29.18
61.	Varanasi	27.80
62.	Mirzapur	17.96
63.	Sonebhadra	14.31

Source: U.P. Annual 1996-97.

The Financial help in the realm of education is very essential as most of the Scheduled Caste students come from economically poor family background. Hence, under the state-sponsored scheme of giving stipend/scholarship to the SC/ST students pursuing their studies up to High School (10th) level, the rates of scholarship have been increased from Rs. 20 to Rs. 40 per month for Junior High School students and from Rs. 30 to Rs. 60 per month for High School students. Thus, a total number of 71, 96679 Scheduled Caste (and also tribe) students got benefited and the total sum of Rs. 292.40 crore was distributed among them during 1997-98. It may, however, be mentioned here that only those Scheduled Caste students studying in High School were eligible earlier for such scholarship whose parents' annual income was not more than Rs. 12,000, but now this income limit has been raised to Rs. 30,000. Besides, under the centrally sponsored scheme, the State Government also provides scholarship to the SC/ST students pursuing their post-metric studies (Uttar Pradesh, Annual, 1996-97).

Under the Scheme of constructing separate hostels for the SC/ST students, with the assistance of the Central Government, 164 hostels (125 for boys and 39 for girls) were constructed in different district head-quarters in the state. Under the scheme of providing financial assistance for purchasing books, stationary, etc. to SC/ST students pursuing engineering/technical/medical and agricultural studies, an assistance of Rs. 0.50 crore was made available to 1,888 SC/ST students during the financial year of 1996-97 (Uttar Pradesh, Annual, 1996-97). Besides, the pre-coaching centres have been set up for helping the SC/ST candidates in their preparation for appearing in the IAS, IPS, PCS, Engineering, Medical and other competitive examinations. One such coaching centre for IAS, 5 centres for PCS and one centre for Engineering are already functioning in the state.

However, an important fact about these facilities provided to the SC/ST students/candidates is that there has been no evaluation of their impact on them. Not even a single study has been conducted about the quality of education imparted to the SC/ST or Dalit students in the government aided schools, Ashram type schools and at the coaching centres. Also, no record is maintained as to how many candidates from these coaching centres have been selected in various services. Moreover, the number of coaching or competitive examinations centres are not adequate enough to meet the demands of the educated number of Dalits in the state, and that too when the bureaucratic jobs are the only channel available for their upward mobility.

The Dalits in UP are not a monolithic whole but are divided into 66 castes, which are given in Table 3.7. Population-wise, Chamars top the list followed by Pasis, Dhobis, Koris and others. As far as economic status of the Dalits in the state is concerned, they are the poorest and own only one per cent of land. The census data and the reports of the Commission for the Scheduled Castes and Tribes reveal the poverty-ridden status of a large majority of the Dalit population clustered in the rank of landless agricultural labours living both in villages and in urban slums. It is they against whom occurs the more insidious form of violence committed by the non-scheduled castes.

TABLE 3.7

Names of Scheduled Castes registered in Uttar Pradesh

Sl. No.	*Name of the Caste*	*Sl. No.*	*Name of the Caste*	*Sl. No.*	*Name of the Caste*
1.	Gariya	2.	Badhik	3.	Badi
4.	Baheliya	5.	Baiga	6.	Baiswar
7.	Bajaniya	8.	Bajgi	9.	Balahar
10.	Balai	11.	Balmiki	12.	Bangali
13.	Banmanus	14.	Bansphor	15.	Barwar
16.	Basor	17.	Bawariya	18.	Beldar
19.	Beriya	20.	Bhantu	21.	Bhuiya
22.	Bhuyiar	23.	Boria	24.	Chamar, Dhusia,

(Contd.)

(Contd.)

25. Chero	26. Dabgar	27. Dhangar
28. Dhanuk	29. Dharkar	30. Dhobi
31. Dom	32. Domar	33. Dusadh
34. Gharami	35. Ghasiya	36. Gond
37. Gual	38. Habura	39. Hari
40. Hela	41. Kalabaz	42. Kanjar
43. Kapariya	44. Karwal	45. Khairha
46. Kharwar (excluding Benbansi)	47. Khatik	48. Khorot
49. Kol	50. Kori	51. Korwa
52. Lalbegi	53. Majhwar	54. Mazhabi
55. Musahar	56. Nat	57. Pankha
58. Parahiya	59. Pasi, Tarmali	60. Patari
61. Rawat	62. Saharya	63. Sanaurhiya
64. Sansiya	65. Shilpkar	66. Turaiha

Source: Census 1981.

The government after independence took policy measures for the upliftment of Dalits by providing opportunities for their mobility. More specifically, through the policy of preferential treatment or protective discrimination justified on the ground of the extreme social discrimination they had suffered for centuries they have been provided a number of opportunities such as reservation in education which we have already discussed, reservation in government jobs and in politics. But such a channel of mobility has provided limited opportunities to the economically and politically mobile groups in certain regions. Reservation in political arena under Article 330 and 332, and in bureaucracy under Article 335 of the Indian Constitution has facilitated some mobility among the Dalits in the state of Uttar Pradesh. Over the years, they have been drawn into greater degree of participation in political life in the state through their election from reserved constituencies. The names of the reserved constituencies for Scheduled Castes in their getting elected to the Parliament and to the State Assembly are given in Table 3.8 and 3.9 respectively.

TABLE 3.8
Parliamentary (Lok Sabha) Constituencies Reserved for the Scheduled Castes in Uttar Pradesh

Sl. No.	*Name of the Constituencies*	*S.No.*	*Name of the Constituencies*
1.	Akbarpur	2.	Barabanki
3.	Banasgaon	4.	Basti
5.	Bijnor	6.	Chail
7.	Firozabad	8.	Ghatampur
9.	Hardoi	10.	Haridwar
11.	Hathras	12.	Jalaun
13.	Khurja	14.	Lalganj
15.	Mishrikh	16.	Mohanlalganj
17.	Robertsganj	18.	Saidpur

Source: Chief Electoral Officer, U.P. 1999.

TABLE 3.9
The Assembly Constituencies Reserved for the Scheduled Castes in Uttar Pradesh

Sl. No.	*Name of Constituency*	*Sl. No.*	*Name of Constituency*
1.	Uttar Kashi	2.	Bageshwar
3.	Khatima	4.	Nagina
5.	Nazibabad	6.	Chandausi
7.	Shahabad	8.	Ganeshwari
9.	Bilsi	10.	Faridpur
11.	Barkhera	12.	Puwanya
13.	Palia	14.	Mohammadi
15.	Bawan	16.	Hargaon
17.	Sihauli	18.	Machhrehta
19.	Beniganj	20.	Ahirori
21.	Malihabad	22.	Mohanlalganj
23.	Safipur	24.	Bachhrawan
25.	Bihar	26.	Salon
27.	Jagdishpur	28.	Kadipur
29.	Jahangirganj	30.	Sohawal
31.	Siddhaur	32.	Fatehpur
33.	Charda	34.	Ikauna
35.	Manakapur	36.	Dixir
37.	Nagareast	38.	Khalilabad
39.	Haisar Bazar	40.	Bansgaon
41.	Munderabazar	42.	Maharajganj
43.	Naurangia	44.	Hata

(Contd.)

(Contd.)

45.	Rasa	46.	Saraimir
47.	Mehnagar	48.	Mohammedabad Gohna
49.	Shahganj	50.	Jakhania
51.	Sadat	52.	Kerakat
53.	Chandauli	54.	Chakia
55.	Duddhi	56.	Robertsganj
57.	Bhadohi	58.	Chhanbey
59.	Meja	60.	Chail
61.	Sirathu	62.	Kishunpur
63.	Manikpur	64.	Charkhari
65.	Mauranipur	66.	Babina
67.	Konch	68.	Bhojnipur
69.	Bilhaur	70.	Sisamau
71.	Ajitmal	72.	Lakhna
73.	Kannarj	74.	Kishni
75.	Jalesar	76.	Tundle
77.	Atmadpur	78.	Agra West
79.	Goverdhan	80.	Sansi
81.	Kali	82.	Jewar
83.	Shikarpur	84.	Hapur
85.	Hastinapur	86.	Siwalkhas
87.	Jansath	88.	Charthawal
89.	Haroora	90.	Nagal

Source: Chief Electoral Officer, U.P. 1996.

The percentage of reservation provided for the Scheduled Castes in the central and state government services since 1970 are 15 and 23 respectively. As far as reservation in the bureaucracy is concerned, the major grievance of the Dalits or the Scheduled Castes in the state has been that the various orders concerning reservation in the government services in the state are deliberately violated. As a result, the reservation quota is seldom filled in. The track record of filling up reservation quota in both the central and state government services has been very poor which is self-evident from Tables 3.10 and 3.11 respectively.

TABLE 3.10

Representation of Scheduled Castes in Central Govt. Services as on 1-1-1999

Group of Services	*Filled in Percentage*	*Unfilled Percentage*
A	11.29	– 3.71
B	12.68	– 2.32
C	15.78	+ .78
D	19.99	+ 4.99

Source: National Commission for the Scheduled Castes and Scheduled Tribes, Sixth Report 1999-2000& 2000-2001, p.182

TABLE 3.11
Representation of Scheduled Castes in State Services, U.P., 1989

Group of Services	*Filled in Percentage*	*Unfilled Percentage*
A	8.16	- 12.84
B	10.12	- 10.88
C	15.76	5.24
D	21.19	+ .19

Source: U.P., Annual, 1996-97, p. 267.

The reservation under Article 335 has seen many ups and downs in Uttar Pradesh. The Janata government during 1977-79 actually suspended reservation in promotion in government jobs for the Dalits. In 1981, the UP government decided that jobs reserved for the Scheduled Castes would be carried forward till the suitable candidates from these castes are found and would not be filled in by the candidates of other castes (Times of India, 6 February 1981, Delhi). In bureaucracy, the Dalits face discrimination and victimization which increases their frustration and retards the rate of their socio-economic development. The representation of Dalits in the judicial services and in the services in various universities in the state is still negligible.

Caste Tensions, Atrocities and Remedial Measures

The structural changes in Indian society have brought socio-political consciousness among Dalits in different parts of the country. This has also created a feeling of resentment and hostility among them against their oppressors. They are no longer prepared to take things lying down. Thus, citing the situation prevalent in Bihar, it has been stated that a socio-psychological climate has ripened for confrontation between the Dalits and the upper castes, on the one hand, and between the Dalits and the other Backward Castes or Classes on the other (Sachchidanand 1988:65). Even in U.P., there has been a tremendous rise in the incidences of atrocities committed on the Dalits. According to the government figures, as high as 34 per cent of incidences of crime or atrocities were committed against the Dalits in U.P during 1981-86. It is interesting to quote Ram (1995:233) here who argues that, "Conflicts (between Dalits and non-Dalits) usually take place on the structural issues. Though some other secular issues such as exercising adult-franchise which are not directly related to the village social structure are not less important, the severity of the conflicts is positively related to the structural issues". Hasan (1998:40) also narrates similar causes by saying that, "Behind the facade of many caste conflicts were thinly veiled attempts to intimidate Dalit voters from freely exercising their franchise. Economic issues such as minimum wages and access to land were equally crucial sources of tension. Attempts by agricultural labourers to press for minimum wages or efforts to raise crops on land allotted to them were seen as threats to the domination of big landowners accustomed to maximizing their profits through a docile labour force... The resistance mounted by privileged groups in rural areas against state-led welfare measures for the rural poor exacerbated the violence". This trend of violence was followed in the urban centres also with the subtle policy of segregation and discrimination by bureaucracy (Ram 1995: 263). The number cases of atrocities committed on the Dalits in the state are given in the Table 3.12.

TABLE 3.12
Atrocities committed on Scheduled Castes in the State

Years	*No.of cases*	*No. of increase/decrease*
1986	18,417	--
1990	17,270	(-) 1147
1995-96	14,966	(-) 2304

Source: UP, Annual, 1996-97, p. 267.

Prevention of Atrocities on the SCs/STs

To deal with the cases of atrocities and provide physical protection to Dalits in the state, the government has adopted certain measures. A Special Investigation Cell headed by a Deputy Inspector General of Police was created in 1973 to check atrocities committed on the people belonging to the Scheduled Castes/Tribes in the state. Realising the importance of the Cell, the government placed it under the control of an Inspector General of Police in 1983. At present, the Cell is functioning under the control of an Additional Director General of Police. In addition, a Special Investigation Cell has been set up in each of the 20 districts,which are considered sensitive from the point of view of atrocities committed on the SC/STs. These districts are Lucknow, Hardoi, Sitapur, Rai Barili, Unnao, Gonda, Bahraich, Barabanki, Sultanpur, Fatehgarh, Etawah, Banda, Jalaun, Basti, Gorakhpur, Azamgarh, Budaun, Meerut, Varanasi and Agra.

The Duties of Each Cell are

1. To immediately investigate the incidents of atrocities committed on the Scheduled Castes/Tribes in the state and report to the DGP and to the Government with necessary administrative suggestions in this connection.
2. To analyse crimes relating to Scheduled Castes/Tribes through making thorough enquiry of these from the people of the affected area(s).
3. To give suggestions from time to time to the Government to control these crimes.
4. To ensure speedy action on the complaints received from the victims of crimes or atrocities.
5. To promptly assess the actual situation on the basis of the reports appearing in the newspapers and inform the Government about it so that necessary action could be taken.
6. To make spot inspection of the incidents and take necessary corrective measures with the local authorities.
7. To get necessary provisions made in the district security plan so that these crimes could effectively be checked.
8. And finally, to prepare a list of such incidents and keep a close watch over them.

Besides, the SC/ST (Prevention of Atrocities) Act, 1989 enacted by the Central Government also came to force in 1990 -91. Special stress was laid on the effective implementation of this Act to curb the incidents of atrocities committed on the SCs/STs in the state. It is, however, interesting to note here that the stress on effective implementation of this Act proved to be instrumental for breaking the coalition government of the BSP and the BJP in the State.

The SC/ST Commission, Uttar Pradesh

The U.P. Scheduled Castes/Tribes Commission has been constituted to safeguard the interest of people belonging to the SCs/STs, in terms of enquiring into the atrocities committed on them and monitoring the schemes being implemented for their welfare, etc. Along with these and implementation of other provisions of the Constitution, the Contingency Action Plan has been prepared to check the incidents of atrocities committed on people of the Scheduled Castes and to rehabilitate the victims socially and economically. Under this plan, state and district level committees have been formed to review and monitor the implementation of the provisions of the Prevention of Atrocities Act,1989. Provisions have also been made for the allotment of agricultural land and house plots to the people of the Scheduled Castes in the state, providing them financial assistance for their self-employment, awarding scholarships to the SC/ST students as stated earlier, giving pensions to dependents, etc. Arrangements have been made to set up special courts for speedy disposal of the cases relating to atrocities. These courts have been set up in twenty districts where maximum cases of atrocities are pending in courts. Besides, workshops are organised to familiarise the officers and employees, 'for the enforcement of this Act.

It is, however, interesting to mention here that the Act became a bone of contention in 1997 between Kalyan Singh, the then Chief Minister of the state and Ms. Mayawati the outgoing Chief Minister. The BSP and the BJP were sharing power under the 'six months formula' during this period. The BJP had alleged that during the six months tenure (from April 1997 to September 1997) of Mayawati's Chief Ministership, this Act was used to harass the people of the upper castes in the state. More specially, it was alleged that many innocent people of the upper castes were booked under this Act only on the pretext of taking revenge on them. It was further alleged that many fraud cases were registered, under this Act, to settle personal scores. Moreover, the government order No. 2039/ 6:PO-15/99 dated 22nd September 1997 stated that Dalits had registered many cases, under this Act, with exaggeration only to gain more compensation from the government. All these allegations created ruptures in the BSP-BJP coalition and the BSP withdrew its support from the government.

The all-round dominance of the upper castes in the state has created a vast gulf between the upper castes and the lower castes, on one hand, and between the dominant Other Backward Castes or Classes and the lower castes, on the other. This separation among the three groups of castes has the potential of social change. Though Pandey (1993) has described this fact in the case of eastern U.P. but the same can be generalised for the whole of Uttar Pradesh. According to Pandey, "It was the implication of social inferiority in the term *razil* (unclean labouring and artisan, castes Ahir, Kurmis) rather than the disadvantage of rent that appears especially to have aroused the resentment of the lower orders in the late nineteenth and early twentieth centuries. With the advance of market forces, bureaucratic procedures and law courts, many of these resentments were to burst forth in the form of social mobility movements for caste uplift and the assertion of self-respect in the face of zamindari (and more generally *Sharif*) oppression" (Pandey 1993:71-72). Further, the qualitative changes in the society have also contributed in positive manner in empowering Dalits after independence. These have enabled them to accept the challenges of the upper strata. Ram (1995:227) notes, "One can accept that the constitutional guarantees of `social equality in principle' have aroused the aspiration levels of the Scheduled Castes. Their urban contact and `induced changes' through the provisions of reservation in the elected political representation, educational institutions and government and semi-government jobs have produced a considerable degree of social consciousness among the Scheduled Castes. More than this, their growing urge through the reference group behaviour for gaining a higher and respectable position in the social order has brought them to a stage where they may easily prepare themselves to face challenges of non-Scheduled castes".

In sum, it may be said that in the given socio-political background the various types of Dalit movements emerged in Uttar Pradesh, which have progressed step by step for amelioration of the Dalit masses. In turn, these movements have thrown a multifaceted Dalit leadership, which has waged an independent battle and in some cases has also taken help from dominant socio-political forces of its time. Now, the militant assertion of Dalits in the state has become a socio-political reality at the present time. Unlike in the past when the Dalit assertion used to emerge from western part of the country, the contemporary Dalit assertion of north India specially in U.P. has shown the way to the Dalits located in different parts of the country.

Socio-personal Background of the Respondents

As already stated in the previous chapter as well as in the beginning of this chapter, the present study is based on the information extracted from 185 respondents who happened to be the Dalit leaders at various levels. Hence, we shall briefly look into their socio-personal background before analysing, in the following chapter, the nature and dynamics of their leadership in particular and that of the Dalit leadership in general in the state. Such explanation of their background is relevant in view of a number of misgivings about the Dalit leadership as a whole. One such misgiving is that the Dalit leaders are not well-educated, hence, unable to articulate the various issues and demands of the Dalits at the appropriate forum. It is also said that the Dalit leaders mostly come from few families drawn from one or two Dalit castes in a given region. Therefore, it is necessary to look at the socio-personal background to clarify some of such misgivings.

Education Status

It was realised in the past that conditions of the weaker sections would be improved, if they were provided education like others. Even Ambedkar had really emphasized as early as in the 1920s and 1930s that only education could liberate Dalits from their traditional bondage and subordination to the upper castes and classes (Ram 1995:22). Since the time of Ambedkar, Dalits in the country and in the state of Uttar Pradesh have come a long way. Yet, they have to go a longer way in achieving especially quality education such as the technical and professional ones. It has, however, been found that most of our respondents- Dalit leaders in the state are literate and some have obtained even professional degrees in Law, etc., besides their graduation degree. A few of them are educated up to High School and Intermediate levels. Not even a single respondent in our sample has been found to be illiterate.

TABLE 3.13
Educational Status of the Respondents

Sl. No.	*Education standard*	*Number of respondents*	*Percentage*
1.	Upto Junior High School	11	5.94
2.	High School	21	11.35
3.	Intermediate/Higher Secondary	67	36.21
4.	Graduation	59	31.81
5.	Graduation with Law Degree	24	12.97
6.	Post Graduation	3	1.62
	Total	185	100.00

This suggests that those respondents or Dalit leaders who have acquired some position or office in the organisation of a few political parties or have got elected to the Legislative Assembly and Parliament or to the different statutory bodies have obtained much better education. Also, no illiterate respondents are found leading any political party at the state, region or national level nor heading any organization at the district level as used to be during the pre-independence period and even during the first few decades after independence. "During the pre-independence era when Dalits were given political rights to represent themselves, the Indian National Congress used to put on front only those Dalit leaders who could listen to the Congress leaders," said Moti Ram Shastri, the prominent Dalit leader from Varanasi, during the 1940-70, in an intensive interview with him.

Age Composition of the Respondents

The contemporary Dalit leadership in UP is very young. Our sample data reveals that most of the respondents - Dalit leaders fall in the age-group of 40-50 years. This means that most of the older generation Dalit leaders have either given up politics or they are not active in political field. Very few Dalit leaders of older generation namely B.P.Maurya, S.P. Gautam, Mata Prasad, Ram Dhan, Chaudhari Chunni Lal, etc. are active in politics, otherwise most of the Dalit leaders in the state are from younger generation as stated above. In fact, it may be argued that the age factor is very much responsible for the qualitative change in the nature of the contemporary Dalit leadership in UP. It is because of this nature the young Dalit leaders want an independent status and prefer a political party established by the Dalits themselves. It is the older generation, which is quite content in the parties dominated by the upper castes and classes. If this trend continues then it may perhaps be difficult for the political parties dominated by upper castes and classes to retain young Dalit leaders in their fold.

Even if the younger generation Dalit leaders enter in their fold, they may not be as submissive as the older lot of Dalit leaders have been. The age composition of the respondents is given in the Table 3.14.

TABLE 3.14
Age Composition of the Respondents

Sl. No.	*Age (years)*	*Number of respondents*	*Percentage*
1.	25-29	8	4.32
2.	30-34	32	17.29
3.	35-39	47	25.40
4.	40-45	93	50.27
5.	Above 45	5	2.70
	Total	185	100.00

Economic Position

As far as the financial condition of the Dalit leaders is concerned, it has been argued that, "There was also ample evidence that the still relatively low socio-economic status of scheduled caste population continues to limit both their short-term ability to influence political decisions and their long-term political mobilization (Joshi 1982:2). This has also been revealed by the present study as most of the respondents in our sample do not receive any financial assistance from their respective families. They also do not get any financial support from their friends and relatives at the time of any exigency or contesting elections. Usually, they are the first generation leaders in their own families without any 'political capital' and leadership tradition. Moreover, majority of these leader respondents on their part are not in position to extend any material gains to their relatives and friends who, in turn, are not yet politically conscious enough to understand and appreciate their (of leaders) worth and commitments. In this type of resource crunch, the Dalit leader remain handicap in performing their expected roles with firm commitment, besides getting hampered their upward mobility in the political arena. Most of the Dalit leaders cannot undertake even routine tour and organise meetings in their constituency in absence of any conveyance owned by them. They also cannot extend hospitality to their supporters the general and the Dalit masses. All these factors have become dominant in the Indian political system but the Dalit leaders have to remain content with their limited resources. The worst sufferers are the Dalit leaders of local panchayats. It is so because they are not paid any remuneration for holding their office. The respondents in our study have also revealed that their condition become all the more difficult as they are forced to entertain their supporters and other individuals who come to them for their work. They have to mobilise and organise on their own the local masses as the political parties to which they belong do not provide them any support for these types of activity.

These aforesaid factors about the financial constraints faced by majority of the respondents-Dalit leaders make them vulnerable to accept any kind of financial help coming from any quarters. Once they accept such assistance from others, they also become dependent on them, which adversely affects their commitment towards the Dalit masses. More so, this has been highlighted by Barbara Joshi who says that, "relatively low economic resources still commonly leave Scheduled Caste candidates effectively out of the race except when they are able to operate as financial dependents of higher caste political patrons. Even in reserved constituencies in which only Scheduled Caste candidates can compete, chances for success are often strongly influenced by the level of backing from parties dominated by higher caste political notables. Thus, even the most effective of Scheduled Caste politician has major problems in developing the campaign staff and finances needed to reach Scheduled Caste voters, in addition to any problems he may have with attitudes of higher caste voters and party leaders" (Joshi 1982:63). Such dependency of the Dalit leaders on the upper castes has cautioned Kansi Ram and Mayawati, the BSP leaders, who time and again argue that, "if you take any body's help then you will have to accept his directions also. Therefore, Dalit leadership has to create and mobilise its own resources" (speeches delivered on 14 April, 1999 at the Maolankar Hall ground, New Delhi). Hence, the BSP leadership has started membership drive for meeting their financial expenses to be incurred on various political activities. Each Legislative Assembly constituency is supposed to collect Rs. 1.50 lakhs as membership fee at the rate of Rs. 10/- from each member. They have a target of recruiting 15000 members from each constituency. Such membership drives goes round the year to maintain a regular flow of finances for the party fund in the state.

On the other hand, the Dalit leaders which get elected to Parliament (Lok sabha) or State Assembly (Vidhan Sabha) or are nominated to Parliament (Rajya Sabha) or Legislative Council (Vidhan Parishad) have a steady flow of income. In fact, this is the monthly remuneration, besides admissible allowances, they get for their services which they render as representatives of the people. This regular income enhances, in some ways, their life chances and helps their family members also. This also enables them in a relatively better way to meet their expenses required for the modern day politics with all its accessories.

Caste Composition of the Respondents

Our data reveals that the Chamars or Jatavs have dominated, in every parts of the state, the Dalit leadership right from its inception. It is more so because they are the most numerous and assertive caste in the state. They have also been the worst sufferer of the caste system and, hence, have ever since taken a lead in doing away with their depressed condition. The Jatav respondents from the western Uttar Pradesh took pride in revealing that they were the most secular and progressive lot because they accepted Babasaheb Ambedkar as their leader even though he was from different caste and region. It is evident from the fact that today the Chamar or Jatav leadership revere him through celebrations of different occasions related to his life. The Congress Party leadership also gave preference to the Chamars/Jatavs in their scheme of politics on the basis of their numerical strength in every constituency, which has also helped the people of this caste to dominate the Dalit leadership in the state.

TABLE 3.15
Caste Composition of the Respondents

Sl. No.	*Caste*	*No. of respondents*	*Percentage*
1.	Chamars/Jatavs	98	52.97
2.	Pasis	42	22.70
3.	Dhobis	18	9.72
4.	Valmikis	7	3.78
5.	Koris	7	3.78
6.	Khatiks	5	2.70
7.	Others	8	4.32
	Total	185	100.00

Now, as the different Dalit castes in the state are becoming politically more conscious, they are also coming to the forefront. One such caste is Pasi, the numerically second largest caste in Uttar Pradesh. But the Pasis have started asserting themselves very lately and that too mostly in the central U.P. They also identify themselves with the Bahujan Samaj Party along with the Chamars. The Valmiki or Balmiki, Dhobi, Kori and other Dalit castes are numerically substantial in some parts of the state but they have not taken active part in the Dalits' struggle for their social and political emancipation. Even now, in many places they support the Bhartiya Janata Party (Mendelsohn & Vicziany 1998:225).

Representation of Dalit Leadership in Different Political Parties

In the present day democratic polity, the Dalit leaders like their counter-parts are not a homogenous group. Instead, they are affiliated to different political parties. Our data also reveals that Dalit leaders in the state are found in different political parties, whether registered as state or national parties. The political parties to which they are affiliated are the Indian National Congress, Bhartiya Janata Party, Bahujan Samaj Party, Samajwadi Party, Janata Dal, Communist Party of India, etc. In fact, it is due to reserved constituencies with the joint electorate system they are found in every political parties. Their party-wise representation in the Assembly and Parliamentary seats are given in table No. 5.16. Apart from the representatives elected from the reversed constituencies, they are also found in the organizational set-ups particularly in the special Cells created for the welfare of the Dalits such as Anusuchit Jati Morcha, Anusuchit Jati Prakoshtha, SC/ST Cell, Dalit Prakoshtha etc. established by the political parties dominated by the upper castes and classes in the state. But their function even in such cells is specific and limited. This proves their secondary status in the various political parties. This also suggests that they do not form the mainstream of these parties. But in the political parties like Bahujan Samaj Party, Republican Party of India, etc. where the Dalit leaders play the vanguard role and are the main organizers of various activities, there is no need of having any special cell for welfare of the Dalits as these parties primarily champion the Dalit cause. The Dalit leaders themselves are responsible for mobilization of the Dalit masses and setting up the agenda for their party. This gives them full freedom and complete independent status which is qualitatively different from their status in other political parties.

TABLE 3.16
Representation of Dalit Leaders in Lok Sabha and State Assembly through Different Political Parties in U.P. Based on 1999 and 1996 General Elections Respectively

Sl. No.	*Political Parties*	*No. of Dalit Leaders in the Parliament*	*Percent-age*	*No. of Dalit leaders in the State Assembly*	*Percent-age*
1.	Bhartiya Janta Party	7	38.88	44	48.88
2.	Bahujan Samaj Party	5	27.77	22	24.44
3.	Congress (I)	—	—	5	5.55
4.	Janata Dal	—	—	5	5.55
5.	Lok Tantrik Congress Party	1	5.55	—	—
6.	Samajwadi Party	5	27.77	14	15.55
	Total	18	100	90	100

Source: Chief Electoral Officer, U.P. 1999, 1996.

We have stated earlier that the Dalit leaders in the state are found in every political party. The main reason for the same is that out of 85 Parliamentary seats in the state, 18 seats are reserved for the Scheduled Castes. Similarly, out of 425 Assembly seats 90 seats are reserved for them. Hence, every political parties woo the Dalit leaders to contest the general elections from these constituencies on their party tickets. This results in the representation of Dalit in every political party. In event of this, one should not get confused that the political leaders from the upper castes or classes have become very benevolent and magnanimous in giving representation to the Dalits in their respective parties.

But the Dalit leaders have had different reasons for their joining a particular party. For instance Lynch in his study of the Jatavs of Agra has found that, "The conservatives consider membership in the Congress Party a matter of survival. The Congress controls to some extent the financial resources and licensing offices upon which they (Dalits) depend...The conservatives' main strategy can be summed up in the phrase, why bite the hand that feeds you?" (Lynch 1974:111). Lynch has further stated that one of the dominant reasons for the elderly Dalit leaders joining the Congress Party was that it was the dominant and the oldest political party, with Gandhi and Jawaharlal as its leaders, in the past. The other reason was that the Scheduled Castes Federation and the Republican Party of India (RPI) were formed very late in the state particularly during the 1940s and 1960s respectively. But as the time progressed, the Dalits' allegiance to the Congress Party was broken because the ideal dreams shown to Dalits at the time of independence could not be realized easily. Secondly, this gap between aspiration and achievement was fulfilled by more misleading and tangent activities of the Rashtriya Sawayam Sevak Sangh (RSS). The Jatavs of Agra, according to Lynch (ibid), had argued that instead of the Congress Party they joined the Jana Sangh - the earlier incarnation of the BJP because they were impressed by the goodwill and gestures of the RSS leaders/workers. The RSS leaders used to perform weekly cleanliness exercise in the Dalit bastis and also organized the 'Sah-Bhoj' (the common community feasts), congregations, etc. among the Dalits. This had attracted many Dalits to join the Jan Sangh, the political wing of the RSS. The RSS volunteers became the link between Dalits and Jana Sangh as most of them used to help it during the general elections in the state.

But the contemporary Dalit leadership in the state is qualitatively different in its ideological pursuit and commitment to the Dalit cause. Our data reveal that most of the Dalit leaders have joined a particular political party because its policies and programmes are distinctly pro-poor and pro-Dalits. The respondents with their affiliation to the BSP and the RPI are of the view that the leadership of these two parties is dominated by the Dalit leaders who make all out effort for realising Dalit interests. Such respondents feel that they are in their own house and these parties are their own parties. They have also added the reasons for not joining the other political parties dominated by the upper castes and classes. They have opined, "It looks that we are living in a rented house, where you have to face so many restrictions. In our parties, we are free to do anything. There we have to moderate our parlance and demands as well". It may be added here that both the BSP and the RPI also give important and key positions to the Dalit leaders in their organizational set up. But other political parties usually keep the Dalit leaders in the insignificant positions.

Thus, a communal and casteist angle of the different political parties has also emerged from the respondents while spelling out the reasons for their joining a particular political party. For instance, the respondents from Agra, Meerut, Bulandshahar, Itawa, etc. have explained that they had joined the Jan Sangh in the past and are now with the BJP because both the RPI and the BSP are dominated and supported by Jatavs and Chamars, and do not give preference to other

Scheduled Castes. Hence, the Gihars, Khatiks, Balmikis, Dhanuks etc. from the western U.P. have joined the other political parties specially the BJP. In eastern U.P. also, the respondents from the Pasi, Hela, Balmiki, Dhobi and Khatik castes have revealed that earlier the Congress Party had played the politics by giving preference to numerically dominant caste (Chamar) and neglected the other Scheduled Castes which were small in numbers. The BSP has also adopted the same policy. Hence, in reaction they have joined the different political parties and not the BSP. Now, the BSP has been hijacked by the Chamars and Jatavs and, to a certain extent, the Pasis have also come closer to it in some parts of the state. Therefore, other Scheduled Castes have joined the political parties like Samajwadi Party, BJP, Congress, Apna Dal, etc. Thus, the Dalit leadership in the state is divided into different political parties as stated earlier.

References

Ahmad, Imtiaz and N.C. Saxena, 1998, "Caste, Land and Political Power in Uttar Pradesh" in K.L.Sharma (ed), *Caste and Class in India*, Rawat Publications, Jaipur and New Delhi.

Chandra, Bipan, 1989, *India's Struggle For Independence*, Penguin Books, New Delhi.

Cohn, B.S., 1992, *Anthropologist among the Historians and Others Essays*, Oxford University Press, Delhi

Dwivedi, D.N., 1973, *Problems and Prospects of Agriculture Taxation in Uttar Pradesh*, People's Publishing House, New Delhi.

Hasan, Zoya, 1998, *Quest for power: Oppositional Movements & Post-Congress Politics in Uttar Pradesh*, Oxford University Press, Delhi.

Joshi Barbara R, 1982, *Demicracy in Search of Equality: Untouchables Politics and Indian Social Changes*, Hindustan Publishing Corporation, Delhi.

Lynch, O.M., 1974, *The Politics of Untouchability: Social Mobility and Social Change in a city of India*, National Publishing House, New Delhi.

Mendelsohn, Oliver and Vicziany Marika, 1998, *The Untouchables: Suborrdination, Poverty, and the State in, Modern India*, Cambridge University Press, New Delhi.

Pandey, Gyan, 1983, "Rallying round the cow: sectarian strife in the Bhojpuri Region, C.1888-1917" in Ranjit Guha (ed), *Subaltern Studies: Writings on South Asian History and Society II*, Oxford University Press, Delhi.

Ram, Nandu, 1995, *Beyond Ambedkar: Essays on Dalits in India*, Har- Anand Publications, New Delhi.

Rudolph L.I.& S. H. Rudolph, 1987, *The Modernity of Tradition: Political Development in India*, Orient Longman, New Delhi.

Shrimali, P.D., 1981, Agrarian Change, Agrarian Tensions, Peasant Movements and Organisations in Uttar Pradesh, Unpublished mimeo, Lucknow University, Lucknow.

Singh, Rajendra, 1982, "Caste, land and power in Uttar Pradesh: 1775-1970" in Gail Omvedt (ed), *Land, Caste & Politics in Indian States*, Department of Political Science, University of Delhi, Delhi.

Singh, Kashi Nath, 1968, "The Territorial Basis of Medieval Town and Village in Uttar Pradesh, India", *Annals of the Association of American Geographer*, LVIII.

Singh, Y., 1994, *Modernization of Indian Tradition*, Rawat Publications, Jaipur.

4

Nature of Dalit Leadership in Uttar Pradesh

In this chapter, we have discussed the nature and social composition of Dalit leadership in Uttar Pradesh. Based on our sampled data, we have examined the nature of Dalit leadership in the state in terms of the issues that the Dalit leaders generally address both in and outside the State Assembly or Parliament, and their style of functioning or the way they interact with the people of the Scheduled and non-Scheduled Castes from their constituencies. In other words, we have tried to examine here the heuristic generalizations about the less effective functioning of the Dalit leaders in the Assembly or Parliament and their alleged excessive favour extended to the people of the non-Scheduled Castes from their reserved constituencies in the joint electorate system.

At the outset, it may be said that most of the Dalit leaders not only in the state but in the entire country hail from rural background. It is so as nearly 80 per cent of India's total population still lives in the rural areas and also around 90 per cent of the Scheduled Caste population in the country is rural (Joshi 1982:22). A large majority of both Dalit and non-Dalit leaders continue to live most of the time in the rural areas and maintain close ties with their parent families, which are generally joint in composition. Sometimes, their families can have more than 20 members. The Dalit leaders visit the State/National capital during the sessions of Assembly or Parliament. Otherwise, they mostly remain confined in their rural constituency which often leaves them without day-to-day knowledge about the fast changing world (ibid: 63). Many supporters both Dalits and non-Dalits not necessarily from their respective constituencies, who need the assistance of the Dalit leaders for solving their problems, accompany them and also stay with them in allotted hostel room for the latter. So also, the Dalit leaders located in the urban centres of the state are not as dominant as are the rural Dalit leaders. This is evident from our data that only a few Dalit leaders have been able, in all these years, to occupy any important position either in a political party (except BSP) or in the Government. Similarly, the urban Dalit leaders have neither contributed, in any significant manner, to the progress and development of the Dalit masses nor promoted their various types of movement in the state. It may also be said that they usually do not have any strong following in the cities so as to get elected comfortably from the urban constituencies.

We have already analysed, in chapter 2, the concept of a leader or leadership. Here, we shall briefly look at who is a Dalit leader in the opinion of our respondents. In the present study, we found that any ordinary worker who listens to and helps the masses in solving their problems is treated as a leader. A leader is one who may or may not be an elected Member of Parliament or State Assembly. But to be a Dalit leader, one should have a clear programme of activities for upliftment of the Dalit masses. He should raise the Dalit issues at proper forum and should not get bogged down under any pressure. In other words, merely taking birth in a Dalit caste or community is not sufficient to become a Dalit leader, though our respondents have remained divided on this issue. But majority of them have asserted that to be a Dalit leader one has to take birth as Dalit. In their opinion, one who is born as a Dalit can truly empathise with the pain, agony, deprivation, humiliation, suppression and day-to-day oppression of the Dalits. He can also effectively work out plan for eradication of these. The respondents have quoted time and again the difference between Gandhi and Ambedkar and also a Hindi proverb from the countryside to prove their point:

"Jake na ho pair biwai
woh kya jane peer pari"
(Only wearer of the shoes knows where it pinches).

In the present study, the Dalit leadership has been defined on the basis of certain important features. These are: nature of issues or demands the Dalit leadership has raised during different periods for amelioration of the Dalits, the form of its functioning and the style of its mobilization of the masses. If the issues were socio-religious and did not have meaningful impact on political system, the stratification system or the caste order then it is termed as socio-religious in nature. The Dalit leaders addressing such issues basically wanted to liberalise the orthodox nature of religious belief of Hinduism and change the Dalit society or community from within, as stated in chapter 1. On the other hand, if the demands of the Dalit leadership were directed towards the state and not against any particular community or the social system as such demanding political and economic rights for the Dalits then the leadership has been termed as political. However, both these categories have, to great extent, not been mutually exclusive.

Second, taking the form or style of functioning of the Dalit leadership, it has been enquired into whether it is assertive or oriented towards direct mass action with confrontationist attitude, or is it persuasive with petition and prayers submitted to the rulers as in the pasts. Third feature deciding the nature of the Dalit leadership has been their style of mobilization of the masses. The Dalit leaders have tried in recent years to mobilize the Dalit masses overtly through organising open meetings and using even harsh language against the exploitative social order or the upper castes and classes whenever and wherever they have wanted, or mobilizing them covertly and clandestinely through close door meetings in insights of the followers. Hence, on the basis of these features the Dalit leadership may be called socio-religious, persuasive and covert in nature, or political assertive and overt in nature.

The Organic Linkages of Dalit Leadership in U.P.

The contemporary Dalit leadership in U.P. specially the leadership of the RPI and the BSP emerged as an inherent outcome of a much wider ongoing Dalit movements in different parts of the country including the state of U.P. For our convenience, we have divided here the Dalit leadership in U.P. in different phases. However, these phases are interrelated and influence each other in more than one ways. In all, we have six epochs or phases of the Dalit leadership at all India level, i.e. before 1920, 1920-1937, 1937-1947, 1947-1970, 1970-1984 and 1984 onwards. As briefly mentioned in chapter 1, in the first phase before 1920 prior to Babasaheb Ambedkar, Dalits were not having any constitutional or political rights what so ever. Though they had got some social rights because of the British intervention, they were not consulted for bringing any reform in their community. Politically, they were represented by the upper castes in the legislative councils at the centre and state level (Zelliot: 1986). This was equally applicable in the case of the Madhya Desh or Central Provinces of Agra and Oudh, the present day Uttar Pradesh.

But during the second epoch, Dalits started consolidating their strength with their different types of organization and socio-political groups. Some Dalits were nominated to the Central Assembly and councils in different presidencies. The most important event of this epoch was the emergence of Dr. B.R. Ambedkar on the horizon of Dalit liberation who had testified before many British commissions and committees constituted to safeguard the interests of the Dalits and suggest various ways and means for their upliftment. Ambedkar had organized and energised Dalit masses by waging number of movements as stated in Chapter 1. Not only that but he also won a number of political and economic rights for them. For instance, he had won the separate electorates for the Dalits which were changed to the reserved constituencies in the joint electorate system, under the Poona Pact in 1932, through his forced negotiation with Mahatma Gandhi. With his highest level of education, vision, tactical moves and dedication, he became the true and sole representative of the Dalits in India.

This had also influenced the Dalit leadership in Uttar Pradesh. Dalits in the state started recognizing him as their leader. According to Lynch, "The struggle between Ambedkar and Gandhi over the issue of separate elections for untouchables was known to the Agra Jatavs. They along with other untouchable groups wired London to insist that Ambedkar, not Gandhi, was their leader. The political importance of this telegram was tremendous. It signalled that Jatavs had become aware of national implications of their problems and activities through a process of analogical identification. That is, their problems, insofar as they were matters peculiar to Agra, were local and unique; but insofar as they were a matter of untouchability, the problem were national and general" (Lynch 1974 :81). In 1936, Ambedkar established the Independent Labour Party (ILP) and directed its campaign against the Indian National Congress for its lip services to Dalits. He had thought of the ILP to be the vehicle through which the constitutional and political provisions for the benefit of the Depressed Classes would be realised (Gokhale 1993:131).

During the third epoch, the Independent Labour Party contested the Bombay Legislative Assembly elections Act 1935. For the first time in Indian society, a political party established by Dalits had won 15 out of the 17 seats (ibid:135). But to what extent the ILP was welcomed by the Dalits in U.P. is not authentically known at this stage. Yet, Ambedkar established the Scheduled Castes Federation in Maharastra in July 1942 which had also influenced the Dalit leadership of Uttar Pradesh particularly the leadership of the Jatavs in Agra "In 1944-45...the formation of the Scheduled Castes Federation (in Agra) was linked to Dr. Ambedkar's All India Scheduled Castes Federation. It was a major turning point in the Jatvas' definition of their social situation. Consequently, their reference group of identification now became the Scheduled Castes with whom they identified as the oppressed, unenlightened and deprived section of the population. These characteristics of the Scheduled Castes became the basis of new Jatav self-image; it was a striking about face from their march to Kshatriyahood (Lynch 1974:86).

The fourth epoch came with the political Independence of India in 1947. The country got its own Constitution with the parliamentary democracy in which Dr. Ambedkar had played the pivotal role as framer of the Constitution. He also became the first Law Minister of the country in the Nehru's cabinet but resigned in 1951 in absence of the assured support for adoption of the Hindu Code Bill piloted by him in the Parliament. But the most dramatic event of this epoch came when Ambedkar converted to Buddhism along with lakhs of his followers on 24th October 1956. These changes affected greatly the Dalits in U.P. also. In the words of Lynch, "First of all in 1956, most of the Agra Jatavs followed Dr. Ambedkar into Buddhism ... Buddhism presented an alternative to the caste system in which Jatavs attempts at social mobility had been unsuccessful" (ibid: 92-93). It is also true that this process of conversion to Buddhism was rampant in other parts of the state (Mendelsohn & Vicziany 1998:116).

Further, Ambedkar's sad demise on 6th December 1956 also occurred during this epoch creating a dearth of All India Dalit leadership. The crisis threw Jagjivan Ram, a Dalit leader from Bihar, as the dominant Dalit leader of the Indian National Congress. In fact, he had opposed Ambedkar during this period on the issue of latter's conversion. He went to Agra in 1956 and tried to persuade the Jatavs for not converting to Buddhism and remain in Hinduism and with the Congress Party (Lynch 1974:145). But contrary to this, the Dalit leaders during this epoch transformed the Scheduled Castes Federation, which was electorally unsuccessful in 1946 and 1952, into the Republican Party of India (RPI) after the Lok Sabha elections of 1957 (Gokhale 1993:215, Mendelsohn & Viczainy1990: 212). The RPI, according to Ambedkar, was to be a political party based on the principles of "liberty, equality and faternity" (Keer 1997-489), and was to represent the downtrodden and disadvantaged class of Indian society irrespective of caste or region.

The formation of the RPI in Maharastra yet again influenced the Dalits of U.P. as they were already in contact with the SCF. Hence, the Republican Party of Agra was formed in 1958 as a branch of the Republican Party of India confirming the belief in the leadership of Dalit leaders in Maharashtra (Lynch1974:95). But in the long run, the RPI became the story of splits, after splits sometimes on the issue of its membership, sometimes on the clash of interests in leadership especially between the older and the younger generations and sometimes because of its support extended to the Congress Party (Gokhale 1993:219-255). Yet, it is a fact that the Republican Party of India Agra branch was always aware of the programmes of the RPI and its leaders had participated in the struggle launched by the later at the national level. "In 1964 march on the Lok Sabha in New Delhi, the party (RPI) claimed that one lakh of people had joined March, which was led by Gaikward, Khobragade and B.P. Maurya, a RPI MP from Aligarh" (ibid: 231). Further split took place in the RPI in 1969, which weakened it more as many of its leaders including the RPI leaders in Agra joined hands with the Congress Party. The Congress Party even highjacked the issues of the RPI and the latter became an appendage to the former. Hence, the Dalit leadership in the state got divided into two streams: of the dependent and independent Dalit leaders. This was practically the end of the fourth epoch of the Dalit leadership in U.P.

The emergence of Dalit Panthers in the early 1970s marked the beginning of the fifth epoch of the Dalit leadership, which continued till 1984 with the emergence of the Bahujan Samaj Party (BSP). Moreover, the beginning of this epoch coincided with the hectic social engineering done by Indira Gandhi, the then Prime Minister of India and leader of the Congress Party. Before going into the general elections in March 1971, she took many significant decisions to woo the Dalits. For instance, "In the fall of 1969, Buddhists became eligible for Scheduled Caste post-matric scholarships. In December the Constitution was amended again, by unanimous vote, to extend reserved seats for another ten years. In January 1970, government proposed to stiffen the Untouchability (Offences) Act. In April, reservations for direct recruitment to the central services were raised from 12.5 to 15 per cent for Scheduled Castes" (Dushkin1998: 208). With these moves, Indira Gandhi successfully won the support of the Dalits and led her Congress Party to an overwhelming victory. This, in turn, left the Dalit leadership without any significant agenda. The RPI leadership in Uttar Pradesh was also subsumed by the Congress Party, which created a vacuum in the Dalit leadership.

The Dalit Panthers movement did galvanize the Dalit masses in Maharastra during 1972-1979 but it also succumbed to the divisive tendencies inherent in the organization besides failure of its leaders in organizing the masses in the rural areas. A good proportion of the Panther leaders got reabsorbed into the Congress Party (Gokhale 1993: 293, Omvedt 1998:156). Though there is no documentary evidence to prove that the Dalit Panthers movement was also active in some regions of Uttar Pradesh but it is a fact that a few Dalit activists came with the Dalit Panthers organization in Kanpur city and had launched some protests there. In our respondents the present study, Dalit leaders have accepted that the Dalit Panthers movement was active in central U.P. even in the rural areas in Lucknow, Malihabad, Mohanlalganj, Barabarki, Pratapgarh, Sultanpur, Faizabad, etc. and it lasted for 5-6 years (from 1980 to 1985).

A different beginning was made by the Dalit leadership in the state with formation of the Backward and Minority Communities Employees Federation (BAMCEF) on 6th December, 1978. Kanshi Ram emerged as the important Dalit leader during this period. He wanted to develop the BAMCEF as the major support organization for a political unit to be set up latter (Omvedt 1998:163). Later on, he established the Dalit Shoshit Samaj Sangharsh Samiti (DS_4) again on 6 Dec., 1981. Not satisfied with these organizations, he launched the (BSP) Bahujan Samaj Party on 14th April, 1984 with a clear political identity, dalit base and militant ideology (Pai, 2000:77). Omvedt has called its formation as "deliberate and not reactive...It has consistently refused a "reactive" agitational stance which has meant, in practice, staying out of many major Dalit struggles" (Onvedt1998:162). During this period, the Congress Party was on the decline and there was an emergence of Rightist forces. Another significant aspect of this epoch was that, unlike the previous movements, which rose in Maharastra and then came to Uttar Pradesh, this time Uttar Pradesh gave the leadership. And till date, the Dalit leadership of the BSP is dominant in Uttar Pradesh changing the course of Dalit action and assertion. Further, many other important events occurred during this period which affected the Dalit leadership in Uttar Pradesh also. For instance, the BSP started contesting elections on its own or in alliance with a few other political parties in U.P. and neighbouring states. "BSP contested Lok Sabha elections in December 1984 and U.P. Vidhan Sabha elections in March (ibid: 94). From then onwards, it has been progressing in positive direction in terms of percentage of its votes, number of seats won both in the Parliament and State Assemblies. The greatest loss in terms of the support base in Dalits and minorities in U.P. was suffered by the Congress Party with such progress of the BSP" (Hasan 1998, Omvedt: 1998).

In the sixth and the last phase of the Dalit leadership since 1984 till date, the BSP has established and stabilized itself as the major Dalit political party in U.P. and a few neighbouring the states. It has become the hallmark of the Dalit leadership in Indian polity also as it has established itself as a national political party. The BSP has been in the Government thrice (1993, 1995, 1997) albeit for brief periods in U.P. It has also created history by elevating Mayawati, a Dalit woman, to the Chief Ministership twice (June 1995 and April 1997) of the most populated state of the country. Not only that, every political party - the Samajwadi Party (SP), the Bhartiya Janata Party (BJP) and the Congress (I) Party have been forced in the recent years to enter in the electoral pact with the BSP. This suggests a qualitative change in the polity of the state as well as in the Dalit politics. Another two important events of this epoch are that the space vacated by Congress Party in the country as well as in U.P. has increasingly been filled in by the BJP through the communal mobilization of the voters (Hasan 1998: 242).

Secondly, the Other Backward Castes or Classes (OBC) have also come in the dominant political position. It has been stated that, "OBC driven political change has radically altered the framework of super-ordination subordination in UP's power structure ...The trend towards greater representation of the OBCs is strikingly manifested in the 1991, 1993, 1996 state assemblies" (Hasan 1998 : 162).

Thus, all the six epochs have remained eventful in the case of the Dalit leadership both at the national and regional levels which directly or indirectly have affected the nature of the Dalit leadership, the issues pursued and the strategies adopted by it for the purpose. Therefore, it is necessary to locate the Dalit leadership in U.P. in the existing socio-political reality to understand and analyse its various moves made in the different epochs. In other words, we shall briefly look here at the various types of issues addressed by the Dalit leadership specially in the state of Uttar Pradesh.

Issues Addressed by the Dalit Leadership in U.P.

As it was difficult to easily locate a living respondent who was born before 1920 to respond to some of the questions relating to the issues addressed by the Dalit leadership since the 1920 till date in the state. Hence, we had to rely exclusively on the written documents about the issues raised by the Dalit leadership and the styles of its functioning in the earlier times. As stated earlier, there were no economic, political and social rights accorded to the Dalits before 1920. In absence of the Dalit leaders in the modern sense of the term, the traditional caste panchayat leaders organised and raised certain issues related to the Dalit community. In fact, the social status and socio-cultural practices within the Dalit community were the core issues. The caste leaders put bans on eating of carrion beef, boycott of meat and liquor, and motivated people for Sanskitisation of their way of life and change their identity. In the case of the eastern Uttar Pradesh, Cohn (1992:278) writes, "At least two generations ago Jaisvara Chamars in the vicinity of Madhopur (in Jaunpur district) began to outlaw the eating of beef and the carting of manure in what proved a futile attempt to gain greater respect for the caste...Thirty years ago in opposition to their own Thakurs, some Chamars of Madhopur declared also that they would no longer carry manure to the

Thakurs' fields...Chamar women in general took further step; they refused any longer to make dung cake for the Thakur's household". This act of self-purification was not limited in the eastern U.P. only but was also prevalent in central U.P. "Thus at a Sabha held in October 1920, the Chamars of Bareilly (central U.P) had decided to forsake meat as well as liquor and other intoxicants; but they were also very forthright in their refusal to do *begar* (unpaid bonded labour) for the district officials on tour and submitted a petition to the Governor" (Amin 1999: 13). The same trend of status enhancement and self-development of a Dalit community could also be observed in the vicinity of western U.P during the same period. For instance, the Jatavs with the help of Swami Atma Ram began to assert in 1900, though unsuccessfully, a claim to the kshatriya status (Lynch1974: 68). Further, the Jatavs' younger generation specially students started organizing their caste people. "In 1917, they banded together and formed the Jatav Men's Association (Jatav Vir Mahasabha). Later the Jatav propaganda circle (Jatav Pracharak Mandal) was formed. These societies were intended to motivate the Jatavs towards education, sanskritisation of their way of life and change of their identity. Education was considered of primary importance" (ibid: 69).

The process of reforms within the Dalit communities was also observed in the urban centres. For instance, in her study of Kanpur, Allahabad, Varanasi and Lucknow , Gooptu has recorded the self-assertion of the Dalits in the form of the a *Bhakti* movement. In her own words, "*bhakti* came to be practiced more extensively by the urban untouchables, from the early twentieth century, as a form of denial of caste distinctions. For the untouchables in the towns, the message of caste equality in *bhakti* gave them a means to question the discrimination and disabilities that they continued to face" (1996:284). The Dalits in the urban centres reconstituted caste panchayats, left non-vegetarian foods, called themselves as *bhagats,* added the suffix or surnames like *Kabirpanthis, Shivnaryani, Raidasi,* etc. Regular *Satsangs* (religious congregations) and *Bhajans* were held in the temples constructed after the names of their Gurus. With all these cultural and religious practices and traditions, they tried to establish a new life-style which was different from their brethren in the countryside. They also tried to improve their caste status without questioning the caste system as such.

The aforesaid issues of self-purification and status enhancement raised earlier by the Chamars and or Jatavs also spread among the other Dalit or untouchable castes during the second epoch (1921-1937). As far as social issues among the Untouchable castes other than Chamar and or Jatavs are concerned, a correspondent from Naugrah in Basti district wrote in *Sandesh* (a Congress Party weekly paper published from Gorakhpur) on 6, Feb 1921, p.8 that, "The Sweepers, Washermen and Barbers of this place met in panchayats of their various *biradaris* (brotherhood) on 27 January 1921. They have decided that anyone who partakes of meat, fish and liquor would be punished by the *biradari* and would have to donate Rs.51 to the gaushala (the cow sheds). The Dhobis and Barbers have also decided not to wash the clothes and cut the hair of any of their patrons who partakes of meat, fish and liquor" (Amin 1999:12-13). Similarly, Cohn wrote in 1952 that, "Chamars are not alone not trying to elevate their caste status. Fifteen years ago representatives of most of the Bhars of Kerakat Tahsil (in Jaunpur district) met to plan ways to raise their status. Several Bhars who were government officials addressed the meeting and told them that they were lowly and despised because they raise pigs. The Bhars gave up pig-raising, yet it is difficult to say they are held in better regard than the Khatiks and Pasis of the area, who still herd Swine" (Cohn 1992:279).

Yet, it is worth mentioning here that during this period, the self-assertion of Chamar community was becoming more frequent and very open in eastern, western and central parts of the state. "By early 1922 indications of a growing restlessness among them (Chamars)...arising out of the general spirit of revolt were reaching the police head-quarters in the districts. The movement for 'self-reform' now revealed 'a tendency to forsake hereditary callings' as well" *(U.P. Police Abstracts of Intelligence,* 1 April 1922). The eight resolutions passed in January 1922 at a large meeting of the Chamars of Azamgarh (in eastern U.P.) followed the standard patterns of social reform about the prevalence among them of child marriage and co-habitation out of wedlock. They also imposed the interdictions on taking toddy and liquor, and on animals sacrifice. What is perhaps equally significant is that they also pledged themselves not to trade in hides and skins, and to discourage their young boys from taking up their ancestral profession (*Sandesh* 8, Jan 1922, p.6). In the western and central U.P. also, Chamars were refusing to skin carcasses and perform *begar* for the landlords and even the government officials. The U.P. Police Abstracts of intelligence (1 April, 1922) also reported that the Chamars refused allowing their women the liberty of movement, an euphemism for the withdrawal of female labour from the homes of the Upper castes" (Amin 1999:13-14).

On the whole, the leaders during this period had adopted the three dimensional approach for social mobility of the Dalit masses. These approaches were: sanskritisation, construction of new history vis-à-vis social order for the Dalits and the use of political means. In the first case, the Dalit leaders tried to imitate the life-style of the dominant caste of their region. For instance, in eastern and western Uttar Pradesh, the Chamars and Jatavs imitated the life-style of Kshtriyas (Cohn 1992), Lynch1974) as stated earlier. Cohn has written that in 1952-1953, "Chamars in nearby villages of Jaunpur district and also in Azamgarh district have started wearing sacred threads, calling themselves 'Harijan Thakurs', but so far Chamars of Madhopur have not joined them" (1992:279). Lynch wrote, "However, the Jatavs did not identify with the Arya Samajists. Their reference group of identification was the Kshatriya Varna...The crucial task was to prove an acceptable genealogy which would legitimise their claim. It was asserted that the Jatavs were of Yadu Race *(Vansh)* and thus were really of Kshatriya Varna" (Lynch 1974:70-71).

In the case of status purification, self-assertion and caste mobility, the Dalit leaders led by Swami Achhutanand in Kanpur district tried to construct a new history and social order for the Dalits. The Adi-Hindu ideology was formulated in the 1920s by a new generation of literate untouchables. "Bhakti resurgence thus produced a generation of literate untouchables who emerged to be the leaders and ideologues of the Adi Hindu movement. Swami Achhutanand (1879-1933), one of the most prominent Adi Hindu leaders in the 1920s and 1930s, was brought up at a military cantonment, where his father worked, and later settled in Kanpur...Ram Charan (1888-1938), an Adi Hindu leader of Lucknow, was born in a slum at Gwaltoli in Kanpur. His parents were casual labourers" (Gooptu 1996:286). Some of the literate Dalit leaders concerned with caste uplift had earlier joined the Arya Samaj, which was promising to uplift the Dalits by allowing them to undergo a process of '*Shuddhi*' (purification). But since the 1920s, they realised that the Arya Samaj was acting as the 'army of high caste Hindus' whose only intention was to rally the Hindu community against the Muslims, and that the Samaj's attempt to uplift the lower castes was merely a part of this strategy (ibid: 287). Swami Achhutanand in a speech claimed that the Samaj aimed 'to make all Hindus slaves of Vedas and the Brahmans' (Jigyasu 1968:9-10).

In the meantime, the British government had also introduced some political reforms. These twin reasons forced Dalit leaders to think that the entry of the untouchables into the Hindu hierarchy through the Arya Samaj would not further their interest (Gooptu 1996:287). Hence, in search of a new ideology to repudiate the Vedic Hinduism and the caste system they drew upon the *bhakti* religion and formulated the ideology of Adi Hinduism as mentioned above. "The Adi Hindu leaders claimed that there had been ancient Adi Hindu Kingdoms, capital cities, forts and a thriving civilization. They alleged that when the Aryans invaded the country, they conquered these Adi Hindus variously by brute force, repression and treachery... Having defeated and subjugated the Adi Hindus, the Aryans forced them to perform 'low' jobs. They then devised the caste system and oppressive social laws, embodied in the Vedas and codified in the *Manu Smriti,* in order to relegate the Adi Hindus to untouchable status and to deprive them of their rights in society. Hinduism, with its caste system, was argued to be a political creation of the Aryans, who called themselves the higher castes" (Gooptu 1996:292). It is further stated, "The Adi Hindu leaders projected the past not only as a period when the forebears of the untouchables were the rulers, but also as a golden age of social equality. In the Vedas and other Hindu religious texts, there are accounts of warfare between Hindu gods and *asuras* or *rakshasas* (demons), in which the latter appear as evil and oppressive, and vanquished by the gods. The Adi Hindu leaders interpreted these stories as references to the process of the conquest of the pre-Aryans by the Aryans...Adi Hindu leaders held that the Aryans deliberately vilified the pre-Aryan rulers as demons in order to justify their conquest of the original races...They then proceeded to condemn the higher castes of the twentieth century as upholders of the tradition of injustice of their Aryan progenitors, for not acknowledging the rights of the untouchables and for continuing to exclude and deprive them" (ibid: 292, 293). Lynch (1974:76) has also mentioned about the Adi Hindu movement prevalent throughout Uttar Pradesh.

Hence, the Adi Hindu leaders tried to construct a separate history for the Dalits and propagate the idea that Dalits could develop themselves if they went outside the Hindu society. Further, they wanted to forge a greater alliance with the Adi movements that were going on in other parts of the country at that point of time. A conference convened by Swami Achhutanand in Delhi in 1926, was attended by the leaders of the Ad Dharma of Punjab and the Adi Hindu leaders of Andhra Pradesh. The purpose of the meeting was to bring unity among the Dalit activists from different parts of the country (Juergensmeyer1982 :38). The meeting displayed a certain amount of agreement on the need for establishing a separate Dalit organization. Though some attempt was made to forge a united front, there was disagreement over the name of the organization and its significance. According to Ad Dharma leaders, Achhutanand wanted the 'Adi' movements to spread all over India whereas the Punjab Dalits thought it proper to attain the regional strength under the separate name and then unite.

Apart from these attempts of social reforms and self-purification, the Dalit leadership in Uttar Pradesh used political means to uplift the Dalit masses, as stated earlier. For instance, for the first time after gaining limited political rights the Jatav Men's Association of Agra lobbied for the inclusion of one of their members in the State Legislative Council. Thus in 1920, Khem Chand Bohare was nominated as member of the Council in the state in which he served two terms (Lynch 1974:78). Later on, Bohare was appointed to the District Board of Agra from 1922 to 1930 and served the Municipal Board of Agra from 1926 to 1928 (ibid:78). Another important political move of the Dalit leadership during this period was that the Dalit leaders testified before the Simon Commission Electoral Committee in 1928. Swami Achhutanand, Khemchand Bohre, Chaudhari Shyamlal and Babu Ram Charanji were a few prominent leaders who were at the forefront of this movement (Kshirsagar 1994:175-346).

Political consciousness was growing among the Dalits of western U.P. at this point of time. The following resolutions passed by the conference of the Jatav Yuvak Mandal (League) in Agra in 1937 and 1938 respectively are testimony to the fact, "The conference takes decision that the aim of league in the future will be to attain political freedom by suitable constitutional and peaceful means. This conference would impress upon the Jatav members of the Provincial Legislative Assemblies that regardless of the political party to which they personally belong, they should vote unanimously on any issue concerning the interests of their community" (Yadvendu 1942:163). The Dalit leadership during this period showing signs of political maturity had supported Dr. Ambedkar's claim and not of Gandhi as their leader at the second London Round Table Conference held at London (Lynch1974:81).

On the other hand, Dalits mainly the Kabirpanthis entered the upper caste dominated politics in Benaras, eastern Uttar Pradesh. Though the Indian National Congress Party was dominant party and a few Dalits also had got entry into it, the Dalits organised their own independent political party. "Increasing realization of their own strength took a new turn, when in 1934, certain *Kabirpanthi* members of Benaras formed a party called Kabir Dal which was to contest elections to realise the egalitarian values in keeping with Kabir's ideology. This party was equally concerned for the independence of India" (Purendu 1999:154). The influence of this party spread to Bihar also where they contested election in 1935 for the District Council. However, their endeavour to establish an alternative to the Congress Party could not succeed and slowly died out. Similarly, the Congress leader Jagjivan Ram was instrumental in mobilizing the Dalits against the call of Dr. Ambedkar for getting converted to some other religion as stated earlier. Even, "In conference of the untouchables held at Lucknow on 22 may 1936, it was however decided at Babuji's initiative that mass conversion of untouchables as proposed by Dr. Ambedkar be postponed for an indefinite period (Kshirsagar 1994: 312).

It may be emphasized here that the Dalit leadership mobilized the Dalit masses on the political terrain to enhance their social, economic and political status. In eastern Uttar Pradesh, the 'Thakurs' (Kshtriya caste) suppressed their tenants and even successfully evicted the latter who had legal rights to permanency over the land cultivated by them. "in 1938 the Chamars made their first large-scale attack upon the Thakurs' position of power. They did so by supporting some Noniyas rather than their own Thakurs" (Cohn1992:275). Similarly, in western U.P. the Jatavs pressurised the government to list them as a separate caste in the

Census. In 1936, their "movement went into full operation with three demands: (1) that in all government papers the caste be listed as Jatav and not as part of the Chamar group of castes; (2) that the caste be listed separately as Jatav in the Census; and (3) that the Uttar Pradesh Government recommend to the British Government the acceptance of the Jatav community as a separate caste in the list of Scheduled Castes...The political manoeuvres undertaken in the push for recognition of their status were not unsophisticated...A deputation of Jatavs put their claims before Govind Vallabh Pant, then premier of the Uttar Pradesh Government. One of the two Jatav members of the Uttar Pradesh Legislative Assembly (elected in 1937) questioned in the Assembly the Uttar Pradesh Minister of Education on the same problem. In addition, a memorial letter, said to bear six thousand Jatav signatures, was sent to the Secretary of State for India in London" (Lynch 1974: 82-83). As stated earlier, the Dalits had limited electoral rights during 1920-1937 because the electorate system was closely limited by the criteria of property and education (Cohn 1992:274). Hence, very few lower caste people were entitled to vote. Later on when the Dalits got the voting rights under the Govt. of India Act, 1935, they had to wait till 1937 general elections to use that and only after their use of the adult franchise, the consciousness started dawning on them to make its use to gain political power.

A new phase of Dalit leadership ushered with the general elections of 1937, as under the Poona Pact seats were reserved for the Dalits and only they could contest elections from the reserved constituencies. As stated earlier, it became mandatory for every political party to give representation to Dalits, which was a new experience to both Dalits and upper castes. Many Dalits contested Assembly elections for the first time in the Indian electoral politics. "Manik Chand Jatav (1897-1956) contested as an independent candidate and won the elections from Agra constituency, Karan Singh Kane contested as a Congress candidate and won. Shyamlal (1894-1959) from Allahabad and Khemchand Bohare from Agra contested independently but both got defeated (Kshirsagar 1994).

It is, however, evident that the Dalit leadership did not have any independent political organization, which could have given to the Dalits a networking throughout the state. There were a few independent organisations here and there but as stated earlier, "In 1944-45 these political undercurrents crystallized into the formation of the Scheduled Castes Federation of Agra which was linked with Dr.Ambedkar's All India Scheduled Castes Federation" (Lynch 1974: 86). This organization tried to unite the Dalit leadership in different regions of Uttar Pradesh under one umbrella. The scattered Dalit leaders got one platform and one leader in Ambedkar. The Dalit leadership, thus, moved steadily from indirect political influence to the direct or active political participation. During this phase of he Dalit leadership, they also raised the issue of reservation to be given to the Dalits in the Government jobs, which was altogether a new type of demand added in the armoury of the Dalit leaders. But it was heard more in western U.P. The second issue for the Dalit leaders was denunciation of Poona Pact. Ambedkar interpreted the Pact as a betrayal of the Dalits by Gandhi, an interpretation which was and still is accepted by a sizable number of Dalits in the state (Lynch 1974:88). Acharya Moti Ram Shastri of Chandauli tehsil of Varanasi district who was an active social reformer and political leaders during the 1950s-70 told that the social and not the political issue had dominated in the eastern region of Uttar Pradesh during 1937-47. Babu Gajadhar Prasad and Babu Bechan Ram from Varanasi were a few prominent Dalit leaders from Chamar community fighting for the Dalit cause. On the other hand, the general elections were held in 1946 and the Scheduled Castes Federation was routed. To certain extent "The defeat of the Scheduled Castes Federation candidates was undoubtedly due in part to its internal factions, lack of organization and lack of money" (ibid: 88). But it did galvanise the demoralized Dalits. The elections further divided the Dalit leaders into the Congress Dalit leadership and the Scheduled Castes Federation Dalit leadership.

After India got Independence in the year 1947, the Dalit masses were also full of expectations along with the socio-political and economic rights bestowed on them with the constitutional safeguards. The changes started occurring at a relatively faster speed. Number of Dalit leaders had emerged by now raising the issues related to the wretched conditions of the Dalits. Acharya Moti Ram Shastri, Ramdhan, Gajadhar Prasad Sankatha Prasad Shastri, Narendra Kumar Shastri, Changur Ram Chaudhry Shyamlal, etc. were important leaders in the early 1950s. It is worth mentioning here that these leaders were active mainly in the rural areas of Azamgarh, Varanasi, Ghazipur, Jaunpur, Allahabad,

Akbarpur and a few other districts in the eastern region. Occasionally, they visited the districts like Lucknow, Unnao, Sitapur, Bareilly, Barabanki, etc. in central U.P. and made their presence felt by the Dalit masses. Besides, the Dalit leaders like Manik Chand Jatav, Sundar Lal Sagar, Chaudhary Nandlalji, Dharm Prakash, Babu Ram Chandraji, Mahadev Prasad, etc. were prominent leaders who led the Dalit masses in their struggles mainly in districts of Agra, Meerut, Bulandshahar, Kanpur, Ghaziabad, etc. in the western Uttar Pradesh.

The social issues raised by the Dalit leadership during this epoch were not very different from those raised in the earlier periods. These included abolition of untouchability, leaving the eating of carrion, giving up the *Hari Begar* (the mandatory unpaid or underpaid works demanded by the Thakurs), giving up the Dai Janai or Nar Biana (asking Dalit women to assist upper caste women at the time of their delivery and cleaning their dirts), raising their voice against the atrocities committed on the Dalits, demanding their rights to enter temples and other public places, attending the common educational institutions, using public wells, etc. Based on his study in 1954 of village Khalapur in the district of Saharanpur, western Uttar Pradesh, Mahar has reported that, "One disability shared in common by ...untouchable castes has been refusal of the village Brahmans, Barbers and Washermen to serve them. Consequently, marriage rites and other ceremonies, performed by Brahman priests for the other castes, have been performed by caste elders within each untouchable group" (Mahar1998: 22). He also informed that the use of gold was forbidden to untouchables (ibid: 23).

Dalits also wanted to change their caste names, which often carried abusive connotations. In the words of Cohn, "the Chamars of Madhopur prefer to designate themselves by other name. Some Chamars call themselves `Raidasi', taking the name of their most famous Saint, Raidas. Other Chamars, of whom there are many in the next district of Azamgarh, style themselves `Harijan Thakur's" as stated earlier (Cohn1992: 264). Similarly, in western U.P. Jatavs started using `Singh' as their surname to run away from their caste stigma even though they had left the process of sanskritisation. The sweeper community also took 'Valmiki' as their surname, after the famous sage Valmiki or Balmiki.

The above-mentioned social disabilities of the Dalits gave ample scope to their leaders to wage a multidimensional struggle for improving the status of their masses. The successful use of political power acquired by the Dalits during this epoch started with the passing of the Uttar Pradesh Panchayati Raj Act, 1947 which replaced the officially appointed panchayats members. Now, members of the Gaon Sabha (village council) and Panchayti Adalat (rural court) were to be elected through the universal adult suffrage. The Dalits organized themselves to oust the dominant caste Thakurs and other castes and captured power in certain areas. "Elections for these new panchayats in 1948 provided the occasion for the first successful of all the lower castes of Madhopur against Thakurs... Chamars were elected to both bodies. The traditional village leadership of the Thakurs had been completely routed from formal control of Madhopur" (Cohn 1992:276-277). In another incidence in Saharanpur, the Dalits adopted a different strategy to assert their demand. For instance, "in 1955, members of the shoemaker caste stated that they would support a candidate for village Pradhan only if he promised to remove the yard used for the disposal of dead animals from their compound to a side outside village settlement. Other Untouchables voiced their desire to acquire more land for housing from an area contingent to their compound that was under the jurisdiction of the village council" (Mahar 1998: 29). With the passage of time, the Dalits were benefited with political power of right to vote which gave them a new status of equal citizen compared to others. Lynch has observed, "By exercising the rights given to them in these new statuses the Jatavs are now trying to gain further entry into the opportunity and power structures of India. Through them, also they are trying to make the politically ascribed status of citizen, and not the religiously ascribed status of caste, the dominant status in cases of conflict or contradiction between interacting Indians" (Lynch 1974: 90).

With the first general elections after Independence in 1952, a change ushered "in the social psychology of people and their social, cultural and political self-awareness. Social scientists have rightly called the elections in India as a measure of 'silent revolution'. It activates new social solidarities, structuration of people's aspirations... It also subordinates the administrative and professional authority to the authority of people's representatives making the system more responsive to needs" (Singh1996: 25-26). This whole process of peoples' representatives with the political patronage and formal institutions of power to cater to the demands of the people relegated the social reformers to the peripheries. Dalit society was no exception to this phenomenon and, hence, the socio-religious Dalit leadership was completely replaced by the Dalit political leadership. The Dalit political leadership was mainly represented by the Scheduled Castes Federation in the state but some of the Dalit leaders were also in the Congress Party as stated earlier. We have also mentioned that in the two general elections of 1952 and 1957, the Scheduled Castes Federation was routed and the Congress Party gained an upper hand in capturing the Dalit votes in the reserved constituencies.

With the conversion of Ambedkar to Buddhism in 1956, the Dalits of Uttar Pradesh especially of Agra region also took the path of religious conversion. Hence, with the passage of time new problems related to conversion emerged. "Therefore, one who openly professes to be Buddhist is (was) not eligible for the special help given by the government to the Scheduled Castes under its "Protective Discrimination" policy. A Buddhist in Uttar Pradesh cannot stand for reserved seats in an election, nor can he apply for government jobs reserved for Scheduled Castes. His children cannot claim eligibility or remission of fees, grants and scholarship given to the Scheduled Castes for educational purposes" (Lynch 1974:147). These along with the persistently pursued issues were taken up by the Dalit leadership during 1956-1969.

The Republican Party of India, Agra branch emphasized the economic, political and social plights of the Dalits in the state. The general policies of the party at the national level were set out in its Election Manifesto, which gives a clear indication of the issues pursued by its leaders during this period. A charter of ten demands was presented to the then Prime Minister Lal Bahadur Shastri. These demands were:

1. "The protrait of Babasahab Dr. B.R. Ambedkar, "The Father of the Indian Constitution" must be given a place in the Central Hall of the Parliament.
2. Let the land of the nation go to the actual tiller of the land.
3. Idle and wasteland must go to the landless labourers.
4. Adequate distribution of food grains and control over the

rising prices.

5. Lot of slum dwellers should be improved.
6. Full implementation of the Minimum Wages Act, 1948.
7. Extension of all privileges guaranteed by the Constitution to those Scheduled Castes have embraced Buddhism.
8. Harassment of the Depressed Classes should cease forthwith.
9. Full justice be done to them under the Untouchability (Offences) Act.
10. Reservation in the services to Scheduled Castes and Scheduled Tribes be completed as soon as possible, not later than 1970.

(Manifesto of the Republican Party of India (Hindi), 1964, and also in Lynch 1974:104).

In addition, the Agra branch of the party included the demand that taxes on shoe-markets should be remitted. This demand reflects the concern of the party with Chamar group of castes, particularly those of Agra and Kanpur as they were involved in this business (ibid:104).

The above-mentioned demands were confirmed by some of our respondents during the interview with them in western Uttar Pradesh. It astonishes here that though these demands were also raised in the eastern Uttar Pradesh, these were scattered, as there was no political party like the Republican Party of India, Agra branch. On the other hand, the Dalit leadership in the Congress Party was not so vocal to raise these issues openly as was revealed by some of the respondents. As such, it may be said that the issue of unity among all the Dalits became the dominant one of the Republican Party of India, Agra branch in the western Uttar Pradesh. "The aim of the Party is to unite all Scheduled Castes against Congress Party" (Lynch 1974:108). This gave birth to a process of horizontal mobilization of the Dalit castes in different regions in the state. By 1962, the Republican Party of India, Agra realised that Dalits could be electorally successful if they organized themselves well. In Aligarh city B.P. Maurya, a firebrand leader from the Jatav community, who was later imprisoned under the Defence of India Rule (DIR) at the time of Chinese intrusion into India, won the Parliamentary elections from a general constituency. Along with him an RPI candidate also won the MLA seat. This means that the Dalits' independent organizing was taking its roots at least in the western part of Uttar Pradeh.

But the independent organizing of the RPI was short-lived and in the 1967 general elections and the 1969 mid-term elections for the State Assembly, the party could not gain any success (Joshi 1982:105). In fact, the Congress Party during this period created factionalism in the state unit of the RPI on the one hand and formulated certain policy to directly influence the Dalits at the national level on the other hand, as stated earlier. But the immediate effect of factionalism was that the RPI became leaderless in Uttar Pradesh. "In a way, Congress snatched agenda of RPI during 1969-70" as revealed by Gulab Shehra, one time Deputy Speaker of Uttar Pradesh Legislative Assembly and Social Welfare Minister of the state during 1984-1989 in the Congress Party regime. "By 1971, Maurya and his major opponent within the party, Ramji Ram, were both returned to the Lok Sabha under the banner of Indira Gandhi's ostensibly left-oriented branch of the Congress. This was the effective end of the Republican Party as a force in Uttar Pradesh" (Mendelsohn & Vicziany 1998:213) as well as the end of this epoch. Today, the RPI exists in Uttar Pradesh mainly into two factions one of Prakash Ambedkar's Bhartiya Republican Party and other of Ram Das Athavale's Republican Party of India. Thus, we may see that this was one of the longest epochs of the Dalit leadership starting from 1947 to the demise of Republican Party of India in 1969.

In effect, with the demise of the Republican Party of India a new epoch of the Dalit leadership emerged which was dominated by the Dalit leaders of the Congress Party. Specially in the eastern Uttar Pradesh, the Congress leadership gave prominence to the Chamar caste and leaders like Ram Dhan, Ganpat Ram, Jai Prasad, Ram Pyare Suman, Baddal Ram, Mata Prasad, Dharamveer and Mahasay Masuriya Din emerged on the scence. Similarly, in the central Uttar Pradesh, Kanhaiyalal Sonkar, Ram Kinkar, Gaya Prasad Prashant, Tilak Chand Kureel, Chaudhry Buddha Dev, Bhagauti Prasad Kureel and Mewalal Sonkar were leading the Dalit movement under the banner of the Congress Party. Finally, in western Uttar Pradesh, Jatav leaders like S.P. Gautam, Ram Lal Rahi, H.L. Azad, Kamal Dariyabadi, B.P. Maurya and Chaudhry Dharam Singh, with the exception of Rameshwar Dayal Valmiki were leading the Dalit politics.

On 5 Dec 1980, the Dalit Panthers movement was born in Lucknow besides in Kanpur as stated earlier. Shyamlal of Jaunpur was its President and D.K.Anand of Sarojini Nagar, Lucknow was its General Secretary. Anand further revealed that a presidium was set with Bharat Singh of Agra, Rahulan Rao Ambavadekar originally from Azamgarh but settled in Kanpur and Satya Priya Manav from Itawa as its members. The Dalit Panthers in Uttar Pradesh were millitant and specially rose against the atrocities on the Dalits since the 1980s when the Congress Party came to power again after a brief gap of two and half years of the Janata Party Government. The main demands of Panthers were that, "in case of a death of the Dalit due to atrocity, he/she should be paid Rs.5 lakh as compensation along with 5 *Bighas* of land, one weapon (a pistol or gun) and service to one person in the family". There is no evidence to prove at this stage whether they had succeeded in forcing the government to pay such compensation. But one thing is clear that the demand itself looked impractical and the Panthers were not in great numbers to amount the required pressure on the government for getting their demands realised. Also, some of their demands were already raised by the RPI in the state, which though promised were not fulfilled by the Congress government, particularly the demand of land to tiller. Later on, the General Secretary of the Panthers was booked under the National Security Act (NSA) because of his provocative speeches and violent demonstrations organized at the district head- quarters in 1986. Thus, with his arrest, the Panthers movement faded out paving the way to the gradual emergence of the BAMCEF in 1979 in Lucknow, the capital of the state.

The BAMCEF emerged after its formal inauguration of the Delhi office on 6th December, 1978 with Kanshi Ram as its Convener. Raj Bahadur, G.R. Khanna, Chhotelal Rahul, Ram Chandra and others helped in developing this organization in Lucknow and adjoining area. Raj Bahadur, the then Convener of the BAMCEF in Uttar Pradesh, told that as he was employed in the department of telecommunication, he could use the government facilities in spreading the message of the organization. The main aim of the organisation was to pay back to the society particularly the Dalit community. Basically, it was an effort of the educated Dalit employees who had benefited from the policy of the 'Protective Discrimination' or reservation on the basis of their caste or community background. A very significant issue raised by the organization was that the Indian society could be divided into two major categories of the Bahujans who constitute nearly 85 per cent of the total population in the country and the upper castes or the Manuvadis with 15 per cent of the population. It was emphasized that the Manuvadis had captured and monopolised every institutions-economic, political, social, bureaucratic, religious and cultural both in the country as well as in the state. Besides holding its annual conventions, one of the most important programmes of the BAMCEF was "Ambedkar Mela on Wheels" which was organised to spread the mission of Dr. Babasaheb Ambedkar. "During the 2 months period, starting on 14th April, 1980, the Mela used to move for two months from place to place in the north Indian states surrounding Delhi and get over on June 14. Thus, covering in all 34 important places of this region through such Mela the BAMCEF was hopeful of removing ignorance about Ambedkar to a great extent. It had also hoped that such activity would help the demoralized Ambedkarites of this region to pick up courage and move ahead enthusiastically" (*Oppressed Indian*, April, 1980). Further, in November 1980, 'Humanity Convention' was organised to demand change in the curricula of education, to appeal to the press to be neutral and to bring about structural changes in the police force (ibid).

As the BAMCEF was non-agitational organization, Kanshi Ram was unable to launch struggle against various types of problems faced by the Dalits, OBC, Minorities and Tribals. He had raised the problems of poverty, landlessness, illiteracy, and non-implementation of laws specially these relating to reservations and physical protection of the aforesaid categories of people. He had argued that these could not be tackled by BAMCEF only, but "The constructive effort of BAMCEF can strengthen the non-political roots of the oppressed and the exploited society and the rest must be left to the others (*Oppressed Indian*, Dec, 1981). He criticized the Dalit leaders in the different political parties and argued to launch another organization to prepare the dedicated Dalit leaders to save the society. "It is with this hope of producing such missionaries that Dalit Shosit Samaj Sangharsh Samiti i.e. DS4 has been (was) launched from Delhi on December 6th, exactly 25 years after Babasaheb Dr. B.R. Ambedkar left us almost orphaned" (ibid).

Immediately after launching the DS4, the process of building up of organization was started in a big way.

The denunciation of Poona Pact was another programe undertaken by the DS4 to critizie the 'Reserved Seats' arrangement imposed by Gandhi on Dalits. The one-month programme started from Poona on 24 September, 1982 ended at Jalandhar on 24 October 1982. The programme's impact was felt by the Dalits of Agra as reported by some of our respondents and a mammoth rally was organised in the Ambedkar Park in which students, youth and women participated in large number. On 14th October 1982, the DS4 took up an ambitious but significant programme of 'People's Parliament'. R.K. Chaudhry from Faizabad district in central U.P, the present General Secretary of the Bahujan Samaj Party, four times cabinet minister and former leader of the upper house of Assembly narrated that, "In a caste ridden society 4 to 5 per cent Brahmins seem to have acquired a grip over the National Parliament through more than 30 per cent MPs they get elected. Our National Parliament does not represent the aspirations of the Dalit and deprived masses". Similarly, many other issues were also debated in this people's parliament in the rural and urban areas in the state.

One can easily draw conclusion from these two programmes that these were organised just to make Dalits and OBCs conscious of the fact that the Congress and other political parties were not effectively taking up their issues. And specially the Congress Party was their real enemy. The last programme of the DS4 was 'Struggle for Equality and Self-Respect' launched on 6th Dec. 1983. Under this, "Social Action propagating the message of struggle for equality and self-respect from Kanyakumari and four other corners of the country, viz. Kargil, Kohima, Puri and Porbandar" (was initiated) (*Oppressed Indian*, 1984). The first phase of social action programme ended on 15th March 1984 that was virtually winding up of both the organizations namely BAMCEF and DS4 and emerging of the Bahujan Samaj Party at the centre stage. This can broadly be seen as end of another epoch (1969-84) of the Dalit leadership in the state.

After galvanizing the sleeping masses of the deprived sections for over a decade (1971 to 1984) through his two organizations, Kanshi Ram launched his political party, the Bahujan Samaj Party on 14th April, 1984, on the birth Anniversary of Babasaheb Dr.

Ambedkar to fulfil the political aspiration of the Bahujan Samaj. Thus, a new epoch (sixth and ongoing) of the Dalit leadership started in Uttar Pradesh from 1984 with the formation of an independent political party where Dalits can play a dominant role. It came to fill the space created by the demise of the Republican Party of India, Agra branch, and incapacity of the Dalit Panthers and other leaders like Ram Dhan, Ram Vilas Paswan, etc. to tap the emerging consciousness among the Dalits in the state. Raj Bahadur, the first President of the Bahujan Samaj Party of Uttar Pradesh told that the two main programmes undertaken by the party in the beginning were agitation for implementation of the Mandal Commission Recommendations and the 'political actions like anti slavery struggle in India'. He told further that, "for this the party launched Anti-slavery Struggle in India on the 15th August, 1984 from all the five corners of the country. The objective behind this was to explain the masses all over the country as to what was their fate after thirty-seven years of independence. Was the Bahujan Samaj really free in this country?" Gandhi Azad, another BSP leader and now a Rajya Sabha member, told that "to attract the imagination of the Dalit masses, we used to raise the issues of 'educate, agitate and organize' and tell about their glorious history". In fact, this version of history is only the history of the 'Adi-Hindus' as narrated earlier in this chapter.

With the establishment of the Bahujan Samaj Party, the BSP has built up a strong Dalit movement making assertion for identity and consciousness of Dalits as its basis in the state which still has a rigid and conservative social structure, and has experienced no anti-caste movement specially in the post-independent period. Still, it has not succeeded in its avowed goal of displacing the Manuvadi forces and introducing social change despite a considerable politicisation of Dalits in the state (Pai 2000:119). Yet, with the emergence of the BSP even the Rashtriya Swayamsevak Sangh (RSS) has felt problems. For instance, Balasaheb Deoras named the BSP as one of the real problems for the RSS in north India (*Illustrated Weekly*, August 14, 1988). Spelling out its success, Kanshi Ram wrote, "The measure of its success in uniting such victims of Brahminism can be assessed from the fears of the RSS. The annual reports of the RSS released on 15th March, 1985 devoted a full Para to such a success of the BSP in uniting the oppressed and exploited caste groups and securing brotherhood amongst them...In the eyes of the RSS, such a success of the BSP is the greatest danger to the Hindu fundamentalist" (*Oppressed Indian,* April 1985).

With its strategy and organizational set up, the BSP contested, for the first time the December 1984, the general elections to the Parliament and qualified for registration in three states including Uttar Pradesh. It officially got elephant as its party symbol and blue colour as its party flag. The Dalit leadership specially the BSP leadership has become further assertive since 1985 with its politics of horizontal aggregation of the lower castes. The BSP first made headway with weaning away the Dalits from the Congress Party in Uttar Pradesh. As stated earlier, the Dalits had a special relationship with the Congress Party in the 1962, 1967, 1971 Parliamentary elections. The shift in the Dalit voting-patterns since 1977 shows, however, that they had voted indiscriminately. The Congress Party since then has not enjoyed a monopoly in representing them (Rudolph & Rudloph 1987: 187-99). This helped the BSP to attract the Dalits towards it as they could easily identify it as a Dalit party playing the dominant role for their amelioration. Their attraction could easily be seen in a bi-election in 1985 for the Lok Sabha seat from Bijnor in which its candidate was Ms. Mayawati. "Her opponents in Bijnor included Ram Vilas Paswan and Meira Kumar, Jagjivan Ram's daughter, representing Congress. Rajiv Gandhi was at the height of his popularity at the time and Meira Kumar won the seat" (Mendelshon & Vicziany 1998:224). But our respondents specially from the BSP described it as their moral victory as their candidate gained 61,000 votes even though BSP was an unknown party. *India today* (Jan 15-31,1986) described the "BSP rising with the sign of a shooting star".

The respondents also told that Kanshi Ram, the BSP supreme, became much after sought person. After this, every leader of the national political parties and the national daily wanted to rub their shoulders with him. "All this hysteria does not merely reflect the rise of BSP, but basically the fears of the big leaders of the national parties. Why should they be afraid of BSP, a little known party? Because the big leaders of all these parties know that the victims of India's social system are rolling around BSP to effect real socio-economic changes in India. These big leaders-the beneficiaries of India's social system know that if real socio-economic changes take place in India, they and their privileged castes will no longer remain rulers of India" (*Oppressed Indian*, Jan.1986). The BSP leaders further told that the "success came because the trained party workers hailed from all parts of the country as it was a bi-election and they were free from political activities in their home states/region. Had it been a general election, it would have not been possible for them to get free from their respective constituency".

By now, the Dalit leadership in Uttar Pradesh led by the BSP and Kanshi Ram understood the real basis of social transformation. Kanshi Ram gave the ideology to the party of "economic emancipation and social transformation through capturing political power", as was revealed by most of the respondents. Mendelsohn & Vicziany wrote the same and explained, "Kanshi Ram's strategy and his larger understanding of social change are now considerably evolved. He no longer believes in the primacy of social reform. Rather, expenditure of effort on any object other than the capture of government is seen to be superfluous. It is administrative power that will bring about desired change, not vice versa" (Mendelsohn & Vicziany 1998:223). By 1989, the BSP had put in five years of solid organizational work in Uttar Pradesh and also in neighbouring states of Madhya Pradesh, Punjab, Delhi and Haryana. The cadre camps were organized to educate the Dalits about the existing socio-political reality of the country and about the programmes of the BSP. This had the tremendous effect on them. The Dalits from different political parties specially the Congress Party joined the BSP's movement "There was a concerted move in 1988-89 to win back scheduled caste voters who were increasingly being alienated from the Congress which faced serious competition from the BSP which was actively mobilizing Dalits, particularly government employees, who were increasingly captivated by the BSP's agenda. The rise of the BSP was a matter of great political significance and one, which affected the Congress most deeply. But the party failed to evolve a tangible strategy to counter the BSP, mainly because it did not have a single reputable Dalit leader with a significant mass base. Moreover, the Scheduled Castes were disenchanted owing to their gross under-representation in the Uttar Pradesh Cabinet" (Hasan 1998:147).

The issue of capturing political power eluded the leadership of the BSP till 1993 during which it shifted its strategy and entered into an alliance with the Samajwadi Party of Mulayam Singh. According to R.K. Chaudhry, the main issue of alliance was that "

The BSP wanted to stop the communal march of the BJP because minorities were also part of the Bahujans. The communal forces comprising of Manuvadis are common enemies of Dalits and Muslims because they have reduced both of them to their present oppressed situation". Hence, a new issue of communalism was attached to the long list of the issues addressed by the BSP. But soon the agenda changed and priority was given to stop the atrocities perpetrated on the Dalits. For instance, Mendelsohn & Vicziany (1998:227) wrote, "There was also concern at the number of 'atrocities' perpetrated against Scheduled Caste people some of them by Yadavs...Accordingly, in June 1995 Kanshi Ram and Mayawati brought the government down". The goal of capturing political power to implement the Dalit agenda soon brought the Dalit leadership in a position to take support of the BJP. It is interesting to note that Kanshi Ram had earlier termed the BJP as "Manuwadi" and even then he took its support to form the government in the state. This shows the preference given by the Dalit leadership to the administrative and political power. In June 1995, Mayawati became the first Dalit woman Chief Minister of Uttar Pradesh and thereby of any state in India. But soon the support was withdrawn by the BJP because the BSP was implementing its own agenda. In March 1997, Mayawati again became the Chief Minister of Uttar Pradesh with the BJP support.

During the second term of her Chief Ministership for 6 months, Mayawati again tried to implement her party agenda instead of raising any demand for the Dalits. Both the times, she became a fearful administrator and proved the point that the Dalits could also govern. It has been stated, "Within the larger administration of the state Mayawati made energetic resort to the device of transfers and disciplinary actions against officers found delinquent in one aspect or another...Quite deliberately she created a climate of fear in order to motivate officials to work to her agenda. She dealt particularly severely with officials judged to have failed to protect the most vulnerable people in a particular district, the Dalits above all. Overwhelmingly condemned in the press, her actions appear to have evoked a sense of satisfaction among people routinely subjected to official arrogance and callousness. And a number of commentators both within the administration and outside believed that Mayawati had administered a powerful and long overdue lesson to bureaucrats that their place was as servant, not master of the people" (ibid: 229).

Anyway, the BSP contested on its own the 1998 and 1999 Parliamentary elections. In 1999, it surprised everyone by winning 14 Parliamentary seats with 22 per cent of votes polled. This success of the BSP proves the consolidation of the Dalit votes by it. One of our respondents told, "they (the BSP leaders) are heading towards a process of participatory democracy in place of the representative democracy because now they themselves are involved in organizing their party and selecting their candidates for contesting elections". Hence, with the different types of achievements in political and administrative realms, the Dalit leadership has grown its strength in Uttar Pradesh. It has monopolized the Dalit votes, and it is very difficult to find any Dalit leader of repute with substantial mass base in other political parties either at the national or state level. In brief, this is the greatest achievement of the BSP leadership particular and the Dalit leadership in general in the contemporary Indian political system.

Style of Functioning of the Dalit Leadership

The Dalit leadership in Uttar Pradesh, like in other states, has a diverse history of its functioning. It used to be persuasive in the 1920s and 1930, as stated earlier, by submitting petition to the upper castes and the respective governments to improve their lot. Our respondents from the eastern Uttar Pradesh have told that such persuasive style of the Dalit leadership prevailed till the 1960s. But as already stated, the assertion of the Dalit leadership in the western Uttar Pradesh had started in the 1920s and the caste like Jatav "gave public demonstration of its offensive stand" (Lynch 1974:82). Again, by the 1940s the Jatav leadership had become assertive and started demonstrative for their demands "The second aggressively defiant act was a parade through the street of Agra. Its main attraction was a wolf symbolizing the Poona Pact...The wolf was publicly burned, and the heat of Jatav anger was not lost to the eyes of the Agra's upper castes who saw themselves symbolically consumed in the flames of long smouldering resentment" (ibid:88). Yet, the Dalit leadership became more assertive after independence. Now, the Dalit leaders could organize their own meetings. Some of the respondents from this region have stated, "earlier, our parents used to go to the Thakurs with folded hand for any type of demand and now with the government's help the Thakurs are no more the rulers over us".

The formation and the consolidation of the Dalit political parties have also strengthened the pressure group strategy and capability of manoeuvering of power of the leadership in the state. With their own mass political base, they can now easily gherao any office and police station if something wrong happens to their people. This trend has increased with the emergence and consolidation of the BSP. Our respondents belonging to the BSP stated that, "now they (Dalits) are respected by most of the village officials, and their applications and complaints are taken up seriously. Today, they (officials) are afraid that tomorrow our party can again come to power and then their position will be delicate". They said further, "earlier our applications use to lie and gather dust. In police station, they never used to write our complaints. But now, things have changed and the police officials even give us seat whenever we go to their office". Thus, the Dalit leadership specially the BSP leadership in the state had addressed social issues and being persuasive in nature in the beginning has now become assertive. The leaders pursue vigorously the political issue leading ultimately to capture power.

Our respondents have further answered that they now do not raise, from the party platform, the social issues like leaving the caste customs, traditional caste occupations, and traditional caste habits like non-judicious expenditure, superstitions, witch-craft, etc. These issues, in effect, were and one are addressed by the caste panchayats or caste associations like Pasi Jagriti Mandal, Jatav Mahasabha, Rajak Sudhar Samiti, Balmiki Mahasabha, Sonkar Samaj Vikas Samiti, Kureel Samaj Sabha, etc. In fact, the traditional panchayats leaders still have hold on many communities. They pass the codes to stop the traditional food habits and impose fine on the caste members who violate the caste rules.

But the leaders usually raise the issues like asking the Dalit masses to pursue their independent livelihood with no inferiority complex. In public meetings, they often argue that 'to be a Dalit is not shame for us'. In the words of a Dalit leader, "For our degraded position the hole Hindu civilization should feel shame, because the Hindus boast that they have given the world a unique civilization but they don't tell it is this civilization which has produced crores of people who are not even treated as human beings". Contrary to this, some of our respondents have admitted that they do not ask the masses to leave their traditional occupations because they have no alternative. But they insist that in the long run, Dalits should leave their traditional occupations and become the rulers of this country. The BSP leadership is also very critical of worship of God. The respondents from the BSP have narrated many stories and they question the very existence of the various gods and goddesses of the Hindu pantheon.

Political Nature of the Dalit Leadership

It was revealed by some of the respondents that the contemporary Dalit leadership in U.P. has turned political in nature. This is evident from the issues the leaders specially from the BSP raise. More often than not, they raise the issues of political rights of the Dalits such as their representation in the various Government organizations, institutions, statutory bodies and committees, various boards, corporations, etc. For achieving these goals, they have tried to unite all the exploited people through their alliance with different socio-political forces and different political parties.

As stated earlier, some of our respondents are of the view that the prime object of the contemporary Dalit leadership in the state is social transformation and also economic emancipation of the Dalits. We have also already noted that such transformation is to be brought through capturing political power. Through such power the Dalits may become the ruling lot and enact laws or social legislations according to their needs, besides those of others, such as laws related to distribution of the surplus land which has remained undistributed even after 45 years of the Zamindari Abolition Act. They can also distribute the quota and licences to the Dalits who have largely remained neglected till date and can encourage them by honouring some of the Dalit personalities who had worked for upliftment of the Dalits at large in the past. In sum, once coming to power, the Dalit leadership can easily adopt agenda, and frame and implement the policies and programmes to ameliorate the conditions of the Dalits. One of our respondents Gulab Sehra, who was the State Convenor of the Nationalist Congress before his death recently, has argued that, "At the grass-root level, the impact of capturing power is very very effective. We do not have to beg for small things from the administrative authorities. One of the most acute problems at the village level is the false implication of the Dalits in the perennial feuds between the upper castes and Dalits, on one hand and between the backward castes and the Dalits on the other. As of now, the Dalits are beaten up and then implicated in false cases. Ironically, the police do not lodge even their FIRs. This was effectively checked when Mayawati was the Chief Minsiter of the state".

Though sometimes the Dalit leadership has acted independently but in the recent years it has entered in the strategic and opportunistic alliances with the different political parties for capturing political power, as stated earlier. The Dalit leadership led specially by the BSP during 1993-94 aligned with the Samajwadi Party (SP) that represents mostly the backward sections of the society such as Yadavs and Muslims. In 1995, it aligned the Bhartiya Janata Party (BJP), a political party said to represent the so-called upper castes and classes specially Brahmins and Banyas. Similarly, in 1996 it aligned with the Congress Party, the oldest party in the country and once represented the upper caste Brahmins. Lastly, it again aligned in March 1997 with the BJP to form the government in the state under the six months formula, as stated earlier.

We have already mentioned that the different political parties have Dalit leaders contesting from the reserved constituency. The Dalit leadership in the state has, thus, always aligned with the dominant socio-political forces of its time. Moreover, the Dalit leadership in the different political parties has been remained averse to forge alliance with the BSP. This may be so as the Dalit leaders from different political parties are afraid of their political existence, though even otherwise it is not much distinctively visible in their respective party. It is important to note here that today every dominant political party is desperately to forge alliance with the BSP. But to reach to this status, the BSP had to wage a relentless battle on its own. This is evident from the fact that the BSP leaders contested many bi-elections and general elections independently, the latest being of the 1999 elections to the Parliament.

The answer to the question whether in the case of alliance with other socio-political forces should the Dalit leadership keep the reigns in their own hands is affirmative. A sizeable number of our respondents have argued that if our leaders do not control the reigns then they cannot guide the government and administration according to their needs and desires. It is all the more important to do so because only they can empathise with the problems specially of the Dalits and other poor masses, and can accordingly formulate the effective and implementable policies and programmes. Their experiences and insights can enrich the day-to-day functioning of the government from the grass-root to the highest level. But Reena Chaudhury, the Dalit Member of Parliament from the Samajwadi Party revealed that, "instead of having opportunistic alliance with the political parties, the Dalit leadership should have alliance directly with the different communities having similar socio-economic and political status. Moreover, they should organize themselves first and become strong enough so that the dominant forces may not be able to break them". She further suggested that, "the independent organizing of the Dalit leadership is necessary because it is not yet prepared to defend itself against the cleverness and unscrupulousness of the dominant socio-political forces". Similarly, Kamal Jayant, the journalist turned politician from Kanpur district lamented that, "the RPI was decimated only because it aligned with the dominant Congress Party and the upper castes captured the important positions of the party organization".

Again, the respondents had divergent views on the issue whether the alliance of the Dalit leadership with socio-political forces of the dominant upper castes and classes has diluted their agenda specially in the light of the BSP's alliance with the BJP. The respondents from the BSP vehemently argued that there was no dilution of the Dalit agenda even after its being allied with the BJP. The party pursued, to great extent, its own and policies programmes without any influence of the BJP. For instance, despite much opposition of the BJP leadership the BSP government organized 'Periyar Mela'. It is worth mentioning here that Periyar had garlanded Lord Rama's (the much revered Hindu God in the north) statue with shoes in Tamil Nadu. Lord Rama is supposed to be very dear to the BJP with the demolition of the Babri Maszid and construction of the Rama Mandir tangle at its core in Ayodhya in the state. Similarly, the SC/ST (Prevention of the Atrocities) Act, 1989 was, for the first time, effectively implemented in spite of the BJP's protest of its abuse. Some was the case with Ambedkar village development scheme. One can quote several such examples to bring the point back home that the BSP's agenda was not diluted with its alliance with the BJP.

Some of our respondents - Dalit leaders from other political parties have argued that, on the one hand, the BSP used to abuse the BJP in the past as Manuvadi party, a party of upper castes representing the status quoits forces but, on the other hand, it aligned with it only for the sake of power. This has created confusion among the Dalits masses regarding where should they go? Ram Pher, member of the Uttar Pradesh Congress Working Committee (UPCWC) and the former Corporator from the Lucknow Cantonment, explains that, "it is difficult to digest and explain the enigma that once you abuse a political party as Manuvadi and then also share the power with it. In effect the impact of the BSP got lost". The difference of opinion was so much diverse on the party line as no satisfactory answer could be ascertained about the alliance of the BSP with the Dalit leaders drawn from the other political parties.

Most of the respondents have agreed unanimously that in the contemporary period, the Dalit leadership has generated greater degree of caste consciousness among the Dalits in the state. It has succeeded in conseintising the Dalit masses about the real enemy for and cause of their degraded conditions. They have also revealed that this consciousness has been termed by the upper castes as caste-hatred which has often been highlighted by the media and a few social scientists. As stated earlier, the Dalit masses have come to realize that there is nothing wrong to be a Dalit because it is none of their fault. Moreover, they know where their salvation lies now. As the confidence among Dalits has grown, they are ready to face day-to-day challenges. Most of our respondents have further informed that upper strata blame the BSP leadership that the speeches of its leaders have created great divide between Dalits and the upper castes. It is more dangerous in the countryside because Dalits are still dependent on the upper castes for their livelihood and survival. The Dalit leaders specially the BSP leaders cannot afford to abuse the upper castes so openly as they will take and they do take revenge from the innocent Dalit masses. Under these conditions, nobody can protect them as they are still not fully organized and are in minority in villages.

As far as the issue of creating casteism among the Dalits themselves is concerned, majority of the respondents have again unanimously replied that this is unfounded. The political mobilization of the Dalits has created relatively more solidarities among the various castes that never used to interact previously. Most of them now sit together, discuss about various issues and chalk out their strategies. Prior to this, only the Dalit political leaders and educated persons used to have commensal relations among themselves. But now even the general masses of these castes have started commensal relations among themselves. Moreover, the Dalit politics is creating more and more Dalit leaders. The BSP leadership in its deliberate attempt has started giving representation to different even numerically smaller Dalit castes rather than relying on and promoting to only the numerically dominant castes like Chamar and Jatav.

Besides, the BSP leadership is very hopeful that whatever success it has achieved in Uttar Pradesh would definitely influence the Dalit politics in other states in the country. But what is needed is that the BSP leadership in these states should be ready and fully equipped to organize itself in the same manner as it has done in Uttar Pradesh. One of our respondents Deenanath Bhaskar, the former Minister in the BSP-SP coalition government in U.P. during 1993-95 and now the Chairman of Scheduled Caste Cell of the Samajwadi Party, tells that, "The SP-BSP alliance in Uttar Pradesh has sent a message throughout the country that if the Scheduled Castes and Backward Castes form an all India alliance, they can rule the nation. They have numbers in their favour as well as effective organizations in other states". Similarly, another respondent Indrajit Saroj, the sitting MLA from the BSP, proudly proclaims that, "with the emergence of the BSP as the strong party representing Dalits, other political parties have started giving due respect to the Dalit members. You see, the BJP has elevated Suraj Bhan as the Governor of Uttar Pradesh, though he comes from Haryana; Congress has made Mata Prasad and Mahavir Prasad as governers of Arunachal Pradesh (now he has relinquished the charge) and Haryana respectively. Even the elevations of K.R. Narayanan to the post of the President of India and now G.M.C. Balayogi to the Lok Sabha Speaker fall in the same line". In addition, other leader respondents argue that the happenings in Uttar Pradesh may guide the Dalit leadership in the country as a whole to get organized and capture power for the development of the Dalits. Moreover, it has broken the myth within the Dalit community and among the general masses that the Dalits cannot rule. It can educate the Dalit masses that they can also form their own government and rule efficiently.

Contrary to this, some of the respondents drawn from other political parties have criticized that whatever has happened in Uttar Pradesh specially the opportunism of the BSP has sent a wrong message at both the state and national levels. It has created a suspected image of the Dalit leadership in general and of the BSP leadership in particular, and the people might think that every Dalit leader is vulnerable and can sell the movement for gaining power. Kaushal Kishore, the General Secretary of Lucknow unit of the CPI explains, "there will be no effect of the BSP in other parts of the country because no effort has been evolved to provide new system of governance in U.P. The Dalit masses here are treated in the same way, as in the past, during Mayawati's regeime. The Dalit ministers forget easily that earlier they themselves were like the Dalit masses. But yes, on the emotional line, Dalits can relate themselves to the achievements of the BSP otherwise there is no other reason for them to celebrate". Ravi Gautam, a BJP MLC from Agra, reminds that, "The BSP succeeded in Uttar Pradesh because there were strong independent organizations here led by the Jatav movements, the Scheduled Castes Federation and the Republican Party of India which are missing in other states except in Maharashtra. Therefore, I doubt that the BSP will have any substantial impact on the other parts of the country". Some respondents have stated categorically that the BSP would have no effect in places like Maharashtra where the RPI is still strong and Ambedkar's grandson is still very active.

It is a well-known fact that since Babasaheb has an all India acceptance, the Dalit leadership in general and the BSP leadership in particular pursues the various issues pertaining to the Dalits within the overall framework of the legacy of Ambedkar's leadership and his ideology. In the light of this, our respondents have opined that the Dalit leadership in Uttar Pradesh is part of the national leadership. To prove this point, they have stated that the BSP has become an All India Party. It is present in every state and has won the seats in the State Assemblies in Bihar, M.P, Karnataka, Jammu and Kashmir, Punjab, Haryana, Rajasthan, U.P., etc. Not only that Kanshi Ram has been accepted as the national leader by the maximum number of Dalits. The following slogans framed by the BSP tell about the strong association of Kanshi Ram and Babasaheb, and, secondly, of Kanshi Ram's effort in making the people conscious:

1. *Baba Tera Mission Adhura*
   Kanshi Ram Karenga Pura (Babasaheb, Kanshi Ram will complete your unfulfilled Mission).
2. *Babasaheb Ka Duasra Nam*
   Kanshi Ram Kanshi Ram, (Kanshi Ram is the second name of Babasaheb)
3. *Kanshi Teri Nek Kamai*
   Tune Soti Kaum Jagai (Kanshi Ram, you have done good job by waking up the sleeping *Quom* {community}).

Though Kanshi Ram's success has been located primarily in Uttar Pradesh, it has also transcended the territorial boundary. Kanshi Ram himself calls Uttar Pradesh as his laboratory (his speech on 14th April, 1999 at Mavlankar Hall Ground, New Delhi) and tries to practices the Uttar Pradesh formula in other states. The biggest advantage of the BSP is that it talks more of Ambedkar's ideology and projects that its leaders are the carriers of Ambedkar's movement. Rest of the Dalit leadership found in other political parties cannot take this liberty. But Acharya Moti Ram Shashtri, Gulab Sehra, Mata Prasad, Ram Dhan and other senior leaders do not accept that there is any association of the BSP leadership in Uttar Pradesh to the national leadership. They reflect that nobody has waged a mass movement like Babasaheb; hence, how can one claim to be of an all India status. To become a part of the national leadership or to be recognized as national leader, a party or the leader has to be recognized at the grass-root level in each state. They also accept that the Dalit leadership both at the state and national levels is divided on the primordial identities like caste, region and language. Ram Nath Kovind, a Rajya Sabha M.P. and President of the Anusuchit Jati Morcha of BJP argues, " In Uttar Pradesh itself, the Dalit leadership is divided because of the socio-political reality of different movements in which they have emerged". But Gandhi Azad, Rajya Sabha member from the BSP differs with this and narrates that, "though the Dalit problems differ from region to region but the Dalits suffer more or less same problems in every parts of the state/country. And, therefore, there is an underlining unity among the Dalit leaders of different parts of the country. It is the lack of the social and political acumen of the Dalit leaders, which create this hurdle for their unity. Moreover, their ego also stops them to accept someone who is not from the same region, as their leader. After all they are also human being."

In sum, we find Dalit leadership in Uttar Pradesh divided into different political parties. It is clear from the above analysis that the earlier Dalit leadership in the state was mainly persuasive and had always relied on the upper castes and classes for its political existence. As a result, the earlier leaders irrespective of their party affiliation neither asserted nor sincerely represented the interest of the Dalit masses. As the political leadership as such in the state took a qualitative turn since the 1970s, so also was the case of Dalit leadership. It is quite clear from our discussion made in this chapter that the Dalit leadership specially the BSP leadership in the state has become quite assertive. Its leaders openly and boldly articulate the interests of the Dalit masses and have become the symbol of aspirations and expectations of the latter. What shape would this leadership take in future may be only a conjecture at this stage that we have not probed in this study.

References

Amin, Shahid, 1999, Gandhi as Mahatma: Gorakhpur District, Eastern U.P., 1921-22, in Ranjit Guha (ed.), *Subaltern Studies III: Writings on South Asian History and Society*, Oxford University Press, Delhi.

Cohn, B.S., 1992, *An Anthropologist among the Historians and Other Essays*, Oxford University Press, Delhi.

Dushkin, Lelah, 1998, Scheduled Caste Politics in J. Michael Mahar (ed.) *The Untouchables in Contemporary India*, Rawat Publications, Jaipur and New Delhi.

Gokhale, J., 1993, *From Concessions to Confrontation: The Politics of an Indian Untouchable Community*, Popular Prakashan, Bombay.

Gooptu, Nandini, 1996, Caste and Labour: Untouchable Social Movement in Urban Uttar Pradesh in the Eearly Twentieth century in Peter Robb (ed.) *Dalit Movements and the Meanings of Labour in India*, Oxford University Press, Delhi.

Hasan, Zoya, 1998, *Quest for Power: Oppositional Movements & Post Congress Politics in Uttar Pradesh*, Oxford University Press, Delhi.

Jigyasu, Chandrika Prasad, 1960, *Shri 108 Swami Achhutanandji Harihar, Hindu Sudhar Karyalay*, Lucknow.

Joshi, Barbara R., 1982, *Democracy in Search of Equality: Untouchables Politics and Indian Social Change*, Hindustan Publishing Corporation, Delhi.

Juergensmeyer, Mark, 1982, *Religion as Social Vision: The Movement against Untouchability in 20th century Punjab*, University of California Press, Barkeley.

Keer, D., 1997, *DR. Ambedkar: Life and Mission*, Popular Prakashan, Mumbai.

Kshirsagar R.K., 1994, *Dalit Movement in India and its Leaders*, M.D. Publications, New Delhi.

Lynch, O.M., 1974, *The Politics of Untouchability: Social Mobility and Social Change in a city of India*, National Publishing House, New Delhi.

Mahar, J. Michael, 1998, Agents of Dharma in a North Indian Village in J. Michael Mahar (ed.) *The Untouchables in Contemporary India,* Rawat Publications, Jaipur & New Delhi.

Mendelsoh, Oliver & Vicziany Marika, 1998, *The Untouchables: Subordination, Poverty and the State in Modern India,* Cambridge University Press, New Delhi.

Omvedt, Gail, 1998, Kanshi Ram and the Bahujan Samaj Party in K.L. Sharma (ed.) *Caste and Class in India,* Rawat Publications, Jaipur and New Delhi.

Pai, Sudha, 2000, *State Politics: New Dimensions,* Shipra Publications, New Delhi.

Ram, Nandu 1995, *Beyond Ambedkar: Essays on Dalits in India,* Har-Anand Publications, New Delhi.

Ranjan, Purendu, 1999, Kabir Panth and Politics in Mithila in Ashish Ghosh (ed.) *Dalits and Peasants: The Emerging Caste-Class Dynamics,* Gyan Sagar Publications, New Delhi.

Singh, Y, 1996, *Social Change in India: Crisis and Resilience,* Har-Anand Publications, New Delhi.

Yaduvendu, 1942, *Yadvendu Ramayan: Yaduvansh Ka Itihas* (Hindi), Navyug Sahitya Niketan, Agra.

5

Dynamics of Dalit Leadership

We shall analyse in this chapter the dynamics of the Dalit leadership which can be identified as a continuous process of interaction of the Dalit leaders with the existing socio-political environments consisting of many actors such as different socio-political groups and their leaders, state and other institutions. Here, the focus would be on the shifting patterns of demands raised by the Dalit leadership, eg. social, economic, political, educational, etc. The dynamics involves the shift of Dalit leadership from social reform to acquiring political power along with the above raised issues over a span of time. In the same manner, the dynamics of Dalit leadership has been analysed here in terms of the dilemma faced by the Dalit leaders in representing both the Dalits and general masses in the reserved constituencies, solution of problems of the Dalits, justice to be accorded to the committed Dalit leaders affiliated to different political parties, the socio-political channelling of the emerging Dalit consciousness, and the birth of the self-aggrandizing leaders and stooges. We have also briefly looked into articulation of a few Dalit leaders regarding the issue of reverting back to the system of the separate electorates. Finally, we have discussed, in this chapter, dynamics of Dalit leadership in terms of formulation of a unified ideology, propagation of a singular identity and the identification of permanent foes and allies. In addition, this chapter also analyses though cursorily the impact of globalisation, liberalisation, privatisation and information revolution on reservations, for the Dalits, the possibility of the inclusion of discrimination and exploitation of the Dalits in the purview of the human rights and failure of the Dalit leadership in garnering the international support for the Dalit problems.

As stated in the preceding chapter, the Dalit leadership before independence of the country had raised the socio-religious issues like putting ban on the practice of untouchability, temple entry and entry to other public places, rights of reading religious scriptures and performing ritual rights, visiting holy places pilgrimages, etc. Through the process of sanskritisation, Dalits tried, on one hand to achieve upward social mobility within the Hindu social order and, on the other, their leaders propagated various Adi-movements to enhance status and gain respectful identity for Dalits outside the Hindu fold. The prominent Dalit leaders who led these movements were Swami Achhutanand in Uttar Pradesh, Narayan Guru Swami (though himself not a Dalit) and Kuran Asan in Kerala, Mangoo Ram in Punjab, Bhagya Reddy Verma in Andhra Pradesh, Jyotiba Phule (a Shudra) and Dr. Ambedkar in Maharashtra, etc. as already stated in Chapter 1 and also in the preceding chapter. Besides, the issues like atrocities and physical violence committed on the Dalits by the upper castes were also raised. These issues were raised as the Untouchables or Dalits did not have the civic rights, they were not allowed to enter common places where general masses walked, sit or gathered. Their entry was allowed only during certain specified period in the day. The Dalit leaders had also waged battle against ban on Dalit women to wear the clothes above the waist (Rudolph and Rudolph 1987:38, Ambedkar 1991:421, 1979:256; Mathew 1986:97-99).

Side by side, the Dalit leadership had also raised educational rights of the Dalits which included admissions of Dalit children in schools and colleges where children of the other upper castes studied, opening of educational institutions and hostels exclusively for Dalit students and instituting number of scholarships for them by the state. The grass-root Dalit leaders before the advent of Ambedkar also tried to mobilise the local resources for propagation of education among the Dalit children by opening up schools and hostels for them. Lynch (1974:79) narrates the educational endeavour of the Dalits in Agra, U.P. by saying, "Education among the Jatavs steadily increased. The first B.A. to a Jatav was awarded in 1926. By 1939 there was an institute called the Jatav Men's Educational Institute, which established and kept under its control five schools for boys and one for girls in Agra district. It also had a library at Raja Mandi in Agra city, which had 229 books and subscription to 16 newspapers and Journals in Hindi, Urdu and English...In 1935 another Jatav girls school, Lady Kailash Girls School was independently established...A hostel for boys at Agra College was established by the Educational Institute in about 1939".

The British government of India helped the Dalits in acquiring their much-needed weapon of education. Even Ambedkar had acknowledged such help and said, "Until the advent of the British, the untouchables were content to remain untouchables. It was a destiny preordained by the Hindu God and enforced by the Hindu state. Fortunately or unfortunately, the East India Company needed soldiers for their army in India and it could find none but the untouchables...In the army of the East India Company there prevailed the system of compulsory education for Indian soldiers and their children, both male and female. The education received by the untouchables in the army...gave them a new vision and a new value. They became conscious that the low esteem in which they had been held was not an inescapable destiny but was a stigma imposed on their personality by the cunning contrivances of the priest" (Ambedkar 1991:189). The army experience of Dalits gave them an extraordinary boost and they forced their off-springs to take education. Ambedkar himself was involved in establishing a chain of educational institutions in every stream of education-Law, Commerce, Arts, and Social Sciences etc. The two most important education societies, which he established, were the "Depressed Classes Educational Society" on 14 July, 1928 and the "Peoples Education Society" on 8 July, 1945. His most famous message "Educate, Agitate and Organize" which has become a common diktat and can be heard in any Dalit conference also emerged during this period.

Yet, the economic issues which attracted attention of the Dalit leadership during the pre-independence period were recruitment of Dalits in state services including army, generation of more employment for them, land reforms and distribution of surplus land, special assistance to the artisan castes, relaxation of taxes in leather industry, etc. It is true that the Dalits especially Mahars, Chamars, Dushads, Paraiyans, etc. joined the British army in a big manner (Lynch 1974, Mendelohn & Vicziany 1998:88). But soon the British stopped recruitment of the Dalits as they came to know that there were some other 'martial races' in Indian society (ibid: 88). Moreover, by that time the upper castes had started entering in the British bureaucracy and army. Gopal Baba Walankar, a retired army officer, of Maharashtra had taken up the issue of retrenchment of the Dalits from the British army. He had filed a petition in 1890 to the Brith officials to consider favourably their recruitment in the army. The same plea was made by Shivram Janba Kamle and Gangaram Krishojee to employ Mahars as police sepoys and soldiers in the British armed forces (Jogdand 1991: 46-47). In Uttar Pradesh, a Jatav Battalion was formed. "During the Second World War, he (Manikchand) cooperated with the British. He called upon his brethren to join the military and defend the country at any cost. It was because of his efforts that the Jatav Battalion was formed, but it was disbanded after the War was over" (Kshirsagar 1994 : 231). After that, the Dalits pursued no such demand.

In certain parts of the country, the agricultural commercialisation also laid the basis for a wide spread rural movement (Omvedt 1994: 114). For instance, the Dalit leaders in the Coastal Andhra and Rayalseema raised the vital issues of the Dalit rights over land, wage, etc. Later, Ambedkar had also raised the issue of Mahar Vatan land in Maharashtra. The RPI in Uttar Pradesh and Maharashtra had raised the issue of distribution of surplus land, and land to the tiller became the national demand (Rosenthal 1986 : 348, Gokhale 1993 : 225). The demands to government for grant-in-aid for sustenance of distributed land were reciprocal to the ownership of the land. Wherever there was land distributed to the Dalits, they made petitions and prayers for the grant-in-aid for sustenance of land allotted to them. But there was very faint voice for distribution of surplus agricultural land and implementation of Minimum Wages Act by the Dalit leadership during the pre-independence era.

After independence, all the aforesaid social, religious, economic and educational issues have been raised by the Dalit leadership. But their efficacy and effectiveness has not been their distinctively visible. Except the RPI, the national and state level Dalit leadership has failed to wage any significant movement articulating the issues discussed in chapter 4. A large majority of our respondents have revealed many causes for the general neglect of these issues. In their opinion, "the Dalit leaders largely lack awareness and do not have relevant data to raise these issues. Secondly, they do not have adequate support on these issues from their respective political parties and they are afraid of their party bosses to compel the latter to endorse their articulation on the issues related to the Dalits. Thirdly, if they raise these issues independently, they might be termed as in disciplined and, hence, may loose their chance of getting ticket for contesting general elections and may not get even party position". Not only this but a respondent was also of the view that "the Dalit leadership has become self-centred and looks for its future only. Since these issues require lot of effort in mobilizing and garnering support of the masses, the Dalit leaders prefer to address relatively smaller issues. Hence, the Dalit leaders across the party line have raised after independence many peripheral issues like fulfilment of reservations, renaming of streets, or institutions including educational ones after Ambedkar or some other leaders, installation of Ambedkar's statue, etc. Many respondents have argued that "as far as naming of the streets and universities, and installation of statues of Ambedkar and other leaders are concerned, the Dalit leadership particularly the BSP leadership in reality wants to pay homage and respect to those leaders who have sacrificed their lives for the Dalits. Their sacrifices went unnoticed earlier. As the Dalit leaders have now got some say and power, they are pushing forward this agenda". A few other respondents are of the view that the "Dalit leaders often play with the emotions of the Dalit masses. They give only psychological satisfaction to the Dalit masses who, in turn, think that their leaders are doing something for them". These respondents are also of the view that though reservation provides instant relief and occupational mobility to the Dalits but since job opportunities in the public sector are shrinking, the reservation is becoming redundant. Yet, the Dalit masses in general and their leaders in particular insist for implementation of reservation provisions as these are enshrined in the Constitution; and for this and other purposes, they take assistance of judiciary and other state machinery. Above all, these types of issues help the Dalit leadership to mobilize easily Dalit masses rather than the social-economic issues".

Shift from Social Reform to Acquiring Political Power

In answer to a question why Dalit leadership has shifted its focus from social reform to capturing political power, most of the respondents have narrated that Babasaheb Ambedkar himself had suggested that, "the Dalits should become a ruling community and political power is the only key to achieve that". Gore (1993:213) also illustrates that, "The importance that Ambedkar attached to a share in political power is reflected in most of his public speeches between 1924 to 1950. In his Barsi Takli speech in May 1924,

Ambedkar had said that in some respects social injustice could be removed only with political leverage. But to get a voice in the polity it was important to organize. Organizational pressure was more telling than the mere enunciation of a principle". In the Round Table Conference held on the 12th November 1930, Ambedkar presented a scheme of political safeguards for the protection of the Depressed Classes (Dalits) in the future Constitution of a self-governing India. In his own words, "...The Depressed Classes must be given sufficient political power to influence legislative and executive action for the purpose of securing their welfare. In view of this, they demand that the following provisions shall be made in the electoral law so as to give them :

(1) Right to adequate representation in the legislature of the country,

Provincial and Central.

(2) Right to elect their own men as their representative (a) by adult Suffrage and

(b) by separate electorates for the first ten years and thereafter by joint electorates and reserved seats, it being understood that joint electorates shall not be forced upon the Depressed Classes against their will unless such joint electorates are accompanied by adult suffrage" (Ambedkar 1991:47). Further, he proposed that the Dalits should be given representation in the Cabinet also. Again, in his own words, "Just as it is necessary that the Depressed Classes should have the power to influence governmental action by seats in the Legislature so also it is desirable that the Depressed Classes should have the opportunity to frame the general policy of the Government. This they can do only if they can find a seat in the Cabinet. The Depressed Classes therefore claim that in common with other minorities, their moral rights to be represented in the Cabinet should be recognized. With this purpose in view the Depressed Classes propose: that in the Instrument of Instructions an obligation shall be placed upon the Governor and the Governor-General to endeavour to secure the representation of the Depressed Classes in his Cabinet (Ambedkar 1991:51-52).

The reiteration of the Dalit leadership on the use of political power as suggested by Ambedkar to wage a struggle against the oppressive social order can further be proved by his speech delivered in Lucknow, "In his Lucknow speech (25 April, 1948), which caused a controversy because he was at that time a member of the Congress Cabinet at the Centre, Ambedkar again reiterated that 'political power is the key of all round progress'. He said that the other backward classes and the Scheduled Castes, if they worked unitedly, would wrest power from the upper classes (Gore 1993:213). It is worth mentioning here that Ambedkar himself made shift from social reforms to political activity. "With the conversion announcement in 1935, the establishment of political party in 1936, and considerable success in the 1937 elections, the shift from attempting to gain status in matter of religion to organising for political activity was nearly complete" (Zelliot 1996:107). Further, Ambedkar in his endeavour of achieving political power to lead the struggle of Dalits, "In 1942, ...decided to consolidate and nationalize his leadership of the Scheduled Castes. Thus in July of that year he founded the All India Scheduled Castes Federation...The bases of the Federation's aim were Ambedkar's fundamental and life-long tenets of political action" (Lynch 1974:135). Hence, the above-mentioned facts are enough to substantiate the arguments given by the Dalit leadership particularly the BSP leadership in their shift from social reform to acquiring political power. The Dalit leaders are largely inspired by Ambedkar's, version and vision about the impact of political power on amelioration of the Dalits.

Some of our respondents have also given another reason for this shift from social reform to political power. According to them, there is now qualitative change in the Indian polity, whereby it is becoming more liberal and democratic. Now, more and more Dalits can participate in the political process that decides their future and enables them to assert their rights. Rudolph & Rudolph (1987:32) have argued, "But as liberal and democratic ideas penetrated to wider sections of the population, the aims of the caste association began to shift from sacred to secular goals. Instead of demanding entry into temples, prestigious caste names, and "honourable" occupations and histories in the Census, the associations began to press for places in the new administrative and educational institutions and for political representation". Lynch also tries to prove this point in Uttar Pradesh. According to him, The change is due to the fact that Sanskritisation is no longer as effective a means as is political participation for achieving a change in style of life and a rise in the Indian social system, now composed of both caste and class elements. The ultimate object of Sanskritisation was to open and legitimise a place in the opportunity and power structures of the caste society. It is hoped that the same objectives can now be achieved by active, but separatist, political participation. No longer is entrance into the power, opportunity and wealth structures of Indian society based solely on ascribed caste status; in the public sector, at least, achievement based on citizenship status is the principle of recruitment to these structures. The Republican Party is the organised response to the majority of Jatavs to gain these ends" (Lynch1974: 97). Indeed, the democratic set up of the country has affected the pattern of mobilization of the Dalit leadership as discussed in the next chapter.

The importance attached to political power by the Dalit masses in general and their leaders in particular is further elaborated by Joshi (1982:123) who," Political power can be seen either as an end in itself, or as a means to other ends. Those who focus upon political power as an end in itself usually expect equality to follow from Scheduled Castes access to power...political power is the sole solution (to inequality). You are treated as an equal if you have political power". Quoting her respondent, Joshi further says, "May be some social and economic inequality will remain, but we can pass legislation to end that if we have political power". In her own words, "political power is regarded as a source of prestige and status equality in itself; use of politics to tackle other facts of inequality was almost an afterthought. In many ways, this is a very realistic outlook" (ibid). Some of our respondents have also argued that power is a means to achieve social transformation at a faster speed. According to them, "No doubt social change will come from social reform also but it is a time taking process. Our ancestors have been involved in doing the same since generations but it has not brought desired result. Nobody knows whether we will be alive to witness the social transformation. Therefore, we need political power to speed up the process of social transformation". The final reason narrated by a leader respondent, drawn from a modest family background, for shifting the priority from social reform to political power was the rights granted to Dalits in the Constitution. He has argued that because of legislations and modern institutions, many of the social problems have been solved on their own. Various provisions and laws have taken note of social discrimination prevalent in the society and have propounded ways and means to check them. Now, what is left is the effective implementation of these constitutional means to eradicate the persisting inequality for which political pressure is very necessary and the same cannot be achieved through social reforms.

Thus, the shift that the Dalit leadership particularly the BSP leadership his made from social reform to acquiring political power is based on many factors. At the outset, Babasaheb Ambedkar's vision sowed the seeds amongst the Dalit leaders on which the structure of their striving for political power is erected. Secondly, there is a qualitative change in the modern polity with Dalits getting constitutional safeguards. Thirdly, Dalits have now developed self-confidence that they can also capture power. Fourthly, they have realized that only social reforms cannot uplift the Dalit masses but to speed it up political power is must. Lastly, an independent assertion of Dalit leadership is mobilizing the Dalits on its own political agenda rather than the one set by others.

Reserved Constituency and Dalit Leadership

Under Articles 330 and 332 of the Constitution, a member of seats vis-à-vis constituencies have been reserved from where only the Scheduled Castes or Dalits can contest elections to the Lok Sabha and the State Assemblies respectively "The political goals of the reserved seat system were two: power and integration. A minority was to have its fair share of power to "secure adequate representation of its political views (and) adequate protection of its interest," and to provide opportunities for its members to participate fully in political life on more honourable terms than before" (Dushkin 1998: 208). But the system of reserved constituency requires the Dalit representative to represent in effect the general masses also, as he / she is also elected by their supports. This factor creates dilemma among the Dalit leaders in performing effectively their expected roles for amelioration of Dalits from their respective constituencies. In the opinion of the majority of our respondents, those Dalit leaders who belong to political parties dominated by the upper castes and classes are bound to work for the upper castes/classes of their constituencies. More specifically, they help them in getting all developmental facilities - approach roads, schools, electricity, toilets, hand pumps, sources of irrigation, etc. to their localities but the Dalits suffer from all these facilities.

In the words of some of the respondents, "they do so because they have to keep the dominant upper castes from their constituency who play decisive role in registering the victory of the Dalit leaders. Not only that but if a leader does not do so then his/her party bosses may get angry resulting into losing the party ticket or seat in the next general elections".

But contrary to this, the leader-respondents from the BSP and the RPI have argued that there is no such dilemma before them. They state that, "we know very well that upper castes have not supported us and they will never cast their votes in our favour. Therefore, we first and foremost look the interests of the Dalits. It is all the more important to give preference to the Dalits in the reserved constituencies because they are the one who need the services most. They have suffered since the ages and have been denied every facilities whatsoever even since the independence". It is also true that with the emergence of an independent Dalit leadership in the form of the BSP leadership, the accessibility of the Dalit leaders to the Dalit masses has increased considerably. Earlier, most of the Dalit leaders specially from the Congress Party were always surrounded by the upper castes and were not accessible to the Dalit masses. As revealed by a sizeable number of the respondents, "even for simple applications for the `ration cards', our brethren used to run from pillar to post". But now, things have changed and the Dalit leaders can be approached easily. On the whole, most of the Dalit-leaders respondents unanimously agree that once they are elected from the reserved constituencies, they represent all citizens of the constituency and take up the cases on their merit. They do not discriminate between higher and lower castes/classes. But they do confess that "somewhere at the subconscious level, we keep the Dalit interests in mind because reality may be sometimes misleading as what is seen with the necked eyes may not be true".

Thus, in the present time there seems to be significant change in the outlook of the Dalit leaders representing the reserved constituencies. Even the Dalit masses have started identifying with the Dalit leaders because the latter have become more accessible, as mentioned above. But it is too early to read much meaning in this change because the present Dalit leadership specially of the BSP is new to the power arena. What would happen in future, may be only a conjecture at this stage.

Impact of Reserved Constituencies

The debate on effectiveness of the reserved constituencies in ameliorating the Dalits through their real representatives goes back to the days of Ambedkar. Ambedkar had opined, "The untouchables demand that their representation shall be by separate electorates. A separate electorate means an electorate composed exclusively of untouchable voters who are to elect an untouchable as their representative to the legislature...But they (Hindus) insist that the untouchable who is to be the representative of the untouchables in the legislature should be elected by a mixed electorate consisting of both of Hindus as well as of the Untouchables and not by an electorate exclusively of the untouchables" (Ambedkar 1991: 412). Ambedkar was convinced that only through separate electorate the reserved constituencies can be made effective because then, "they (Dalits) would be in a position to elect a man in whom they have complete confidence and who would be independent to fight the battle of the untouchables on the floor of the Legislature against the representative of the Hindus" (ibid: 414). Further, narrating the dysfunction of joint electorate, he wrote that, "If…there is a joint electorate in these constituencies, the representative of the Untouchables would be only a nominal representative and not a real representative, for no Untouchable who did not agree to be a nominee of the Hindus and a tool in their hands could be elected in a joint electorate in which the Untouchable voter was out numbered in ratio of 1 to 24 or in some cases 1 to 49. The joint electorate is from the point of the Hindus to use a familiar phrase a "rotten borough" in which the Hindus get the right to nominate an Untouchable to set nominally as a representative of the Untouchables but really as a tool of the Hindus" (ibid: 414). In true sense of the term, if an upper caste "is made to concede power, he must not lose control over it. This is secured by joint electorates and frustrated by separate electorates" (ibid: 414).

In the light of the above discussion, if we evaluate the impact of the reserved seats vis-à-vis constituencies on conditions of the Dalits in general and the Dalit leaders in particular then we have two different and juxtaposed views. One, some of the respondents have revealed that, "with this representation, Dalits have got at least opportunity to sit in the legislature and know the reality. They can influence the legislature in formulating the policies and programmes in favour of Dalits. It has created special role for Dalits assuring at least some attention to be paid to the Dalit interests". In this regard, Joshi says that, "The political representation policy proved particularly important in maintaining government support for Untouchable development programmes in the face of increasingly well-organized violent opposition to untouchable mobility as well as competition for development resources from groups better equipped for electoral combat...Further, Scheduled Caste representatives, whose presence in substantial numbers at such major points of political power as party organizations and legislatures has been largely the result of the political representation policy, proved to be a built-in source of support for certain types of policies favouring all individuals at the lower end of the socio-economic scale (Joshi 1982:2). Interestingly, this process has also led to greater intensity of political participation of Dalit masses. Writing in the 1970s, Beteille brought this point to fore. In his own words, "...young Harijans with ambition, drive and initiative are in demand all round. They are sought by every political party; for, they are not only valuable as vote banks, but can also be put up as candidates for reserved seats from the Zilla Parishad right up to Parliament" (Beteille 1997: 132).

The opposite scenario is equally important wherein it has been stated that the reserved constituencies did not contribute in any significant manner for development of the Dalits in the past. "While the Scheduled Castes were drawn into government and legislatures, their induction did not contribute to the development of their distinct political identity" (Hasan 1998:129). In fact, these were used mostly by the dominant Congress Party for increasing its strength but not for giving proportionate power to Dalits. Some of our respondents expressed their views by saying that, "Within Congress the importance of the untouchable votes did not translate itself into great influence for individual untouchables in either the organization or the ministry. In particular, the building of the compensatory discrimination system arose more from the arithmetic of elections and the goodwill of sections of the elite than from the efforts of Dalit parliamentarians". They further stated that, "The prediction of Babasaheb Ambedkar is proving right because the real Dalit representatives are not given ticket to contest the elections and only yes men are promoted".

In this context, referring to vertical mobilizations (Rudolph & Rudloph 1987:24), Dushkin (1998:209) has argued that, "If we apply these types to scheduled caste politics, the first would require the untouchable leader to play the part of the loyal "Harijan" analogous to the "Uncle Tom" of American parlance. Under this arrangement, locally powerful upper-caste notables mobilize the votes to fill the reserved seats with their own men, whom they manipulate and control. These men are bound to them by traditional ties, as well as political debts, and the kind of leadership expected of them is good followership. Their reward for loyalty is the opportunity to distribute the Scheduled Caste benefits to their own followers". The same fact is highlighted by Lynch (1974:107) in his study of Jatavs of Agra in western Uttar Pradesh who says, "The `Radicals' maintain that because of the present system of reservations, Congress "yes men" are elected from the Scheduled Castes rather than men who will represent and fight the "real" interests of the Scheduled Castes". Even in the eastern Uttar Pradesh, our respondent Acharya Moti Ram Shastri lamented, "The labourers of the land lords were promoted to contest elections from the reserved seats. Once a "*Bhand*" (male dancer) was given ticket and he won the election. The *Halwahas* (ploughmen of upper castes), *Charwahas* (cowherds), *Nachanians* (male dancers), *Gavayias* (singers), etc. were in the good list of the Congressmen. One cannot expect anything from them". Reiterating the fact, Brass also wrote, "The Scheduled Caste leaders who have been given tickets in the reserved constituencies are non militant and have no power in the local or state Congress organizations. The numerous organizations in Uttar Pradesh for the advancement of the Scheduled Castes and `depressed classes' have been content to serve as agencies for the distribution of Congress patronage" (Brass 1965: 105).

But in the 1970s the Dalit leadership highlighted the dysfunctions of the reserved constituencies and the Dalit leaders suggested these constituencies to be abandoned. For instance, B.P.Maurya, ex-M.P. from Aligarh besides then being an important leader of the Republican Party of India but now a General Secretary of the BJP had once remarked, "This system does the Scheduled Castes no good because the people in the reserved seats belong to the party in power and are often incapable persons. Although they are educated, they dare not speak out against the party in power. They do not represent their people to the party and government, but represent the party in power to their people" (Isaacs 1965: 125-126). The Jatavs of Agra had also agreed to abandon this system though on different ground. According to (Lynch 1974:107), "The policy of `protective discrimination' is, the radicals say, a Congress trick to divide and rule the Scheduled Castes; if it is abandoned, then the Scheduled Castes will be forced to unite as a matter of political survival".

Further, the Dalit leadership in Uttar Pradesh warned the Congress leadership against its 'cunning manipulations'. Dalit leaders cautioned it that if Dalits were not given proper recognition, they would turn against it. Addressing a large Scheduled Caste rally in Kanpur, Gulab Sehra what Dalits had got in return for restoring the Congress to office time and again. In his own words, 'It is due to us that the party is ruling the country and the state. Are we getting proportional representation in the government?" (*India Today*, 31, Oct, 984). Even Mata Prasad, a senior Congress leader from eastern Uttar Pradesh, complained in the same manner to Congress leadership. But nothing could get materialized and the Congress leadership continued the same policy towards the Dalits.

For keeping a tenacious check on the growing assertion of the Dalit leadership, the Congress leadership did not digest any assertive Dalit leader in its fold. "Jagjivan Ram was alone as a Scheduled Caste politician in becoming a genuinely national figure through Congress. There have been a couple of Chief Ministers - one of them was Bhola Paswan Shastri, who three times held his position in Bihar for very brief periods in the 1950s. Bhola Paswan was respected for his modesty, dignity and probity but he made no deep mark on even state politics...A small number of other state and national politicians have gained a measure of ministerial seniority, but none has had either a long period at the apex of ministerial service or any substantial political base" (Mendelsohn & Vicziany 1998:206).

The organizational set up of the Congress Party which was dominated by the upper castes (Hasan 1998:133) could never accept Scheduled Castes as a social group with distinct agenda and aspiration for power. So, whosoever rose against the party leadership with an independent agenda was sidelined and it happened from local level leadership to national level. "One new recruit to politics...who served as a city councilman in Kanpur, learned that the local practice of excluding Scheduled Caste college students from common dormitories and mess hall was strictly illegal. When he persisted in complaining to local colleges and the city council and party officials, he also learned that he could be denied a Congress Party nomination for "breaking party discipline" (Joshi 1982:23). At the national level, this policy of exclusion of assertive Dalit leadership was quite evident. "There are persistent suggestions that Dalit politicians have not thrived within Congress, if they have too strenuously promoted the cause of their own people. This is an explanation sometimes offered in relation to Yogendra Makwana, a talented and energetic Minister of the early 1980s whose career did not prosper under either Indira or Rajiv Gandhi. Makwana can be contrasted with Buta Singh...who rose to the position of Home Minister under the same Prime Minister. Buta Singh...was known for his political savoir-faire and his loyalty to the Nehru family rather than for any particular zeal for the problems of scheduled castes" (Mendelsohn & Vicziany1998:207).

Thus, the reserved seats intended to uplift the Dalit masses through their own representatives have not brought the desired results. Many of our respondents have pleaded for reverting back to the demand of the system of the separate electorates for effective representation of the Dalits. But the Dalit leadership specially the BSP leadership has argued that there is no need for the same as the 'stooges' have now been exposed and only true representatives will be able to enter in Parliament and State Assembly in future. Kanshi Ram, the BSP supremo wrote a book 'Chamcha Age' (Era of Stooges) and criticized that the educated elite of the Dalit community have turned *Chamchas* (stooges) because of the Poona Pact. He advised them to reject this role and, instead; direct their services, loyalty and talent towards organization of the Dalit community. According to him, this would help in breaking the hegemony of upper castes and class which dominate in every institution of society (Kanshi Ram 1998:79-123).

Even a large majority of our respondents have remained critical to the Congress Party in which the upper castes play dominant role unlike the RPI and the BSP in which Dalits play a vanguard role and the relationship of subordination and super-ordination based on caste background of the leaders does not exist. As already stated in the previous chapter, Dalit leaders are free in their own parties to raise openly and effectively any issue concerning the Dalits. Not only that but they also occupy dominant and significant position in the party organization and also in the Cabinet whenever these parties come to power. In replying to a question whether they find the Dalit leadership optimistic with respect to breaking the upper castes, dominated Congress and other political parties manipulating the reserved seats, a sizeable number of our respondents have stated that, "with the emergence of the BSP, the number of stooges in other parties is declining. See for example, the Congress Party does not have any Dalit representative in Parliament since the last four elections".

Formulation and Implementation of the Dalit Ideology

Before examining the Dalit ideology, it is necessary to have a brief look at what ideology means. Ideology has been seen as a system of ideas underlining and informing social and political action. It has also been seen as a system of ideas that justifies or legitimates the subordination of one group by another (Collins Dictionary of Sociology 1995:306). According to Gore (1993:29-30), "Thus a broad definition of `ideology' as a system of ideas which gives legitimacy to an existing or proposed system of relationships, and correspondingly supports an action programme to sustain or subvert the prevailing system, may prove more useful." Taking a clue from Edward Shils (1968), he argues further, "An ideology is a relatively comprehensive and organized pattern of values, beliefs and cognitive perceptions. These perceptions seek to interpret and explain the nature of existing social relations in terms of certain values and goals, judge them for their efficacy in achieving the desired goal, and either help to defend the existing system or spell out the inadequacies or inequities of the existing order and the desired system of relationships. ...Ideology...serves not only as an explanation of life's phenomena but also as a goal-setter and an inspiration behind movements of social action...an ideology has to be a set of relatively integrated ideas, a system and not just a collection of disparate ideas" (ibid: 30).

Seen in the light of the above, the Dalit leadership since its inception had crisis of a concrete and crystallized ideology of its own. For the liberation of the Dalit masses, the Dalit leadership used two types of ideology in its formative years. First, it adopted what is known in Marxian terminology as, "Ideology of the ruling class". In this period, the Dalit leaders imitated the life-style and traits of people of the upper castes which M.N. Srinivas has termed sanskritisation. According to him, "Sanskritisation is the process by which a low Hindu caste or tribal or other group changes its customs, rituals, ideology and way of life in the direction of a high and frequently "twice-born" caste" (Srinivas 1995:6). But, contrary to this, Swami Achhutanand in Uttar Pradesh invented the `Adi' ideology for struggle of the Dalit in the 1920s as stated in the previous chapter. This ideology explains that Dalits are original inhabitants of the Indian society. It was also prevalent in south Indian in the form of the Adi-Dravida, Adi-Andhra, Adi-Karnataka, around which the Dalits had organized movements in these areas.

Second, with the emergence of Ambedkar a new ideology emerged which remained in an evolutionary state till the fag end of his life. After his demise, many sociologists have tried to put his 'ideology' in a proper paradigm. For instance, Gore (1993:30-70) defines that, "Ambedkar's ideology is primarily an ideology of protest against the existing unequal social order and of protest movement for radically altering it". He also tells, "This ideology is existentially related to the problems of inequality built into every system of social stratification, but specially it is related to the denial of human dignity and material opportunity to the untouchables in the traditional Hindu structure. The Ambedkar-ideology simultaneously straddles the areas of religious belief, social practice, economic, civic and political deprivation as an existential reality...it identifies specific demands, points out the kind of changes of attitude that would be necessary both among the oppressors and the oppressed, and spells out the means whereby the ends may be realized" (ibid: 223). Nandu Ram states that Gore's definition of Ambedkar's ideology is to be further substantiated to comprehend it in its totality. In his own words, "In fact, his (Ambedkar's) ideology with a 'universal and perennial function in society' needs to be substantiated by recognizing his almost equal importance given in his thoughts and actions to the nation-building and social-transformation, to his vision for forming a modern and democratic society in India, and to certain viable ways and means that he suggested for the purpose. His ideology is to be primarily looked in his understanding and pursuance of equality, liberty, fraternity and justice which he was looking for not only in the traditional and contemporary Indian society but even in society to emerge in future" (Ram 1995:35-36). Till Ambedkar was alive, the

Dalit movement was guided more or less by the aforesaid elements of his ideology. But after his demise, his ideology has been termed 'Ambedkarism' (Omvedt 1994:223-259) in the words of Ram (1995) though it has to be theoretically integrated.

The contemporary Dalit leadership, specially the BSP leadership claims to adhere to 'Ambedkarism' as its guiding principle. It was, to a certain extent, present during the time of the Republican Party of India (Rosenthal 1986:346). With the emergence of the Dalit Panther, movement in Maharashtra in the 1970s, "While the Panther's continued to draw inspiration from Ambedkar, an attempt was made in the manifesto to formulate an ideology-drawing inspiration from Marxism, to guide the movement with a broader orientation. It was even said that the manifesto was based on the Communist Manifesto of 1848 and that it drew inspiration from that of the Black Panthers" (Murugkar 1991:115). Further, the Dalit leadership represented by the Bahujan Samaj Party also draws its inspiration from "Ambedkarism" but it also proclaims that, "Economic emancipation and social transformation" as part of its ideology which we shall see in the following section.

The BSP leaders believe in the parliamentary democracy, so dear to Ambedkar, which can be proved by their slogans, *"Vote se lenge PM, CM; Arakshan se lenge SP, DM"* (From vote we will have Prime Minister and Chief Minister, and from reservation the Superintendents of Police and District Magistrates); *Vote hamara, raj tumhara! nahi chalega, nahi chalega* (Our votes and your rule, No more, No more). But it is difficult to assess that these leaders fully endorse 'Ambedkarism', especially in event of their neglect of 'Buddhism' as a religious revolution-a tool for mobility of the Dalits. The BSP appears to be too much engrossed with capturing political power. Hence, we find difference between the ideology of the Dalit Panthers and of the Bahujan Samaj Party. For instance, in its initial phase the Dalit Panthers did not believe at all in the parliamentary democracy and boycotted elections also. Later on, they had a mixture of Marxism and Ambedkarism as their ideology as stated above. But contrary to this, the BSP leadership has believed in the parliamentary democracy right from its inception. The problem of common ideology of the Dalit leadership across the party lines becomes more acute when we take the 'dependent' Dalit leadership into consideration. Though most of the Dalit leaders found in different political parties being a Dalit want to have 'Ambedkarism' or Ambedkar's ideology as their ideology but their respective 'party ideology' and so-called party-discipline do not permit them to profess and implement it for the liberation of Dalits.

It is, thus, evident that the Dalit leadership at the national level and in the state of Uttar Pradesh does not have any common ideology for amelioration of the Dalit masses. It is not much difficult to delineate the reasons for this even though the Dalits face, more or less, similar problems throughout the country. Few reasons cited by our respondents are, "There is different socio-political reality of every region and the Dalit leadership found in different political parties acts according to that only. The Dalit leaders are more concern with their immediate goals and demands. Moreover, Dalit leadership is lacking a broad vision unlike the one which Babasaheb had". Nandu Ram also explains the reason why the Dalit leadership throughout the length and breath of the country may not have accepted `Ambedkarism' in its totality. According to him, "The Dalits have accepted this (Ambedkar's ideology) and they seek guidance from it in their thoughts and actions. This is, however, not to suggest that all Dalits have fully understood and grasped his ideology...various Dalit movements have sought to address the local issues and use the local idioms but they definitely derive their strength and legitimacy from Ambedkar's ideology in whatsoever version it has reached to them" (Ram 1995). Therefore, only drawing legitimacy from "Ambedkarism" would not help the Dalit leadership in establishing a unified ideology acceptable to all the Dalit leaders across the party lines and even to the Dalit masses.

Yet, the Dalit leadership is well versed with the ideologies of the national leadership in general and that of its own in particular. A number of our respondents have informed that the Congress Party is based on the mixture of Gandhism, secularism, socialism, etc. The BJP is based on the 'Hindu nationalism', and the communist parties are based on communism or socialism. The leaders-respondents have also added that, "these ideologies are propagated only in theory but at the practical level, all these political parties are Manuvadis. They practise Brahminism and casteism, and are supporters of the *status quoism*. They want to maintain their dominance and, hence, want to capture power". In Uttar Pradesh, these parties have always maintained their dominance by capturing political power, which can easily be proved. For instance, at the time of the first general elections in 1952, around 28 per cent of the

Congress MLAs were from Brahmin and 13 per cent from the Thakur castes. In 1962, the figures had risen to 30 and 19 respectively. In fact in 1962, the strength of the representatives in the Legislative Assembly showed that of all the political parties the Congress Party was having the least number of representatives from the Other Backward Castes or Classes (OBCs). Similarly in 1971, of the 70 Congress Presidents functioning at the various levels, 42 were either Brahmins or Thakurs. "The six U.P. cabinets formed between 1952 and 1974 were similarly dominated by Brahmins, Thakurs and Vaishyas. In the Sampurnanand, C.B.Gupta and Sucheta Kripalani ministries, nearly half the ministers belonged to upper castes...In Kamlapati Tripathi's government, 50 per cent of ministers were Brahmins. Brahmin dominance was maintained during the chief ministership of Bahuguna, Sripat Misra and N.D. Tiwari in the 1970s and 1980s"(Hasan 1998:133-134). As far as communists are concerned, their rule in West Bengal had similar dominance of the upper castes. "In the case of Government led by the Communist Party of India (Marxist) between 1977 and 1982, there were even more Brahmins than in the Congress Government. In West Bengal between 1952-1962, the number of Brahmins (over 35 per cent), Kayasthas (31 per cent) and Vaishyas (23 per cent) was almost the same as in the Congress Government, while Scheduled Castes, representation was marginally lower at 1.5 per cent. These figures must be read in the context of a state which has the highest concentration of Scheduled Caste people in the country-now almost 24 per cent" (Mendelsohn & Vicziany1998:209). To prove further the upper caste bias and dominance, we can easily show that most of the political parties in the country have their President and General Secretary from the upper castes. In few cases, they do nominate some Dalits as Vice-President or some insignificant posts. It is, thus, clear that the ideology of the general leadership in the country propagated through the manifestoes of different political parties is just an eye wash. At the implementation level, these parties dominated by the upper castes and classes have always been furthering the interests of their respective castes and classes.

As stated earlier, ideology of the Dalit leadership is based on "Ambedkarism" which argues for the establishment of a social order based on equality, liberty and fraternity. But some of our respondents have said that "Ambedkar's name has been used to gain legitimacy and nothing substantive has been done for the Dalit masses". Ambedkar's name is a means to achieve their ends (Parvathamma 1973:22-34). Our respondents have further stated that, "the Dalit leaders from the different political parties in Uttar Pradesh are generally guided by the ideology of their own respective party. But only the Bahujan Samaj Party which represents another brand of Dalit leadership has its own ideology".

Yet, all this has not been a smooth sailing specially for the BSP leadership since its inception. It has faced many problems in the past and still continues to face many newer problems. Some of the major problems of the Dalit leadership as such have remained perennial for them though some have already been solved. The unresolved problems, as stated earlier, are formulation of a unified ideology, formation, implementation and propagation of a common political agenda, forging of a common identity for all Dalits in the country, identification of permanent allies, the various types of crisis in Dalit leadership, etc. Since we have discussed about the problems of forming a unified ideology and various types of crisis in the Dalit leadership, we shall examine briefly here adoption of a common political agenda, the forging of a common identity and the permanent or otherwise allies of the Dalit leadership in the state of Uttar Pradesh.

Adoption of a Common Political Agenda

We have already mentioned that adopting and pursuing of a common political agenda by the Dalit leadership across the party lines either at the national or state level is a difficult proposition. We have also stated about both general and specific reasons for that. It is worth to bring back one or two important reasons here. One such reason is that the Dalit leaders found in other political parties do not have their own manifest agenda; instead, they are bound to pursue the agenda set by their respective political parties, though they may have their unpursued latent agenda for amelioration of the Dalits. Secondly, even if they wish to pursue their own agenda, they are often controlled by their party bosses. It is only the RPI and the BSP who formulated their own socio-political agenda for amelioration of the Dalits but the former could not take it to the logical end due to the reasons stated earlier. But the BSP has formulated and pursued, to some extent its own socio-political agenda particularly in U.P. Such pursuit of the BSP has manifested throughout these years, though unlike other political parties, it does not come out with a printed manifesto of its own. Yet, its pursuit has well taken note of by the people at large in the state and in neighbouring states, and the social scientists as well both in the country and abroad.

Kanshi Ram, the BSP supremo also wrote, "I made it clear that BSP has its agenda of "social transformation' and economic emancipation" (Akhtar 1999). To achieve this agenda, the BSP leadership has formulated a five-fold strategy of struggle for social transformation and the five-fold programme for economic emancipation of the Dalits. These are struggle against, (i) Untouchability, (ii) Inhumanity, (iii) Injustice, (iv) Insecurity, and (v) Inequality for social transformation. Similarly, the five-fold programme for economic emancipation of the Dalits are, i) Bhartiya Kisan Mazdoor Andolan (Peasant Movement), ii) Bhartiya Safi Mazdoor Andolan (Cleaner's Movement), iii) Bhartiya Dastakar Andolan (Artisan Movement), iv) Bhartiya Sharanarthi Andolan (Refugees of slums), and v) Bhartiya Bhagedari Andolan (Sharing Movement) (Atey 1997:158:60).

One important aspect of the socio-political agenda of the Dalit leadership is to forge a common identity of the Dalits in the country. The Identity or social identity points to an individual's link with the unique values fastened by a unique history of his/her people. Besides expressing a mutual relation, it also connotes both a persistent sameness within one-self (self sameness) and a persistent sharing of the same kind of essential characters with others (Erikson 1960:68). According to this definition, one can easily make out that Dalits through out the country though share the same values of stigma and deprivation of rights and privileges as fostered by a unique history of the Hindu social order, yet they are identified with different nomenclatures in different parts of the country. The identity of the Dalits who now number a little over 150 millions has a chequered history. The Dalits have acquired by now a peculiar combination of their social, political and constitutional identities besides their localized primordial or caste identities that emerged at different points of time. Their well-known primordial or caste identities, as recorded in the history, are of *Chandalas, Avarnas, Achhuts, Antyajas, Nishads, Namshudra, Pariahs*, etc. These identities were formalised and legitimised by the theory of Karma and rebirth with the help of the religious scriptures (Oommen1994).

We have already mentioned in chapters 1 and 2 that in the 1920s, the identities like Adi-Hindu, Adi-Dravida, Adi-Andhra, Adi-Kannada and Ad-Dharmi emerged for the Dalits claiming their original inhabitants' status in the Indian society. But a unique thing about these identities was that these were coined and adopted by the Dalits themselves as a mark of their assertion against the oppressive Hindu social order. During the same period, other terms used by the officials and the social reformers for the Dalits were Depressed Classes, Suppressed Classes, Oppressed Hindus, Exterior Castes and Untouchables. These identities of the Dalits in the official records did not last long. Babasaheb Ambedkar and Rao Bahadur R. Srinivasn in their supplementary Memorandum to the Round Table Conference (R.T.C.) wrote, "we would like to point out that the existing nomenclature of Depressed Classes is objected to by members of the Depressed Classes who have given thought to it and also by outsiders who take the interest in them. It is degrading and contemptuous and advantage may be of this occasion for drafting the new constitution to alter for official purposes the existing nomenclature. We think that they should be called Non-Caste Hindus," "Protestant Hindus," or "Non-Conformist Hindus," or some such designation, instead of "Depressed Classes" (Ambedkar 1991:306). However, Ambedkar himself used in all his writings and speeches the Depressed Classes, Untouchables and later the Scheduled Castes as the nomenclature for Dalits.

Again, the nomenclature 'Harijan' originally coined by Narsinha Mehta - a Gujarati saint-poet was popularised in the 1930s by Gandhi for the Dalits. The members of the Dalit community specially educated ones hated and rejected it. Lynch gives the specific reasons for this reaction that also speak the minds of millions of the Dalits. According to him, "Literally the word means 'Child of God' but figuratively its connotations are quite different. My Jatav informants showed dislike-at times (when the term was popularised by Gandhi) and intense dislike for the word. They felt, it connoted the idea of being bastard and also brought to mind patronizing and upper caste benevolence" (Lynch 1974:128). Under the Gov. of India Act.1935, Government gave a new identity to the Dalits as of the 'Scheduled Castes' for providing constitutional safeguards to them. Though the same term has been adopted as a legal nomenclature in the Indian Constitution, it does not contain any operational definition. In fact, it remains only the legal or constitutional identity for the Dalits for providing them benefits for their welfare, protection and development.

However, at the level of their religious identity other than their traditionally being considered Hindus, they came with a new identity of Buddhist along with the Babasaheb Ambedkar's conversion and the conversion movement to Buddhism in October 1956. According to Gokhale (1993:156), "With the conversion of Mahars to Buddhism, the Mahar movement under Ambedkar took the ultimate step in establishing its new and separate identity apart from Hindu society and its ideology. By becoming Buddhist, the Untouchables demonstrated that they had progressed beyond Hindu scriptures; they would no longer see themselves, through Hindu eyes, as Untouchables, nor would they perform those menial and polluting tasks which has been assigned to them". It is true that at that time it was confined to nearly a million Dalits mostly Mahars in Maharashtra, besides hundreds of Dalits who had embraced Buddhism in South India much earlier to the 1956 conversion. It provided opportunity to the Dalits in north India particularly in Uttar Pradesh to adopt their identity of being Buddhist. Thus, the Buddhist identity of the Dalits though originated in Maharashtra has travelled throughout the country. More and more Dalits have converted to Buddhism with the passage of time and the process is becoming rampant in the contemporary Indian society.

In the 1970s, a new identity of being Dalit was popularised by the Dalit Panthers' Movement in Maharashtra as stated earlier, though the word Dalit was in vogue since long. According to the Dalit leadership, "this identity provides a sense of pride and self-assertion". To be a Dalit, it feels, is no more a shameful thing. 'Dalitness' is a source of confrontation and is a matter of appreciating the probability of one's total being (Murugkar 1991:54). In the contemporary Indian society, this identity is gaining ground in every part of the country including Uttar Pradesh-locale of the present study. Majority of our respondents have stated, "we like this identity more than any other identity because Dalits themselves have coined it". We have already stated that the Dalit Panthers in Maharashtra gave a very broad definition to it by including "Members of Scheduled Castes and Tribes, Neo-Buddhists, the working people, the landless and poor peasants, women and all those who are being exploited politically, economically and in the name of religion" (ibid: 237). But according to Ram (1995:18), "contrary to a heuristic understanding, the term Dalit is currently used only for and by untouchable castes all over the country. Even social scientists have started referring to the Dalits and untouchables or the scheduled castes inter-changeably".

Against this socio-political background, a major section of the Dalit leadership led by the Bahujan Samaj Party has propounded a new identity for the Dalits and that is the Bahujan which of course is inclusive of the lower echelons of the OBCs, and the Muslim, which no doubt are poor and toiling masses. This means, the leadership of the Bahujan Samaj Party as a political movement has tried to include almost the same social categories in their definition of the term Bahujans as were done by the Dalit Panthers during the early 1970s, as mentioned above. But it is a fact that Dalits were the first, and so is the even today, to accept it as their new identity. The movement has tried to spread this identity at the pan-India level, but it is still restricted to the northern and the western regions of the country as the case of the movement of the Bahujan Samaj Party for the purpose specially in Uttar Pradesh.

Thus, the Dalits in the country and even in the state of the U.P. have had eight types of identities since the earlier period. These are Chandalas, the regional identities with the Adi-prefix, Depressed-Classes, 'Harijans', Scheduled Castes, Buddhists, Dalits and now Bahujans, and nobody knows how many more identities will they forge in future. Because of these different types of identities of the Dalits all through the phases as mentioned in the previous chapter, the strength of Dalit movements has also got fragmented. Therefore, for Dalits, a unified identity is must. In this regard, Gore (1993:53) explains the impact of a unified identity by stating that, "The problem of defining the identity of the group on whose behalf one is playing the leadership and advocacy role is thus a complex one. In Indian Pre-independence politics, Jinnah claimed to speak on behalf of all Muslims and Gandhi, as a leader of the Indian National Congress, claimed to speak on behalf of all Indians. Their claims came to be tested in different ways-sometimes borne out, sometimes disproved. Mass mobilization, mass movements, street riots on command, limited *satyagrahas* were different ways of assessing and demonstrating the strength of one's following as well as widening the circle of one's followers." Further, he says that Ambedkar was knowing the problems involved in propounding a common identity for the Dalits. "He was aware that bringing on to a common platform all the various sub-castes among the untouchables within Maharashtra and then all the untouchables distributed throughout India who differed in language, cultural context and sometimes in economic standing, was in itself an immense task. It needed the creation of a sense of common identity among relatively distinct groups who, though they suffered from the stigma of untouchability and from the same social and economic privation vis-à-vis caste Hindus, yet prided themselves on their distinct community identities and on their own status in the internal hierarchy which was sub-caste" (ibid: 52-53). Therefore, at this point of time when the divisions among Dalits have grown, is it possible to have a common identity? Whether the modern political system would permit to do so? These are moot questions to be pursued by the Dalit leadership in the country as well as in the state of Uttar Pradesh. But as of now, it has retarded the progress of the Dalit movements by not allowing the Dalit masses to come under the rubric of one identity.

Another important issue to be addressed here is the political and social allies of the Dalit leadership in the state as well as in the country. No doubt, the Dalit leadership has faced an acute crisis in the past of finding its permanent or even temporary allies. However, such allies can broadly be classified into two categories: one, in the form of political party or parties in the realm of political power and, two, in the form of social groups in the social realm. In the political realm, the Dalit leadership had never have experience of having an alliance at the national level. It might be so as no political party led by Dalits had reached to the level of becoming a national party. Yet, the Bahujan Samaj Party is the first political party, organized by the Dalits themselves, to achieve since the recent times the status of being a national party. Before that, all political parties like the Independent Labour Party and the Scheduled Castes Federation both formed by Ambedkar as stated earlier, and the Republican Party of India conceived of by him but formed after his demise and the Dalit Panthers had some regional following but never proved their significant political existence at the national level. The case of the RPI is slightly different which for a brief period during the 1960s had its following in the states of Maharashtra and Uttar Pradesh.

Nevertheless, these political parties had some regional political forces as their alliance partners. According to Gokhale (1993:133), "During the 1930s, the class model seems to have dominated the Mahar Movement. The ILP (Independent Labour Party) sought to establish itself as a spokesman for the working classes and peasants, championing issues that had immediate relevance to these elements. There was also brief rapprochement with the left parties and the ILP seemed to be constructing a political front without any regard to caste or creed". Further, Ambedkar in particular emerged as a vigorous defender of the rights of the working class in the Assembly during the debate on the Industrial Disputes Bill of 1938 which curtailed the right of workers to strike. Similarly, he also participated in the peasant demonstration in Bombay in the same year (ibid:137-8). But soon this class dimension of the ILP broke when Ambedkar realised that the interests of the Dalits and other touchable caste workers were qualitatively different. Before that, the Hindu Mahasabha leader Veer Sarvakar and Dr. Munje had attempted unsuccessfully to persuade the upper castes to open the temples for the Dalits. But such attempt(s) to aid the Dalits was not for having a genuine alliance with them or their political empowerment, though it might have been guided by its political competition with the Congress (ibid: 104-5).

As stated earlier there was no independent Dalit leadership of political nature during the pre-independence period in Uttar Pradesh. Hence, there was no alliance of Dalits with any political force or party. Instead, they were taken for granted by every political parties operating in the state. The formation of the All India Scheduled Castes Federation in the early 1940s in Maharashtra and during 1944-45 in Agra, Uttar Pradesh kept itself away from forging any alliance. "This strategy was based on the premise that untouchables could not rely on non-untouchables for support and solidarity in their political movement, but had to develop an independent organization which would be concerned almost exclusively with issues peculiar to them. The assumption was that the interests of the untouchable communities were unique and distinct from those of the caste-Hindus, and that the untouchables all over India shared a set of common interests despite the particularities of region and language" (ibid: 142). But later on specially after the demise of Ambedkar and with the formation of the Republican Party of India (RPI) in the year 1957 in Maharshtra and the Republican Party of India, Agra branch in 1958, the alliance partners came into existence. Before his death, Ambedkar had envisaged the alliance with socialists as stated earlier. According to Kshirsagar (1979:36), Ambedkar's particular concern was the potential appeal of the Communist Party to the Dalits. He feared that in the absence of an organizational alternative, the political loyalties of the Dalits might easily be captured by Communists. Thus before his death, he had talked to various socialist leaders such as Ram Mahahar Lohia, P.K. Atre and S.M. Joshi regarding his plans for a new political party and had expressed the hope that these leaders could join him in this endeavour. Although the RPI had a class approach with a caste-neutral name as stated earlier, but even then it was stigmatised as casteist political party as it had maximum following among the Dalits. By 1966, the Dalit leadership saw split after split and ultimately one of the splinter group joined the Congress on the plea that, "They (Dalits) had to operate within the limits set by Congress and, hence, had to rely on it for whatever concessions that they could wrest from it. Therefore, the wisest political course for the Dalits...was to act as a pressure group within the Congress and try to influence its policies as members of the Congress" (Gokhle 1993:230-31). Hence, the Dalit leadership in Maharashtra had alligned with Congress in the 1960s.

Contrary to that, the Dalit leadership in Agra, Uttar Pradesh had an alliance with the Muslims in 1962. In fact, A Muslim was nominated for the Parliament seat and three Republicans including a doctor of the Vaisya caste ran for the state legislature (Lynch 1974:120). Not only that but it also was propagated that the Republicans had popularised a communal slogan symbolising their alliance with the Muslims: "Jatav Muslim Bhai-Bhai Hindu Kaum Kahan Se Aye" (Jatavs and Muslims were brothers, but where from the Hindus had come) (ibid: 102). It is interesting to note here that, on the one hand, Dalits were having alliance with the Muslims at the community level and, on the other; they were also having political alliance with the Jan Sangh. The Jan Sangh was the political wing of the Rashtriya Swayamsevak Sangh (RSS) at that time and the predecessor of the Bhartiya Janata Party of now. This all was done to keep the Dalits away from the Indian National Congress (ibid: 115-117). Yet, this alliance of the Republican Party of India with the Jan Sangh was criticized vehemently by the then the Dalit leadership of the Dalit Varg Sangh in the state on the ground that, "...the scheduled castes who are in position of power...want to sell their Jatav brothers...It is because of this that they have entered into a contract with the Jan Sangh, those communal, narrow-minded and primitive sloganeers of the Brahmanical Hindu State. These leaders have not even consulted the voters, their Jatav brothers. We cannot understand how there can be a union of straw with fire. These devotees of Brahminism, these priests, these primitive Jan Sanghis and their kind have continually been inflicting all sorts of tyranny, injustice, insults and disrespect upon us, according to the laws of Manu Smriti". The lust for power slowly led the Jatavs to another ally, i.e. Congress in Uttar Pradesh in due course of time specially after 1970 (Mendelsohn & Vicziany 1998:213).

In recent years, with the Bahujan Samaj Party (BSP), the phenomenon of searching of permanent allies in the political realm has again gained prominence. The BSP had entered in the electoral alliance with the Samajwadi Party (SP) in U.P. and with the Congress both in U.P. and Madhya Pradesh and with the Akali Dal in Punjab for a brief period in 16 years of its history. It has also allied with the Rashtriya Janata Dal in the recent Assembly elections in Bihar. Also, it has formed 3 governments in U.P. one in coalition with the S.P. and two with the BJP as stated in the previous chapter. All these alliances and coalitions have been unstable with the ideological differences. On the practical side, our respondents from the BSP leadership have opined, "the coalition politics has not benefited the party because there is no mutual transference of votes. Our votes get transferred to the other party candidates but their votes are not transferred in favour of our candidates". Secondly, in their opinion "in the formation of a coalition government after the elections, the BSP has a greater bargaining power. On its strength, it can dictate its terms which it has done till now". In the social realm also, the BSP leadership has preferred alliance with a few castes and communities like Muslim and the Most Backward Castes or Classes. In the words of our respondents from the BSP, "We are now going for direct alliance with communities, and we have chosen the most backward castes for this. Their socio-political condition is very similar to that of the Dalits and as of now they have not got any political space for assertion also." It is difficult to predict at this stage the result of such alliance of the BSP in future. But as of now, has reaped the rich dividends from such alliance.

The causes of failure of the alliance of Dalit leadership with other social groups located in the Hindu social organization were critically viewed long back by Ambedkar. He had opined that the Shudras and the Criminal and Primitive Tribes would have been natural allies of the Untouchables or Dalits. There is every ground for them to combine, but they have not (Ambedkar 1989:115). Further, pointing out the exact antecedent of this lack of alliance between the OBCs, Tribes and Dalits, he had argued that, "The reasons for this want of solidarity is not far to seek. It is to be found in the system of graded-inequality whereby the Brahmin is above everybody; the Shudra is below the Brahmin and above the Untouchables. If the Hindu Social Order was based on inequality, it would have been over-thrown long ago. But it is based on graded-inequality so that the Shudra, while he is anxious to pull down the Brahmin, is not prepared to see the Untouchables raised to his level. He prefers to suffer the indignities heaped upon him by the Brahmins to join the Untouchables for a general levelling down of the social order. The result is that there is nobody to join the Untouchable in his struggle. He is completely isolated. Not only is he isolated, he is opposed by the very classes who ought to be his natural allies" (ibid: 116). The causes of failures of having a genuine alliance of the Dalit leadership with other social groups has also been narrated by Dushkin (1998:201) on the basis of her data on the RPI. According to her, "Normally, they (Dalits) must win caste Hindu support as well as mobilizing their own members. The risk they run is that the very activities must engage into mobilize their own supporters that alienate the caste Hindu voters, as the Republicans did in earlier elections. Second, opposition alliances run the risk that, if successful in one election, the Congress will accommodate them, so the issue that made them possible will disappear by next election...Third, more stable inter-caste alliances based on common class interests are extremely difficult to effect under untouchable leadership... Non-untouchable labourers are unlikely to follow untouchable leadership."

Thus, we find that a genuine alliance of the Dalit leadership either in political or social realm with other political and social forces is a difficult proposition. This is so as its both social and political interests are qualitatively and quantitatively different from other social and political forces, groups or parties. The Dalit leadership particularly of the BSP in U.P. intends to use the political power for ameliorating socio-economic conditions of the Dalits and bringing social transformation in general. It is in this respect, the BSP leadership is qualitatively different from its few allies.

Functioning of the Dalit Leadership in Uttar Pradesh

Another aspect of analysing the dynamics of the Dalit leadership is to examine how it has been functioning in the state since the early times. From the sociological perspective, leadership is the exercise of power or influence over a collectivity such as a group, organization or a nation. This power may be addressed to any or all the three and even related functions of establishing the goals, purposes or objectives of the collectivity, creating the structures through which the purposes of the collectivity are fulfilled and maintaining or enhancing these structures (Akinchan 1995:295). Seen in this light, the Dalit leadership of pre and post independence periods seems to be similar in its fundamental function of mobilizing people around certain goals to be achieved, and to evolve and maintain certain type of socio-political structure. But during all these years, it has undergone changes in its other functions. It has given up some traditional functions and added some new ones. We shall analyse here these functions in detail.

In the pre independence period, recruitment of the Dalit leadership used to be more on particularistic traits as hereditary panchayats were order of the day. Every caste used to have its own panchayat with a *Chaudhry* at the helm of affairs. These *Chaudhries* with their hereditary rights guided the castes both on their internal and external matters. They also used to be the senior or more able members of the lineage which traditionally supplied the jati or caste leadership (Rudolph & Rudolph 1987 : 34). It is interesting to mention here that the caste panchayats used to be a localized phenomenon and were more effective in the caste affairs. The caste *Chaudheries* at the most interacted with their upper caste landlords for certain rights. These rights were asked through prayers and their grant depended on the benevolence of the latter. This leadership never questioned the oppression in an overt manner and was mostly dependent on the dominant socio-political force of the day.

Things changed a little bit during the 1920s when a number

of sanskritization movements emerged, as discussed in chapter 4 and earlier in this chapter. "One result of the Jatav- as Kshatriyas movement (in Agra in Uttar Pradesh) was the rise of new leaders parallel to the old hereditary caste leaders (*Chaudhries*). These "Big Men" were better equipped to handle the problems which sanskitisation had brought to the Jatavs. Many of them were literate, although not necessarily educated and many, too, were possessed of a worldly confidence developed in business; such confidence the older leaders lacked" (Lynch 1974:77). In this era, the Dalit leadership came out of their exclusive traditional functions. Lynch further argues, "The "big men" (leaders) used their influence both within the caste and without it, with other castes and the local administration" (ibid: 77).

According to Lynch, these leaders used to perform three functions of 1. Translators, 2. Problem solvers, and 3. Political entrepreneurs. As translators, they tried to influence the values, rituals and behaviour patterns of the caste brethren, which they had acquired from the orthogenetic and heterogenetic sources. They were, in a sense, pivots between the inner world of the caste and the outer world of the society. As problem solvers, they interacted with persons of other castes, representatives of the courts and administration. Finally, as political entrepreneurs, they performed duties of coercion, manipulation and advice (ibid:77-78). This shows that the Dalit leadership in the 1920s was multifaceted and had taken up the new functions or roles to ameliorate the Dalit masses. The independent organizing had taken birth but it did not wish to come out of the existing social order. The leaders wanted social mobility within the Hindu social order. Hence, their functions or roles remained, more or less, of social reformers though these had spread to a wider territory.

With the advent of Ambedkar, the Dalit leadership in Uttar Pradesh accepted him as its leader, which in turn, increased its scope and placed it in the national perspective (Lynch 1974). Its function also became more political. As already stated, it had testified before many British Commissions committees and thereafter started contesting elections. By now, a significant segment of Dalit leadership in the sate shelved its dependence on the dominant socio-political forces and started organizing independently. A new era of independent political functioning started with the formation of the Scheduled Castes Federation in

1944-45. Such segment of the Dalit leadership both in the country and in the state changed the course of its action and also aspired, through the 'political participation, for upward social mobility out side the Hindu social order. But as a fall out of the modern day polity, such Dalit leadership with its independent organizing was also subsumed by the dominant political forces like the Congress Party and could not pursue its agenda of amelioration of the Dalit masses to the logical end.

Then, with political independence of the country, the new socio-political reality also emerged. The adoption of the democratic polity and the constitutional safeguards guaranteed to the Dalits changed the function or role of the Dalit leadership. Now, most of the Dalit leaders had to confront directly with the state for the speedy implementation of the constitutional safeguards granted to the Dalits. More and more Dalits took politics as vocation. It was because, "the new political system has thrown open many possibilities of advancement to people from Scheduled Tribes, the Scheduled Castes and the Other Backward Classes...The adoption of a democratic political order in a highly particularistic society ensures that people from every major section of it can aspire position of power and authority" (Beteille 1997:179-180). The Dalit leadership, therefore, became synonymous to the politicians as these politicians occupied elected offices in the government and wielded power. "It is these elected men who form today the *de facto* Jatav elite...As members of these assemblies, they serve on various committees and are thereby in positions of structural observability" (Lynch 1974: 114-115). Even today, this is true and the Dalit leadership which actually organizes people at the grassroots becomes secondary or unimportant. The social activists and reformers are nowhere seen and not even considered for any purpose either by government or by the people themselves. They usually remain at the grassroots level and do their work of awakening the masses. They act as appendage to the state and national level leadership.

The activities of the 'politicians' clubbed by Lynch can throw further light on the role of the Dalit leadership after independence. He has categorised these activities into three types: goal achievement, interest articulation and better organization. By goal achievement, it is meant that the 'politicians' have made substantial gain for their party through the political participation and representation of their caste people. The interest articulation involves making the party's demands and views known in the local, state and national legislatures as well as in the government administration. It also includes the airing of the complaints, desires and wants of the Dalit communities at the public meetings from the party platforms. In certain cases, this can also be done through the party newspapers, pamphlets, booklets, etc. Finally, better organization consists of bringing together both party and caste people when specific political actions require it. Thus, the various acts of Dharnas (sit ups), Pradarshans (protests), rallies, meetings, etc. throughout the year depend upon the decisions and organizational skills of the politicians for their success (ibid: 118-121). Though Lynch has articulated his views on such functions in the case of a smaller party like the RPI and that too in a particular context, these functions of leadership can also be applied to the contemporary Dalit leadership. But the only difference is that today the Dalit leadership especially of the BSP has expanded its boundaries and covers most of the Uttar Pradesh. It also includes many castes other than Jatavs and or Chamars and communities like Muslims, Sikhs, etc.

Besides this, many of our informants have argued that the major difference between the functions of the Dalit leadership of the pre and post-independence periods is that, "the former was more for social reform and social rights and the latter is committed more for political power" along with social rights". Such leaders-respondents want to have share in every aspect of social and political life and that too on equal basis. The respondents have also opined that, " the upper castes have no right to give us; we are not begging from them. We will take it through struggle and political power". Further, the post independent Dalit leadership particularly of the BSP acts more as protector of the Dalit community because it has become strong enough to defend its cadres and file. A simple case of atrocity in any place can create law and order problem for the state machinery.

Globalisation, Dalit Leadership and the Constitutional Safeguards for the Dalits

The constitutional safeguards better known as provision of reservation has been provided for the Dalits systematically, since independence, in the three areas: political reservation of seats in the Parliament (Lok Sabha) and the State Assemblies (State Legislatures), reservation in public jobs, and reservation of seats in admission and related facilities in educational institutions. It may be mentioned here that it has produced by now the significant results, though the evaluation of its precise impact on the Dalits in the country and in the state of Uttar Pradesh is an overdue. In between, with the onslaught of the processes like globalisation and economic liberalization, privatisation of jobs and the information revolution, the Dalit leadership has a lurching fear that apart from the political reservation the other two types of reservation, i.e. reservation in jobs and in educational institutions would be adversely affected. A simple explanation given by the most of our respondents was that the new outcome of these processes would curtail the government's roles in different realms of the people's life specially the Dalits in the country. The government is 'rolling back' and would confine itself a very limited sphere of life of the people as it intends to play the role only of facilitator. This means, the job opportunities in the public sector would go on shrinking heavily and in the same proportion, the number of reserved seats heavily be cut down. This would virtually finish the reservation for the Dalits under Article 335 or make it insignificant. Even though there may be more jobs in private sector, the Dalits would not be able to take any advantage of that because of their inability to meet the highly competitive and specialized technical and professional qualifications for such jobs.

More precisely, the greater number of technocrats with specialized knowledge of management, and computers and electronic engineers would be required to cater to the needs of the upcoming Multi National Corporations (MNCs) and big business houses. As these business houses are profit- oriented, they would prefer a 'meritocratic' regime without caring for any reservation for the Dalits and other weaker sections in the Indian society. The situation might aggravate further in view of the fact that as of now the educational level of Dalits is very low. The literacy among them in the country is 37.41 per cent and in U.P it is 26.85 per cent only. The Dalit students are enrolled for their higher education mostly in the conventional subjects like History, Sociology, Political Science, Hindi, Geography and so on. These subjects are loosing rapidly their saleability in the job-market. Today, even if a Dalit student wishes to acquire technical and professional expertise, he/

she does not have purchasing power. Hence, he/she is left with no option other than going for conventional degrees like Bachelor of Arts (B.A.) Master of Arts (M.A.) and utmost Bachelor or Master of Law (L.L.B. or L.L.M). These degrees remain now ornamental pieces only.

Under these hard pressing circumstances, the Dalit leadership is forced to demand reservation in the private sector also. Though in Uttar Pradesh there is a very faint voice for this demand and only a few Dalit leaders of the national stature are able to comprehend the impact of the earlier stated processes, the voices for reservation of jobs in private sector are becoming louder. The Dalit leadership in Maharashtra has again shown the way. For instance, the Dalit leader Ramdas Athavale of the RPI recently organised a rally and demanded reservation in jobs in the private sector. Gail Omvedt argues that, "while some believe that reservation in the private sector is impossible, this is simply wrong. Most of the affirmative action programmes in the U.S. in fact work in the private sector. One basic reason is that there is no simplified division between public and private sectors. Any sector that is regulated and/or funded by the Government is open to Government directives. In the U.S., to take a specific example, colleges and universities are all by Indian standards "private" since they are not directly controlled by the Government; they raise their own budgets, charge students fees, make their own decisions, appoint their own teachers, and so on. Yet, because they get some Government aid and are subject to Government regulation, "affirmative action" programmes can operate; if they do not fulfil the criteria, the Government aid will be withdrawn..."affirmative action" means that a certain proportion of black (or other minority) people are supposed to be there" (Omvedt, *The Hindu* Jan., 2000). Then, with the Government action, the Dalit leadership has to put extra social and political pressures in the country as well as in the state of U.P. and not just a political rhetoric. The Dalit leaders can easily quote the American example and ask for reservation in jobs in the private sector.

Atrocities on Dalits and Human Rights

Yet another important role of the Dalit leadership has been analysed here in regard to the numerous forms of atrocities inflicted on Dalits in Uttar Pradesh, which stands one of a few top states where the number of cases of atrocities committed on the Dalits are maximum. According to almost all of our respondents, the number of cases of atrocities on Dalits are increasing not only in the state but all over the country. Dalits suffer violence of caste Hindus because of their changed socio-political consciousness (in the present time) (Beleille 1997:183, Ram1995:219-347, Mendelsohn & Vicziany1998:44-76). Ram (1995:346) argues that, "Atrocities are committed more on those Scheduled Castes or some sections, or particular Scheduled Castes which are socially and economically more developed or at least have more urge to develop than others". The worst part is that, "...in event of their (Dalits') conflict or confrontation with caste Hindus and others the Scheduled Castes and other weaker sections are isolated and made target of atrocities by the latter. Even the police and the civil administration become partisan against them depending upon the issues and situations involved in the cases" (ibid:263). This has been a general trend in the country against which the Dalit leaders had raised many movements in the past but till date they have not been successful in curbing its intensity.

The majority of our respondents drawn from all the three regions-eastern, central and western in Uttar Pradesh were in general ignorant about the fact that the atrocities committed on Dalits should be brought under the Human Rights violation. Only a few respondents, both sitting and former member of Parliament and former ministers, had answered favourably. They had stated that, "It should be done more than merely putting the cases of atrocities on Dalits under their human rights violation simply so because the state plays a very partisan role and sides with the dominant castes." But the Dalit leaders have failed so far to raise effectively this issue at any international platform. A sizeable number of our respondents explained the failure of the Dalit leadership for not succeeding in doing so because of lack of an effective international forum for the Dalits. When probed further, they told that, "We have to have a strong centralised leadership and acquire a lot of resources. We have also to capture power at the centre and in the state so that we can go and plead our case in the United Nations".

However, the National Campaign on the Dalits' Human Rights a group of voluntary organizations and persons with its headquarters at Secunderbad in Andhra Pradesh, has taken an initiative in this direction. Running a national campaign on the Dalits' human rights from December 10, 1998 to 15 August, 1999 through their manifesto, they appealed to the United Nations by stating, "We therefore, demand that in the 50th year of the Declaration of the Universal Declarations of Human Rights all the international human rights organizations give an assurance to all the Dalits of Asia that the violations of their rights will be considered as violations of Human Rights and that the UN in particular will respond seriously to such violations through the appointment of a special Rapporteur or Working Group on the practice of untouchability in Asia and include caste discrimination in Article 1 of the "Convention on the Elimination of Racial Discrimination" (National Champaign Manifesto:34). A sizeable number of our respondents have also shown their will to endorse this demand. They have questioned, "When atrocities against Muslims in Kashmir and Sikhs in Punjab committed by the police can be included in the purview of the human rights then why not atrocities committed on the Dalits have been included in it ? If we compare these two sections of minorities with the Dalits, the number of the former is far less." To a question which countries can help Dalits in their struggle for liberation, they were unanimous in their reply and said that, "all the Buddhist countries or where Buddhism as a religion survives can help the Dalits in their cause. Moreover, South Africa can also help us because people there themselves have suffered racism".

In sum, the contemporary Dalit leadership specially of the BSP in U.P. is quite dynamic and is well informed about the empirical reality pertaining to the Dalits both in rural and urban areas. The Dalit leaders drawn mostly from the rural areas are now quite vocal unlike in the past, and articulate the Dalit interests in a relatively more systematic and comprehensive manner. They largely derive inspiration from the life and mission of Dr. Ambedkar, and try to analyse and resolve the problems of the Dalits in the state within the broad framework of Ambedkar's mission. It is also worth mentioning here that they are aware of the negative consequences of the more recent processes of globalisation, liberalization, etc, as stated above, which appear to be in high currency now in the Indian society. Contesting the trickle down effects or benefits of these processes to the toiling masses specially the Dalits, they insist though not in well-organized manner for reservation to be given to the Dalits in jobs in the private sector including the multinational corporations. As stated above, on the issue of perennial cases of atrocities committed on Dalits specially in the rural areas in the state, they wish to mobilize the international public opinion but they do not find at the moment any organized effort(s) made for the purpose.

References

Akinchan, S., 1995, *Caste, Class and Politics : Emerging Horizons of Political Sociology*, Gyan Publishing House, New Delhi.

Ambedkar, B.R., 1976, Caste In India, Annihilition of Caste, in Dr. Babasaheb Ambedkar: *Writings and Speeches, Vol.1*, Education Department, Govt. of Maharashtra, Bombay.

________, 1989, Untouchables or the Children of India's Ghetto and other Essays On Untouchables and Untouchability: Socio-Political-Religious, in Dr. Babasaheb Ambedkar: *Writings and Speeches, Vol. 5*, Education Department, Govt. of Maharashtra, Bombay.

________, 1991, 'What Congress and Gandhi have done to the Untouchables', MR. Gandhi and Emancipation of Untouchables, in Dr. Babasaheb Ambedkar: *Writings and Speeches, Vol. 9*, Education Department, Govt. of Maharashtra, Bombay.

Beteille, A., 1997, *Society and Politics in India: Essays in Comparative Perspective*, Oxford University Press, Delhi.

Brass, Paul R., 1965 *Factional Politics in an Indian State : The Congress Party in Uttar Pradesh, University* of California Press, Berkeley.

Dushkin, Lelah, 1998, Scheduled Caste Politics in J.Michael Mahar (ed.) *The Untouchables in Contemporary India*, Rawat Publications, Jaipur & New Delhi.

Ericson, Eric., 1960, The Problems of Ego Identity in Arthur Vidich and David While (eds.) *Identity and Anxiety*, Free Press, New York.

Gokhale, J., 1993, *From Concessions to Confrontation: The Politics of an Indian Untouchable Community*, Popular Prakashan, Bombay.

Gore, M.S., 1993, *The Context of an Ideology: Ambedkar's Political and Social Thought*, Sage Publications, New Delhi.

Hasan, Zoya, 1998, *Quest for Power : Oppositional Movements & Post-Congress Politics in Uttar Pradesh*, Oxford University Press, Delhi.

Jogdand, P.G, 1991, *Dalit Movement in Maharastra*, Kanak Publications, New Delhi.

Joshi, Barbara, R., 1982, *Democracy in Search of Equality : Untouchable Politics and Indian Social Change*, Hindustan Publishing Corporation, Delhi.

Kshirsagar, R. K., 1976, *Bhartiya Republican Pakha* (Marathi), Aurangabad,

________, 1994, *Dalit Movement In India and its Leaders*, M.D. Publications, New Delhi.

Lynch, O.M., 1974, *The Politics of Untouchability : Social Mobility and Social Change in a city of India*, National Publishing House, New Delhi.

Mathew, Joseph, 1986, *Ideology, Protest and Social Mobility: Case study of Mahars and Pulayas*, Inter-India Publications, New Delhi.

Mendelsohn, Oliver & Marika Vicziany, 1998, *The Untouchables: Subordination, Poverty and the State in Modern India*, Cambridge University Press, New Delhi.

Murugkar, Lata, 1993, *Dalit Panthers Movement in Maharashtra: A Sociological Appraisal*, Popular Prakashan, Bombay.

Omvedt, Gail, 1994, *Dalit and the Democratic Revolution : Dr. Ambedkar and the Dalit Movement in Colonial India,* Sage Publications, New Delhi.

Parvathamma, C., 1973. 'Ambedkar and After: The Position and Future of Indian Scheduled Caste Masses and Classes', *Eastern Anthropologist,* 26(3), pp. 221-34.

Ram, Kanshi, 1998, *Chamcha Age* (Hindi) translated by Ram Gopal Azad, Samta Prakashan, Nagpur.

Ram, Nandu, 1995, *Beyond Ambedkar: Essays on Dalits in India,* Har-Anand Publications, New Delhi.

Rosenthal, D.B., 1986, Caste and Political Participation in Two Cities in Rajni Kothari (ed.) *Caste in Indian Politics,* Orient Longman, New Delhi.

Rudolph, L.I. & S.H. Rudolph, 1987, *The Modernity of Tradition : Political Development in India,* Orient Longman, Delhi.

Srinivas, M.N., 1995, *Social Change in Modern India,* Orient Longman, New Delhi.

Zelliot, E, 1996, *From Untouchable to Dalit: Essays on the Ambedkar Movement,* Manohar Publishers, New Delhi.

6

Socio-Political Mobilisation and Empowerment

Social mobilisation refers to a process of change affecting substantial chunk of population in the society, showing sign of shift from traditional to modern views. It brackets together a number of specific processes of change, including the need for new patterns of group affiliation and new images of personal identity. Karl Deutch argues that by this process, major cluster of old social, economic and psychological commitments are eroded or broken and people become available for new patterns of socialization and behaviour (Deutch 1961 : 493-514). But according to Weiner (1962), social mobilisation in India is not likely to lead homogeneity but it already seems to have aggregated some small groups into somewhat greater size. Social mobilization, therefore, does not necessarily freeze the traditional system at the pre-existing level of social cleavage. It may reinvigorate a social cleavage at a high level of interest aggregation. Further, Rudolph and Rudolph (1987:24-28) have conceptualised the process of socio-political mobilisation of the people in India through the basic institution of caste. They also explain that the process of mobilisation is found in the three forms: vertical, horizontal and differential.

Besides, Lelah Dushkin (1998) has analysed the functioning of these processes in the realm of Dalit politics. She explains, "If we apply these types or forms of mobilisation to the scheduled caste politics, the first would require the untouchable leaders to play the part of the loyal 'Harijan', analogous to the "Uncle Tom" of American parlance. Under this arrangement, locally powerful upper-caste notables mobilize the voters - both Dalits and non-Dalits to fill the reserved seats with their own Dalit men or women whom they manipulate and control in regard to performing the political roles by the latter. These men and women are bound to the upper caste man through the traditional ties. But contrary to this, the legal model of the protective discrimination policy seems, in fact, to call for the second and third forms of political mobilisation of the voters". According to Dushkin, it suggests more or less a stage theory, as follows: Stage 1: the British created a category of the Scheduled Castes, which, through the horizontal mobilisation of its component groups, presses it for upward mobility en-bloc. The leadership skills called for here are those needed to turn the legal category into an organized bloc, no small task. The tactics would presumably include emphasis on the Scheduled Castes' communal loyalties, symbols and objectives overriding those of locality, party and birth in a particular caste. Stage 2: as the members move into new fields of endeavour and gain differentially economic prosperity, education including the higher one, and more favourable links with a larger society. Thus, develops an 'elongated' structure, and with it a tendency to mobilize on the basis of economic, ideological, and personal interests through political parties and factions that cut across caste affiliation (Dushkin 1998:209).

Rudolph and Rudolph's (1987:144-145) analysis of political mobilisation of the people in general and of the Dalits in particular are quite in time with that of Dushkin. They visualize the use of horizontal and differential process of mobilisation by the Dalits in politics. According to them, "The Scheduled Castes Federation, founded by Ambedkar in 1942, contested the general elections in 1952 and 1957. It expressed in its name and politics a sense of communal separateness, and it pursued, for the most part, a strategy of horizontal rather than differential mobilisation by appealing to and organizing Mahars (in Maharashtra). The more radical and ideological Republican Party of India, which Ambedkar established after the second general election of 1957, attempted to move toward differential mobilisation by combining appeals to the poor and dispossessed with efforts to broaden the party's community base". Pai (2000:122) puts it differently and argues about the mobilisation pattern of the Bahujan Samaj Party, specially in U.P. In her words, "During an early phase between 1985 to 1989, the BSP attempted to be both a radical movement and party using all its three mobilisation strategies: socio-cultural, agitational and electoral. It was a phase of militant vertical mobilisation of the poor and exploited, ideologisation of caste as a tool to break the existing social order and strident criticism of mainstream parties".

It is, thus, clear that all the processes of mobilisation have been operating simultaneously in the Indian polity particularly at the time of general elections. But a fact may be mentioned have that the different processes of mobilisation have been used to mobilize the various socio-political groups in different geographical settings with several permutations and combinations. Yet, it is a fact that if one process of mobilisation is operative in a particular region, the other process or processes of mobilisation are also present though these may not be as effective as the first one. In the case of Dalits, for example, their mobilisation in rural areas has seen of all the three processes of mobilisation at work-somewhere differential, somewhere horizontal and still somewhere vertical. Still, Dalits are often terrorized and patronized by the upper castes to cast their votes in their favour or in the favour of candidates sponsored by them who contest elections especially from the reserved constituencies. But in urban areas differential mobilisation is the dominant trend.

Secondly, the process of political mobilisation of Dalits specially during the voting period wherein they are lured or intimidated by the upper castes to cast their votes in their favour or in the favour of candidate sponsored by them has not been put in any specific type of mobilisation. There is need of either stretching three to four types of mobilisation or to find a new nomenclature for this process. I would prefer to call it 'contemptuous mobilization' because it snatches the democratic rights of a citizen to exercise his/her will to choose a representative. Thirdly, Pai's explanation that the BSP has used vertical mobilisation for the mobilisation of Dalit masses does not fit in basic definition of vertical mobilisation analysed by Rudolph and Rudolph, as stated above. They have defined it as a process of "marshalling of political support by traditional notables in local societies that are organized by rank, mutual dependence and the legitimacy of traditional authority" (Rudolph & Rudolph 1987:24). If we go by this logic then the BSP's mobilisation cannot be described as vertical mobilisation because the BSP leaders who were/are neither notables nor had they have legitimacy of traditional authority playing dominant role in mobilizing the masses. Moreover, they also mobilize the so-called superior castes to whom they cannot provide any protection or patronage which is also an essential part of vertical mobilisation.

Some authors may call the BSP's mobilisation as differential mobilisation because the BSP is a political party with an ideology of the economic and social emancipation of the 'Bahujans'. But that is only partially correct as at its core, the BSP has had organized all the Dalit castes horizontally. It is true that at the initial stage, the Chamars and a few other Dalit castes came to its fold. But today, it intends to distribute power according to the population percentage of each and every caste specially of the Dalits and the Most Backward Castes in the state as well as in the country as stated in the previous chapter. Hence, it has propagated the slogan: *Jiski Jitni Sankhya Bhari, Uski Utni Bhagedari* (each caste has to share power according to its numbers). Therefore, we may put the BSP's mobilisation in both the categories of differential and horizontal mobilisations.

Mobilisation of Dalits in U.P.

It is distinctly clear that the Dalit leadership in the contemporary times has shifted its focus from bringing various types of social reform among Dalits to attainment of political power, as stated in the previous chapter, through mobilizing them for the latter. There have remained different issues on the basis of which Dalit and non-Dalit masses have been mobilized during the pre- and post-independence periods. As stated in the previous chapter, the Dalits after independence have gained the constitutional provisions and safeguards which have yet to be fully and effectively implemented. The Dalit leaders, as informed by many of our respondents, rally around this point to get these benefits delivered in favour of the Dalit masses. They mobilize the Dalit masses by informing them about the various socio-economic programmes launched by the Government for upliftment of the Dalits. In the process, they also take credit by saying that these programmes have been implemented because of their efforts. They further impress upon the Dalit masses that if the latter keep on supporting their leadership, more such benefits would be made available to them.

On the other hand, a sizeable number of our respondents have remained of the view that the Dalit leaders in U.P. also try to convince other political parties dominated by upper castes and classes that they have a following which can benefit their parties in terms of votes and supports; therefore, they should be given proper representation in their party organization, in the cabinet and in other important establishments. Our respondents specially from the BSP have informed us that the Dalit leaders from the BSP criticize, from their platform, the exploitative attitude of the upper castes and classes to influence their voters. The provocative speeches help the Dalit leaders to energise the Dalit masses. The atrocities, coercion and oppression of the Dalits are highlighted by these leaders who ask and convince them (Dalits) that it is through the political power that they can overcome their subordinated social, economic, educational and political status in the society.

It is also a fact that the mobilisation of the Dalit masses on the basis of their gaining (or gaining in future) political power has increased political consciousness among them. They have realized by now the value of their votes and numbers. It has brought greater participation of the Dalits in the political arena. More and more of Dalits have come out and voted for the BSP (see Tables 6.1-6.2). More and more Dalit political leaders are seen contesting elections from the reserve constituencies. As stated in the previous chapter, every political party has been forced now to field, in the reserved constituencies, an effective, educated, socially and politically conscious Dalit leaders who can raise and speak with conviction on the Dalit issues.

TABLE 6.1

The BSP's Progress in the U.P. Assembly Elections

Sl. No.	*Years*	*No. of Seats Contested*	*No. of Seats Won*	*% of votes polled*
1.	1989	373	13	9.83
2.	1991	386	12	9.2
3.	1993	166	67	11.2
4.	1996	299	67	20.06
5	2002	403	98	23.00

Source: Chief Electoral Officer, U.P., Lucknow.

TABLE 6.2

The BSP's Progress in UP Lok Sabha Elections

S.No.	*Years*	*No. of seats won*	*% of votes polled*
1.	1985	- 2.6	
2.	1989	29	.5
3.	1991	11	.0
4.	1996	6	20 .6
5.	1998	4	20 .91
6.	1999	14	22.08

Source : Chief Electoral Officer, U.P., Lucknow.

This is contrary to the pre-independence Dalit leadership and also Dalit leadership in first three decades after independence in the state as well as in the country when mute, dumb and uneducated Dalit leaders were given tickets to contest the general elections from the reserved constituencies as already mentioned in the previous chapter. "Most of the untouchable candidates for Congress in the thirties and forties were figures of no prominence and often of little education" (Mendelson & Vicziany 1998:110). This fact was also endorsed by the Dalit leader Acharya Moti Ram Shastri who in interview had narrated few names of the leaders with such credentials as mentioned in the previous chapter. No doubt, such Dalit leadership of the first three or four decades after independence had mobilised the Dalit masses on the whims and fancies of their political bosses. Ambedkar had highlighted this fact very early when the controversy for over separate versus joint electorate was on (Ambedkar 1991:44).

Usually, during the election times, the Dalit masses were bribed by the upper castes with gifts like liquor, blankets, food packets, some clothes, etc. and were asked to cast their votes in favour of both the Dalits and non-Dalit candidates of their respective parties. And if they wanted to cast their votes independently, the various types of coercion, harassment and violence were used against them. In fact, the upper castes in the rural areas kept full vigil on the Dalits' exercising their votes in favour of a particular candidate. Gould found, for example, that in Faizabad constituency in U.P. the Scheduled Caste "landless menials are sill too economically dependent upon the Thakurs..." to vote independently. Many Scheduled Caste people were gathered together in little groups by their Thakur overlords and marched to the rolls under Thakur supervision in order to ensure that they voted for the Jan Sangh. They were able to impose their will, in this way, by threatening these impoverished folk with such economic sanctions as the denial of opportunities for field labour, withdrawal of sharecropping privileges and the calling in of loans" (Gould 1965:175). Moreover, there was no evaluation of effectiveness and competence of the Dalit leadership of that era specially in absence of competition and opposition among the Dalit leaders.

For more than three decades after independence, Jagjivan Ram dominated the Dalit leadership in north India and attracted Dalit masses towards the Congress Party, except for a brief period in 1969 when the Republican Party of India under the leadership of B.P. Maurya challenged him in some western districts like Agra and Aligarh in Uttar Pradesh.

The style of mobilisation of the Dalit leadership used to be persuasive in the early years of its inception and before independence, as stated in the previous chapter. We have also mentioned that the Dalit leaders used to even submit petitions and prayers to the rulers for granting social and political rights to the Dalits. They usually carried the reforms within the Dalit community and educated them in regard to the benefits of unity, education, cleanliness, and leaving the bad habits like carrion eating, consuming liquor, pursuing the traditional and hereditary occupation, etc. They petitioned the bureaucracy against the Dalits' doing *begar* (or forced labour) for the bureaucratic officials and upper castes especially in the rural areas. But we do not come across any authentic data or cases of direct action or confrontation of the Dalit leadership against the oppression and suppression of the Dalits by the upper castes and officials during this period. Anyway, it is interesting to note here a unique way of mobilisation of the Dalits for their freedom from the traditional shackles of caste system and economic exploitation. This can be seen in the revival of the Bhakti movement of the mediaeval period during the first decades of the twentieth century as mentioned in the preceding chapters. The Dalits organised themselves in different sects named after the different poet-saints like Kabir Das and Ravi Das or Raidas calling themselves as Kabir Panthis and Ravidasis, during the 1920s, in some parts of Uttar Pradesh specially in Kanpur, Allahabad, Varanasi and Lucknow. Only Ambedkar had launched the first mass action programme at Mahad in the year 1927 and at Kala Ram temple in 1930 in Maharashtra during this period.

But after independence, the Dalit leaders both in U.P. and in the country have changed their *modus operandi* of mobilisation of the Dalit masses and even others. Now, the direct mass actions and confrontations have been adopted to deal with the officials and the upper castes in the cases of high handedness by the latter.

The Dharnas (sit ups), gheraos, strikes, violent demonstrations, open criticism of government, etc. have increased tremendously now in the state. The Dalit leaders have formed their own organizations and raise their voices against the atrocities and un-fulfilment of reservation quota in the government jobs. They have also formed political parties to mobilize the Dalit masses in greater numbers. Since the 1980s till now, there is a qualitative change in the nature of Dalit leadership, as discussed in the previous chapter, which has also affected the nature and rate of their political mobilisation of the Dalit masses. Earlier, there used to be Dalit ministers from the various political parties in the governments. However, with the emergence of the Bahujan Samaj Party, the Dalit leaders found in different political parties in the state have been overshadowed. Even though the sharing of power in different governments for a brief period, the speed of mobilisation of the Dalits by the BSP leadership in the state has increased all these years. This has been augmented all the more because of Mayawati's (a Dalit woman leader) becoming the Chief Minister for the first time in the history of the state. Every conscious Dalit has now started identifying himself/herself directly with the Dalit leadership or that of the BSP which has an independent status unlike the other type of Dalit leadership dependent on their party bosses. The phenomenon of Mayawati becoming Chief Minister and with a BSP Government having the Dalit agenda in the core of the governance gave the Dalits of the state new aspirations and hopes which has been rightly brought out by Jens Lerche. In the words of Lerche, "Chamars commonly said that they had acquired 'courage' and 'self-esteem', or that they were 'not afraid any longer', that they now dared to stand up for what they perceived as their rights. This change was encapsulated symbolically in the change that many Thakurs pointed to as central: that Chamars no longer showed them respect. Most Chamars would no longer participate in various festivals and rituals which, among other things, emphasised their inferiority, and they would answer the Thakurs back" (Lerche 1999:213).

Thus, the Dalits in the state have come out of their pre-conceived 'object' status and socialized themselves as the 'subject' status or as an active player. The notion that the Dalits cannot rule and manage their own the political affairs was dismantled for the first time and the construction of a new era began. The neo-rich and the middle class among the Dalits, who had benefited from the policy of the protective discrimination and the process of modernisation, contributed in a significant manner in the initial stages of mobilisation of the Dalit masses by the Dalit leadership of BAMCEF and DS4. As the time progressed, this mobilisation also covered the new terrain in the countryside. For the first time in the state politics, the Dalit leadership specially of the BSP went independently, so deep in the villages, with a programme of their own. Even mobilisation of the RPI was restricted to some western parts of the state and that of Dalit Panthers' in the central part of the state - Lucknow, Barabanki, Sitapur, Hardoi and other adjoining areas of the state, as stated in the earlier chapter. The rural presence of the BSP has been highlighted by Lerche who suggests that, "This study agrees that the emergence of the BSP on to the political scene is important but for different reasons : namely because of its influence on rural class struggles. Although the BSP has not raised major class issues such as land reforms, it has, nevertheless, influenced local agrarian struggles and labour relations through changes in how the local state apparatuses relate to them" (ibid: 183).

We have already stated in the previous two chapters that during the pre-independence period, the Dalit leadership could not organize inter-regional or even intra-regional conferences for the purpose of the mobilizing the Dalit masses in the state. Only local level meetings or congregations were organised and that too with the help of the leadership of the traditional caste Panchayats. Yet, there were one or two successful conferences organised by the Dalit leaders in the state. One such conference was organised when Ambedkar came to Lucknow in 1948 to mobilize the Dalits for capturing political power (Gore 1993:213). Again in 1956, he came to Agra second time to mobilize and educate the Dalit masses about his plans for conversion to Buddhism (Lynch 1974:145). Contrary to this, the Dalit leadership of the Congress Party organised regional conference to stop the Dalits to follow the act of conversion to Buddhism led by Babasaheb Ambedkar. For instance, Jagjivan Ram organised a meeting in Subhas Park in Agra to stop the Dalits to convert to Buddhism (ibid:145). Before that

Achhutanand, the leader of the Adi Hindu movement, had organised an inter-regional meeting in the 1920s of the Dalit leaders drawn from all over the country to unite the Dalit movements organised in the name of the Adi-Hindu, Ad-dharm, Adi-Andhra, Adi-Karnataka, etc. as mentioned in the previous chapters. This conference ended in a failure as the propagators of the different movements did not agree to unite their respective movements under one name (Juergensmeyer 1982:38). However, after independence the Dalit leadership has increased the frequency of organising local, regional and inter-regional conferences for the mobilisation of the Dalits. Even they have gone to organise the inter -state conferences. For instance, the BSP organized the Ambedkar Mela in Lucknow in April 1995 in which the Dalits from different parts of the country had participated. Similarly, the Sahuji Maharaja Mela was organised in Kanpur in which again the Dalits from different states had participated and performed cultural activities. Now, big rallies with lakhs of people attending them have become part and partial of the strategy of mobilisation of the Dalits in Uttar Pradesh, like in other states. The regional and state level conferences are regularly organized to assess progress of activities of the party workers.

Another strategy for mobilising the Dalits is to raise their vital issues in the Parliament and in the State Assembly. It has been revealed by the majority of our respondents that Dalit leaders raise socio-economic, educational and other types of issues related to Dalit masses in the Parliament and the State Assembly to mobilize them. But a chance to raise the questions depends on many factors. Since a political party is allotted limited time to raise a particular issue, the party bosses entrust responsibility to a particular member to raise the issue in the house. Our respondents have also argued that the impact of raising of question in Parliament and State Assembly depends on the extent it is advertised by both the electronic and print media, or by the party's publicity machinery. But as has been seen time and again, the Dalit issues raised in the house by the Dalit leaders rarely become a news item. Hence, there is very remote chance that the raising of Dalit issues in different houses really helps mobilisation of the Dalits.

As far as the above mentioned style of mobilisation by the BSP leadership largely representing the Dalit leadership in U.P. is concerned, many respondents want change in it. For instance, they do not wish the caste provocative language to be used by the leaders because, in their opinion, it creates lot of animosity in the society. Moreover, they argue that because the Dalit masses are fatalistic and vulnerable, they always want a charismatic personality to lead them and take out from their miserable conditions. They also do not want to wage their struggle or protest longer as it may prove to be counter-productive. A point may be mentioned here that their understanding of the charismatic leadership is somewhat different from that characterised by Max Weber (1958) where a charismatic leader be a traditional one. In fact, in their frame of reference a charismatic leader is the one who is well educated, articulate logical-rational, and has a full commitment and conviction for the Dalit cause. Another point is that due to their existential condition specially in the rural areas, they seem to be well aware of the fact that waging struggle or confrontation with the upper castes and classes means not only getting their subsistence sources blocked but also loosing their life and destruction of their meagre belongings including their houses or thatched shelters. Further, they do not want a particular caste to politically dominate the Dalit leadership in the state; hence, they demand that collective leadership should be developed. They also argue that single party cannot claim to represent the total Dalit community. Therefore, the Dalit leaders should remain in different political parties but on the issue of the Dalits' interests, they should come on one platform and unitedly press their demands. In their opinion, pressurising the government to implement the constitutional provisions would help the Dalit masses to gain the benefits, and would also facilitate the Dalit leadership in easily mobilizing the former.

The majority of our respondents have also expressed their opinion that while mobilizing the general masses in spreading their party base, the Dalit leadership should be cautious about their not sacrificing the Dalit cause. In other words, the leaders drawn from the upper castes and classes within the Dalit leadership should not be given important and significant portfolios in the government formed by it and also key positions in the party organisation. Rather, they should be used as instruments for attracting votes from the masses of their community as other political parties do and use the Dalits for the electoral purposes only. Our respondents have further revealed that, "If the upper castes and others are given important position in the organizational set up, they can sabotage the movement of the Dalits as they are basically *status quoits* and want to perpetuate the existing social-order".

Socio-cultural Mobilization

Another strategy suggested by our respondents for mobilisation of the Dalit masses is to form a number of cultural and social organizations playing the role of shadow organizations. In their opinion, "If the Dalit leadership wants its political roots to be stronger and masses do not get alienated then they have to establish a strong cultural and other shadow organizations. Even if the Dalits come to power, these organizations can work at the grass-root level to educate the masses. The enlightened leaders should be accommodated in these shadow organizations so as they do not feel alienated. They will get some satisfaction that they are also being given some importance". To prepare the leadership at the grass-root level, more and more Dalits should be given some positions in these organizations to keep them involved with the Dalit agenda. This is extremely necessary, in their opinion, as the upper caste dominated political parties and other organizations attract the petty Dalit leaders by offering them insignificant post in them. This retards the rate of Dalit mobilisation, on the one hand, and hampers the growth and development of the independent Dalit leadership, on the other. The Dalit masses are also confused by the presence of these leaders in the parties dominated by the so-called upper castes and classes.

Our respondents have further opined that, "to emerge an effective and committed Dalit leadership, it is *sine qua non* for the Dalit leaders to leave their personal ambitions. They cannot afford to function like power brokers and agents of different socio-political forces. The disciplinary action against the erring Dalit leaders have to be sharper so as to bring them under control. This is necessary as the Dalit leaders, as evidences suggest, are often vulnerable to indiscipline in absence of a proper mechanism of control". But a sizeable number of respondents have also confessed that, "in the BSP because of strict disciplinary actions and extra-regimentation, a few fragmentations have taken place. Therefore, the BSP leadership has to be somewhat flexible and the top level leaders have to forego their personal ambitions".

Another interesting point to mention here is that the political leaders irrespective of their party affiliation generally take up the day-to-day problems of the people of their constituency and thereby mobilize their support in the electoral politics. Occasionally, they address the long-term agenda either in piloting some bills or supporting others and thus getting legislations enacted in the Parliament and the State Legislature, as may be the case. Only a few political parties like the communist parties-CPI, CPI (M) and CPI (ML), and the BJP have adopted the long-term agenda, besides addressing the short-term issues, which of course have got diluted over a period of time due to situational compulsions. The Dalit leadership in the state as well as in the country has also followed the same suit, except Dr. Ambedkar who had consistently pursued the long-term agenda of bringing transformation in the Indian society but at the same time not undermining the day-to-day problems of the Dalits. Hence, the Dalit leadership in the state has to chalk out its both the long and short term goals for the better mobilisation of the Dalits and other weaker sections. It has also to take cognisance of the ongoing processes like globalisation, privatisation, liberalisation and information revolution. Otherwise, Dalits would again be left in lurch because they are still not equipped with the technical and managerial skills needed to get employment in the multinational companies or corporations operating and going to operate in big way in India as mentioned in the previous chapter. Our respondents are of the strong view that the Dalit leadership has to guide the masses to come out of the shadow of the traditional type of education, and go for the modern technical and managerial skills needed for getting employment in the contemporary job market. Moreover, the Dalit leadership has also to come out of their narrow perspective of the 'good of the Dalits only'. They have to add the national issues for mobilisation of the other sections of the society. To get more strength, they have to take every sections of the society into their fold.

Further, the Dalit leadership in the state if wants to increase its mobilising capacity, it would have to pursue the social reforms within the Dalit community and in the country as well along with the goal of capturing political power. Some of our respondents have argued that, "Without a strong cultural and social movement, the political movement may loose its sight. It would be without any restrain and can easily be misguided". As far as cultural movement is considered, the "whole history of India is to be questioned and rewritten because the contributions of the Dalits have grossly been undermined by the historians. There has to be proper evaluation of the Dalit labour which produces food grains, industrial products, constructs roads, rails, houses for others, etc. Why their labour has been degraded and not considered worth mentioning with respect in the annals of academics? The whole literature, which is literature of the upper castes and classes, does not devote required space for the Dalits. Therefore, the respondents suggest that the Dalit literature should be produced which can narrate the sufferings of the Dalits and expose the true nature of the exploitative social order. This, in turn, would make the Dalits conscious of their exploitation also. It can have the same effect as in Maharashtra where the leaders of the Dalit Panthers' wrote Dalit literature and instigated the violent Dalit struggle. For this, Dalit scholars should be awarded special scholarships, grants and awards to motivate them for more creative writing of the Dalits and for the Dalits as well as for others. The school curriculum which propagates superstition among the masses in general and Dalits in particular should be changed. More progressive curriculum has to be regulated in the schools".

Retrospectively, the Dalit leadership also mobilise Dalit masses in the state by distributing the literature related to the Dalit movements, their ideology and strategy. This is done with the view that the local level people like to know what is happening at the national level and how do their leaders react to that. This literature answers their queries and easily educates them in absence of their direct interaction with the higher level of their leadership. The literature of this type is all the more important because the media is dominated by the upper castes and classes, which mainly caters to their needs. The Dalit perspective seldom appears in the print media. The television is another strong electronic medium of putting across the views of Dalit leaders, but somehow very few Dalit leaders are seen on the television. Their absence is more astonishing when the television channels are multiplying. Hence, the majority of our respondents are of the view that, "Dalit leadership should give away its `media shy' nature and face the challenges of the era of 'information revolution'. This would enhance their image and aura, as the reach of the television has gone deep into villages with increased hours of transmission, and also Dalits have gained access to watch the national channels, if not the cables".

The Dalit leadership irrespective of party affiliation has to be more democratic in nature. Most of our respondents have revealed that though the "BSP mostly represents the Dalit leadership in the state because it has maximum percentage of Dalit votes, it has only two main leaders and there is no second line leadership. Also, there is no democracy within the party as most of local leaders are not allowed to speak freely. The organisational elections are not held democratically. The different party functionaries are nominated and chucked out on the whims and fancies of the two party leaders. In Uttar Pradesh, Mayawati has been the sole in-charge and others have only to follow her. In other political parties also, "the Dalit leaders once established become egoistic and self -aggrandizing. They never allow other stream of Dalit leadership to emerge so that they do not loose their dominant position in the party". In other words, our respondents cited the cases of late Jagjivan Ram of the Congress Party and Ramvilas Paswan of the Janata Dal, besides Kanshi Ram and Mayawati of the BSP. It is interesting to note that, except Jagjivan Ram who is no more alive, the other said leaders enjoy the maximum support of the Dlits in Bihar and Uttar Pradesh respectively.

Empowerment and Dalit Leadership

The concept of empowerment in its current usage is very new as it does not find place in the Encyclopaedia, a number of dictionaries and glossaries of sociology textbooks. According to Beteille (1999:589), empowerment is related to certain context in Indian society. In his own words, "in a nutshell, that context is the contradiction between a hierarchical social order and a democratic political system". He opines further, "the idea of empowerment may be invoked in virtually any context: in speaking about human rights, about basic needs, about economic security, about capacity building, about skill formation or about the conditions of a dignified social existence" (ibid: 590). It is also seen as a way of addressing the problems of rights that remain un-enforced. In economic context, it is invoked in capacity building particularly of marginalized, unorganised and other disadvantaged groups, classes and categories. Beteille elaborates by saying that, "Implicit in the idea of empowerment is certain theory of social change in particular of change from a hierarchical to an egalitarian type of society (Beteille 1983), or in a slightly different language, from an aristocratic to democratic type of it (Tocqueville 1956). The main point behind empowerment is that it seeks to change through a rearrangement of power" (Beteille 1999: 591). Beteille gives a concrete proposal of empowerment by suggesting a radical change in social composition of the strategic institutions of society, in particular the various organs of the state. He opines that the institutions of society with diverse social groups will be more open and more sensitive in its approach to the larger problems of society (ibid: 596). For achieving empowerment in the society, he suggests two paths: one, there is a laborious and unexciting process through expansion of the civic, political and social rights of citizenship. Second is by providing as extensively as possible quota to the un-empowered on the basis community, caste and gender. But in this case, we have to compromise with the ideals of our Constitution which assigns the rights and capacities to the citizens as individuals, and not to castes and communities or men and women separately (ibid: 597).

If we analyse the empowerment of Dalits in the sense described above, we find that the government has already provided both the paths for the purpose: one, through granting them civic, political and social rights which were denied to them earlier. Secondly, it has provided them special quota in different spheres of their life. Yet, Dalits are powerless and are unable to set their own agenda as stated in the preceding chapter. They have to largely look for the benefits of the policies and programmes adopted and implemented by the government of the day. The main hurdle in their empowerment, according to most of our respondents, is the "existing value system of the Indian society. The traditional hierarchy does not allow the Dalits to have their access to the strategic positions of the authority in the public domain and to the decision making". Therefore, the Dalit leaders want to capture power so that they can change the social composition of the state machinery. We have already mentioned in this as well as in the preceding chapters that this was done in Uttar Pradesh soon after Mayawati became the Chief Minister in June 1995 and again in April 1997. In was reported in the media that, "The Emancipatory campaigns and fierce of anti-upper caste rhetoric gain credibility and substance through BSP's attempt to change the staffing of state by unprecedented transfers of government officials, placing Dalit cadres in key posts with the public administration (*India Today*, September, 1997:46-8; *Frontline*, 1 December, 1995:30-31; 18 April 1997:18). Our respondents also have stated that, "for the first time in the history of the state, the Chief Secretary is a Dalit and the Director General of Police is also a Dalit. Whether they do anything for us positively or not but they will not do anything negatively for us. Moreover, the entire upper caste bureaucracy in the state was afraid of the fact that a Dalit was their boss; and if anything went wrong, there would be no one to save them. Half of our problems were solved by their mere presence".

The implementation of the Scheduled Castes and Scheduled Tribes (Prevention of Atrocities) Act, 1989 is another testimony of the fact that how things change where Dalits themselves become the custodian of law. Anyway, under this Act, a person committing atrocities on the SCs/STs can be sent to jail, while cases are investigated. Similarly, the victim is awarded Rs. 6,000 to enable him/her to fight the case in a court of law. During Mayawati's Chief Ministership, these provisions of the Act were implemented with seriousness as revealed by many of our respondents. Not only that but the power of investigation in the cases of atrocities was delegated to police station in-charge/sub inspector, with posting of the SC/ST candidates as in-charge at 25 percent of the *Thanas* in all the districts in the state. Besides, the BSP government also facilitated the Dalits to take possession of land already allotted to them, and, on its own, initiated only limited number of minor new allotments of government land to the Dalits (Department of Information and Public Relations, U.P.). Further, it provided tangible improvement to some Dalit groups through channelling of government funds to the programmes benefiting primarily to the Dalits. The focus of such programmes was implementation of the Ambedkar Village Development Scheme in the villages, with major concentration of the Dalit population. Under the Scheme, in all 37 programmes were to be implemented so that the Dalits with their economic development could be brought above the poverty line. The most important programmes under this Scheme included construction of link roads, rural electrification, construction of brick-paved roads, drains, rural sanitation programme, opening of primary schools/building construction, and free-boring, Integrated Rural Development Programme, Indira Housing

Scheme, making clean drinking water available, Kisan Pension Scheme, Widow Pension Scheme, etc. There is a long list which can prove that the process of empowerment of Dalits in the state was initiated when the BSP leadership had ruled the state and the Dalits occupied key positions in the different institutions (Department of Information and Public Relations, U.P.)

In a nutshell, the empowerment of Dalits as reported by Lerche (1999:213) in his study in eastern U.P. brings the point home. According to him, "whereas generation before Thakurs could summon their Chamar workers for duty by yelling at them from the outskirts of the Thakur hamlet (a distance of 500 metres), this changed during the 1970s and 1980s when it became common for Thakurs to go to their labourers' homesteads in the Chamar hamlet to call them when needed. However, since 1995-96 they have even stopped doing this as they might now suffer the humiliation that Chamar workers would not stand up straight away when they arrived; the workers might ask the Thakur to sit down on the same charpoy (string-bed) as them, or even offer tea, thereby emphasising the egalitarian relationship between them. They might also claim not to be available for work, so that the landowners would have to go to several labourers' households to procure workers. To avoid such humiliations, Thakurs now send their children to call the Chamars instead".

Thus, the conventional forms of political mobilisation of the people in the state in particular and in the country in general has undergone change in the recent decades. Instead, the money and muscle power plays more significant role in mobilising the people specially at the time of general elections. The Dalits also have been governed by such process of mobilisation. The repeated threats from the Elections Commissions to counter-manned elections through such practices and reprimand the persons violating the elections norms and considerable degree of assertion of the Dalits have, however, changed the political scenario during the recent years. We have already stated in this as well as in the earlier chapters that in spite of playing electoral politics, the BSP, in the opinion of its leadership, is an ongoing movement for the amelioration of Dalits in the state as well as in the country. It is true also as, apart from playing the electoral politics as mentioned above, it addresses the wider issues of empowering the Dalits in terms of bringing qualitative changes in their socio-economic status, educational level, power position, in their attitudes, behaviour, consciousness, etc. It is clear by now that it has been successful, to some extent, in its endeavour. But ironically, the Dalit leaders in other political parties still follow the conventional form of political mobilisation of the Dalit voters and are unable to play any significant role in empowering Dalits in the state.

References

Beteille, Andre, 1999, Empowerment, *Economic and Political Weekly*, March 6-13.

_______, 1983, *The Idea of Natural Inequality and Other Essays*, Oxford University Press, Delhi.

Deutch, Karl, 1961, Social Mobilisation and Political Development, *American Political Science Review*, 55.

Dushkin, Lelah, 1998, Scheduled Caste Politic, in J. Michael Mahar (ed.) *The Untouchables in Contemporary India*, Rawat Publications, Jaipur and New Delhi.

Gore, M.S., 1993, *Social Context of an Ideology: Ambedkar's Political and Social Thought*, Sage, Publication, New Delhi.

Gould, Harold, 1965, Traditionalism and Modernism in U.P. in Myron Weiner and Rajni Kothari (eds.), *Indian Voting Behaviour*, Firma K.L. Mukhopadhyaya, Calcutta

Juergensmeyer, Mark, 1982, *Religion as Social Vision: The Movement against Untouchability in 20th century Punjab*, University of California Press, Barkeley.

Lerche, Jens, 1999, Politics of the Poor: Agricultural labours and Political Transformation in Uttar Pradesh in Jens Lerche et.al *Rural Labour Relations in India*, Frank Class, London.

Pai, Sudha, 2000, *State Politics: New Dimensions*, Shipra Publications, New Delhi.

Rudolph & Rudolph, 1987, *The Modernity of Tradition: Political Developoment in India*, Orient Longman, Delhi.

Tocqueville, Alex de, 1956, *Democracy in America*, Alfred Knopf, New York, 2 vol.

Weiner, Myron, 1962, *The Politics of Scarcity*, Chicago University Press, Chicago

7

Conclusion

The Dalit leadership has been conceptualised in this study as a collective process through which individuals initiate activities for delivering the common objectives of the community by working together, stimulating each other, supplementing abilities and resources and evolving an effective organisational or hierarchical pattern. Going by such framework, it may be said that the Dalit leadership has emerged from the basic premise that the Dalit leaders are born in the Dalit or Untouchable community, and have worked for upliftment of the people of their castes or communities either being part of the various socio-political forces or independently. We have not accepted those leaders as Dalit leaders who are born in the Other Backward Castes or Classes (OBCs), or are non-Dalits and have worked for uplift of the Dalit masses. We have done this simply because almost all of our respondents have suggested that individuals born in the Dalit community have first hand experience of oppression, suppression and exploitation of the Hindu social order and the caste system. They have quoted time and again a Hindi proverb, "Jake na ho pair biwai, woh kya jane peer parayee!!" (only those who have hurt in their feet, know the pain). Moreover, they have also argued that the section of the people who have suffered maximum from an exploitative system would only want to change and not those who have ever enjoyed all privileges of the system. Therefore, Dalits and only Dalits can be their true representative and can give a lead in their struggle.

At the outset, we have categorised, in this study, the Dalit leadership according to temporal and spatial bases. On the temporal basis, the Dalit leadership has been perceived in the time-frame keeping Ambedkar's leadership as the rallying point. We have, thus, divided the Dalit leadership into three epochs: Dalit leadership before Ambedkar, during his time and after him or the contemporary Dalit leadeship. As far as the spatial basis is concerned, the Dalit leadership has been categorised in this study at the national, state, district and panchayat levels though we have concentrated only at the state level Dalit leadership.

There is a general misconception that the Dalit leadership started with the emergence of Ambedkar on the socio-political scene sometimes in the early 1920s. But there are evidences as mentioned in details in chapters 1 and 2 that the Dalit leadership of various types had existed in different parts of the country before Ambedkar took up the struggle of Dalits in his own hand. For instance, a number of Adi-movements, the Mahar movement, etc. had emerged before Ambedkar. All these movements raised significant socio-political issues related to the Dalits. Therefore, when Ambedkar started his struggle for the upliftment of Dalits, he had enough cultivated ground though half-baked political material before him. The human resource of the Dalits was politically in the semi-conscious state and there was need of only energising them to stage a combat against the tyrannical Hindu social order. We have, further, divided in chapter one, Ambedkar's leadership into three interrelated phases because of his changing stances or strategies for upliftment of the Dalit masses. These are strife for social reforms, for acquiring political power, and role of lawgiver and emancipator from Hindu religion. In the first phase, he wanted to bring social reforms both within the Hindu social order and among the Dalits. He waged certain exaltations to energise the Dalit masses and also change the hearts of people of the upper strata. He opined, "In order to bring about the uplift of outcastes, it is first necessary to awaken them. Any community before it can progress must develop a consciousness. As someone has put it while the poor are certainly handicapped by their poverty, the real obstacle in their path is their inertia and indifference. To overcome this inertia and indifference, it is necessary that they should become charged with resentment of the injustice of their own condition. Without it, they cannot get rid of the factors that obstruct their progress. And even this is not enough, while on the one hand the obstruction must be removed, one must also simultaneously promote conditions which will ensure their prosperity" (Ganaveer 1985: 21). In his role of a social reformer, he vehemently criticised the Congress leadership and also other nationalist leaders for their not taking up the Dalit issues effectively. But when he realised that social reforms were not possible in the

Hindu social order or were not proving much beneficial to the Dalits, he left it and started attacking the former from a more secular angle.

The second phase of Ambedkar's leadership started in the 1930s and continued till his resigning from the Nehru Cabinet in 1951 after framing and getting adopted the Constitution of free India. During this phase, Ambedkar resorted to the political weapon to get over the age old disabilities, degradation and exploitation of the Dalits. But he took this step only as a last resort. He argued, "when the untouchables lost all hope for their salvation through social reform, they were forced to seek political means for protecting themselves" (Ambedkar 1991:190). He went on to achieve many political rights for the Dalits. He acted as the 'Father of the Indian Constitution', as mentioned above, during this period. But when he saw nothing much was coming out of the political means, he took to another instrument - religious conversion for uplifting the Dalit brethren. We have discussed in details, in chapter 5, his rational for adopting of political stance for uplift of the Dalits.

The third phase of Ambedkar's leadership saw him as religious leader. He embraced Buddhism along with lakhs of his followers and thereby gave them new identity and religion so that they could come out of their stigmatised identity in the Hindu social order and lead a liberated life. Praising Buddhism, Ambedkar narrated that, "it is a religion based on moral principles...unlike the founders of other religions, who consider themselves the emissaries of god, the Buddha regarded himself only as a guide and gave a revolutionary meaning to the concept of religion. He said that Buddhism stands for equality...Buddhism preached working for the well-being of all, for their happiness and for fostering the love of all. That which promised equal opportunity to all was the true religion" (Gore 1993:249-51).

It is a bitter truth that after the demise of Ambedkar in 1956 there has been no Untouchable or Dalit leader of his stature, integrity and dedication. But there have been many leaders leading the movements of the Dalits either independently or being in various political parties. In their presence and struggle, "while the condition of some of the Untouchable groups particularly in the urban-industrial areas has improved, the condition of the others has probably worsened as a result of fear and the effort of the upper castes to screw the lid tight against the possibility of new aspirations raising their head among the untouchable, captive workers on land" (ibid:225). Similarly, Beteille (1997:201) argues, "A case study of the untouchables in India clearly shows that disabilities cannot be abolished...Nobody would seriously claim, thirty-six years after the Constitution was adopted, that untouchables enjoy in the average Indian village the same rights as the other members of the community". These inequalities exist even after 50 years of adoption and working of the Constitution. Yet, the assertion of the Dalits for achieving equality and other rights has increased over all these years. More precisely, the independent Dalit leadership led by the Republican Party of India, Dalit Panthers and now BSP have shown the increasing level of consciousness among the Dalits for their rights as discussed in details in the preceding chapters. Though these three Dalit organizations or political parties rose, at different intervals, addressing the wider range of issues and having their cross-section followings specially in the case of the RPI and the BSP, these may be placed in the linear process of the evolution of the Dalits' consciousness and assertion.

Against this background, we have examined the nature and dynamics of the Dalit leadership drawn from the three selected regions namely eastern, central and western of Uttar Pradesh. Chapter 2 covers the conceptual explanations of the terms, used in the present research, specially leadership, Dalit leadership, socio-political mobilisation, etc. Besides, this chapter also describes briefly the methodology adopted for the present study. Chapter 5 draws the brief socio-historical profile of the universe, i.e. selected regions of Uttar Pradesh. We have discussed, in this chapter, the existing social arrangement or stratification in the state and compared it briefly with that found in other states particularly in the southern states of the country. Generally speaking, the caste-hierarchy in southern India is quite sharp and there are no *dvija jatis* (twice-born castes) other than the Brahmin. Hence, the caste-hierarchy in south India is discrete. But in north India, the hierarchy is continuous because of presence of the twice-born castes like Kshatriya and Vaishya, besides the Brahman. But the state of UP has been overpowered by the dominance of certain twice-born castes in every realms of society - land ownership, bureaucracy, political power, etc. They have cumulative dominance over the polity and society. For example, the Thakurs and Brahmins have owned 57 per cent of the land in the whole state. "The Indian

Administrative Service (IAS), Indian Police Service (IPS) and Provincial Services in UP have been dominated by the upper castes and classes; so also have been political institutions, the legislatures and party organizations" (Hasan 1998:9). The state is still predominantly rural in nature. As far as population concentration is concerned, around 75 per cent of the people still live in villages. The rural work force also contributes to the same percentage, i.e. they are engaged in agricultural and allied activities.

Against this backdrop, the Dalits constitute 21 per cent of the total population in the state. They have really suffered cumulative deprivation. This has happened so as "...from the outset the ruling party restricted the access of lower castes to positions in government and successive Congress regimes were dominated by upper castes" (ibid:19). The various forms of atrocities inflicted by the upper and middle castes and classes on the Dalits increased. The successive governments neither implemented fully and properly the public policy which might have neither benefited the Dalits in the state nor showed any sensitivity to the questions of social justice, alleviation of poverty or more equitable distribution of income. It was natural because the rulers were from the upper castes and classes; and, hence, they never wanted to change the structure of the society in the state.

Against this exploitative socio-political conditions emerged the Dalit leadership in Uttar Pradesh. Though it took a relatively long time for Dalit movement to emerge in the state, the answer for this is not far to seek. Rudolph and Rudolph (1987:78-79) explain that the "Anti-Brahmanism seems to have flourished in regions characterized by steep and discontinuous traditional social hierarchies, and it in turn seems to have fostered the political mobilization of castes still lower in the ritual hierarchy. At the other extreme, regions with relatively higher proportions of twice-born castes and more gradual and continuous social landscapes seem to be less susceptible to horizontal mobilizations from below of ritually deprived castes seeking opportunities, status and political power". This has been applicable equally to the different regions in the country as well as in the state. However, in course of time the gap between twice-born castes and lower castes increased because the former dominated in every aspects of life which, in turn, led to growth of feeling of deprivation among the Dalits.

Consequent upon that, they started mobilising horizonantally against their exploitation.

The nature of the Dalit leadership in the state has been discussed in details in chapter 6. Before analysing nature of the Dalit leadership, we have also analysed briefly the social and economic profile of the respondents - Dalit leaders selected for the present study. We have found most of them belonging to economically weaker sections, except those who have been elected to the Parliament or State Legislature either at present or earlier. The educational level of the respondents - Dalit leaders is satisfactory, as most of them have achieved education up to graduation and post graduation levels. As far as their age composition is concerned, they are quite young and most of them are between 25-45 years of age. It may, thus, be inferred that the first and even second generation Dalit leadership has either left politics or is no more active. It also gives an idea of the mind-set of the young Dalit leadership that is often an independent in nature to which we shall come a little later. It is, however, true that the Dalit leadership in the country as well as in the state is not totally unified; instead, Dalit leaders are found in most of the dominant political parties. For our convenience, in this chapter we have divided the emergence and growth of the Dalit leadership in six inter-related epochs. These epochs are based on certain specific socio-political conditions and the resultant Dalit movements prevailing at that point of time in the Indian society. These, in turn, had also influenced the Dalit movements and leadership in Uttar Pradesh.

Yet, we have found in the present study that, the nature of the Dalit leadership in the state has mostly been determined on the basis of the types of issues and demands pursued by the Dalit leaders. Their style of assertion for rights of the Dalits has also been an important factor in determining the nature of Dalit leadership. Accordingly, Dalit leadership in the state falls into two broad categories: socio-religious and political. The first type of leadership had mobilised the Dalit masses, during the first quarter of the twentieth century, on the basis of social-religious issues as discussed in this chapter. The processes of sanskritisation and de-sanskritisation were dominant during this period, which had provided the space to the Dalits for their status upliftment. The socio-religious Dalit leadership may further be divided into two categories: one which wanted to uplift the Dalits within the Hindu social order and the other insisted for Dalit upliftment outside the pale of it. A number of the Adi-movements discussed in this chapter fall in this category. Similarly, the religious conversion of Dalits to Buddhism led by Ambedkar and even prior to him specially in the southern states, and to other religions such as Islam, Christianity, Sikhism, etc. may also be bracketed within this category. But there was not much scope for the Dalits to upliftment their social status through their Adi movements or even religious conversions because the dominant Hindu social order was very rigid at least in the case of the Dalits. Also, this type of leadership did not question the existing social structure of the Hindu society, except the political and religious leadership of Ambedkar.

Gradually, the socio-religious leadership started getting displaced by the second type of the Dalit leadership, i.e. their political leadership. Our study reveals that there were several reasons for emergence of their political leadership. One, the issues raised by the socio-religious leadership among the Dalits in the past had already aroused aspirations of the Dalit masses and made them conscious enough to take up their problems at different plains. Secondly, the British rule in India had extended political rights to them, which helped them to be an equal citizen and to assert against their exploitation. Thirdly, by that time Ambedkar himself had changed his stance and started attacking the Hindu social order through more secular ideas and strategies. He was of the opinion that the socio-religious reforms were to perform some specific purpose and could bring about only limited change. Therefore, the socio-religious leadership was restricted to charge the Dalits with the resentment of their exploitation and social degradation but the political leadership became an effective instrument in promoting their interests, which ensured improvement in their socio-economic conditions.

We have already discussed in this chapter that as the Dalit political leadership developed, it got divided into two streams. We have named the first one as dependent Dalit political leadership and the other one as independent Dalit political leadership. As already stated, the first type of Dalit leadership was present in the different political parties dominated by the upper castes and classes. They were mostly guided by their political bosses without freedom of pursuing any independent agenda of their own. They spoke the language of their party and seldom raised the issues related to the Dalits. That is why, many of the respondents - Dalit leaders, called them as psychophants and stooges. In any case, their numbers went on multiplying because of the reserved constituencies, under the joint electorates system, from where they used to get elected. But the second type of Dalit leadership had established its own political parties at different points of time and played the vanguard role in setting up their agenda which kept the Dalits at the centre stage. The leadership of the Scheduled Castes Federation, the Republican Party of India, Dalit Panthers and now the Bahujan Samaj Party (BSP) may be kept in this category. This leadership has its own lexicon and parlance and criticizes vehemently the Hindu social order constructing it as "other" or the BSP's calling it 'Manuvadi' against which the battle could be pitched for liberation of the Dalits.

As far as the issues raised by the Dalit political leadership is concerned, the Dalit leaders had demanded, in the early decades of the twentieth century, the grant of political rights for the Dalits. They had testified in front of the commissions and committees of the British government of India, contested elections, demanded rights of Dalits in the surplus land, tried to get the untouchable castes included in or excluded from the list of the Scheduled Castes, and succeeded in obtaining representation of the Dalits in Legislative Assemblies, Parliament and in different statutory bodies. After independence, the political demands of the Dalits took the shape of fulfilment of reservation for them as enshrined in the Indian Constitution. The RPI had raised the slogan - "*Jo jamin Sarkari Hai, Woh Zamin Hamari Hai* (the government land belongs to us - the Dalits). Its leaders had also demanded for installation of the portrait of Babasaheb Ambedkar in the Central Hall of Parliament and his statue in its compound, renaming of streets and buildings after him, capturing power, etc.

The impact of the Dalit political leadership on the Dalit community was both positive and negative. On the positive side, Dalits were now categorised as a separate political group which attracted different political parties. Therefore, these political parties started taking up their issues, even though for namesake. Secondly, the bargaining power of the Dalit leadership got increased. The pressure mounted by the 'independent Dalit political leadership' has got reflected, in the present time, in the elevation of the Dalit leaders to various offices within the organisation of the different political parties, in the Cabinet of Ministers, to the posts of Governors, Speaker of State Assembly or of Parliament, and even the President of India. Yet, a new notion of sharing of political power emerged in the 1980s among the independent Dalit political leaders. For instance, with the rise of the BSP, the aspiration of the independent Dalit political leaders along with Dalit masses has reached to an altogether different plain. They have started aspiring for and succeeded to, to some extent, in occupying new political offices, which has affected significantly the state agenda. On the negative side of the Dalit political leadership, Dalit leaders of the dominant political parties attracted Dalit masses through enrolling them. Therefore, factionalism and division in the Dalit political leadership prevalent since the pre-independence period has also confused the Dalit masses even today and affected negatively their assertion for rights.

We have also discussed, in this chapter, the style of functioning of the Dalit leadership. As already mentioned in details, the Dalit leaders relied in the beginning on submitting petitions and prayers to the British government in India for achieving rights, and getting the miseries of the Dalit masses conveyed to the upper castes and classes and to the government officials. But after 1937 or so, they became assertive and organised open demonstrations for achieving their rights. Hence, the Dalit leadership changed its nature from persuasive to assertive and confrontationist. It happened more so when Ambedkar articulated their problems, made them conscious of their rights and of social identity, and organised open demonstrations against the tyranny of the Hindu orthodoxy. This chapter has also analysed the caste background of the Dalit leaders who had played the dominant role in raising the Dalit problems and led their struggle since the early decades of the twentieth century.

It is a fact that the Chamars or Jatavs in the central and western Uttar Pradesh had spear-headed their struggles in the beginning. Since they along with the Dalit masses had faced the cruelty of the Hindu social order, they retaliated against it. For instance, in the eastern Uttar Pradesh, the Chamars had organised themselves since the late 1940s onward when Ambedkar visited Varanasi and Lucknow. But with the growth and development of the democratic polity specially in the contemporary period, we have observed in our study that the different political parties have different Dalit castes as their vote banks. Even the BSP has desperately been trying to give representation to other Dalit castes in its fold, though Chamars and or Jatavs still form its base-vote. In fact, we have also seen in chapter 4 that the Congress Party manipulated in the past the different Dalit castes to take the political mileage. It mobilised the numerically dominant castes and neglected the castes with smaller numbers. That is why, most of the castes which are smaller in number have shifted to the BJP now. They have got a political space there which, was denied to them by the Congress Party. Anyway, we have found that the Dalit struggle in the recent times has remained situated mostly in the eastern and western parts of the state, and the central Uttar Pradesh has produced relatively less important Dalit leadership unlike that in the past.

We have analysed dynamics of the Dalit leadership in chapter 7. The dynamics of Dalit leadership in the present study has been defined as the shifting patterns of demands raised by the Dalit leaders. The major focus of this chapter is on the shift made by the Dalit leadership from social reform to the acquisition of political power. More specifically, we have elucidated in this chapter the status of the Dalit leaders in different political parties, and the role played by them in uplift of the Dalit masses, the nature of allies of the Dalit leadership, the issue of reservation dealt with by the Dalit leaders specially in the light of the on slot of the processes of globalisation, privatisation, liberalisation and information revolution. In the beginning of the chapter, we have analysed a few social, economic and educational issues raised by the Dalit leadership prior to independence. We have also explained that the Dalit leaders could not raise these issues very effectively as they themselves were not well organised. More peripheral demands like renaming of the streets and buildings after Babasaheb Ambedkar, fulfillment of the reservation quota for the Dalits, etc. became the core of the political demands of the Dalit leadership during the first two decades after independence.

But soon after, as discussed in this chapter, the Dalit leaders both in the country and in the state of Uttar Pradesh took clue from Babasaheb Ambedkar's scathing attack on the exploitative Hindu social order and sought for more secular options, i.e. political and educational avenues for uplift of the Dalit masses. Capturing political power and implementation of the legal provisions for their representations in different statuary bodies became the main aims of the Dalit leadership. Most of the respondents have quoted Babasaheb when asked, why the Dalit leadership has shifted its focus from social reform to political power. They have stated that it was Babasaheb who had told the Dalit leaders and the masses that, "Dalits should become the ruling community and political power is the only key to achieve that". Hence, the different strategies of Ambedkar for gaining political power have been dealt at length in this chapter. Apart from his relevant writings and speeches, his presentations of memorandum to a number of commissions and committees of the British government of India for the protection of political rights of the Dalits have also been highlighted in this regard. He had emphasized that Dalits should not only get reserved seats and voting rights but also be properly represented in the Cabinets (Ambedkar 1991:41-42). He had educated them and demanded for political rights for them at the pracucal level also. His establishment of a few independent political parties at different points of time and organisation of intra- and inter-regional conferences are testimony to the aforesaid fact.

The shift of Dalit leadership from social reform to achieving political power has also been substantiated by many social scientists. For instance, Rudolph and Rudolph (1987), Lynch (1974), Joshi (1982), etc. have given different versions for this shift of Dalit leadership and they have argued that this has occurred because of the development of liberal and democratic values fostered by the Constitution. The Dalits have, therefore, taken politics as their weapon for their struggle. Our informants have also endorsed this. They have also argued that the social transformation through the use of political power is a speedy process. Mendelsohn and Vicziany (1998:223) tend to capture the mood of the contemporary Dalit leadership in the state and say that, " Kanshi Ram's strategy and his larger understanding of social change are now considerably evolved. He no longer believes in the primacy of social reform. Rather, expenditure of effort on any object other than the capture of government is seen to be superfluous. It is administrative power that will bring about desired social change".

We have also analysed, in this chapter, the dynamics of the Dalit leadership in terms of roles played by the Dalit leaders in the reserved constituencies and have found that the present arrangement of seats in these constituencies has also affected the Dalits in both positive and negative manner. The positive effect of such arrangement is that the Dalits have got opportunity to influence the policies and programmes formulated for them. They can also very well utilise their experiences and social sensitivity, in the governance which is ordinarily missing from the administration. The reserved seats no doubt has integrated the Dalit masses with the democratic electoral process but has also affected them negatively. We have already discussed in this chapter that a sizeable number of Dalit leaders in the state like in other states have become captive in different political parties. These political parties use the Dalit leaders to mobilised supports of the Dalit voters and thereby to perpetuate political hegemony of the upper castes and classes. They groom the Dalit leaders to attract the Dalit votes, and because of the vote-share and psyche of the general masses these leaders win the elections. This, in turn, creates hurdle in getting the committed Dalit leaders elected; and, hence, retards their emerging consciousness. They feel defeated, as they know that even their hard work and dedication could not get them elected; instead, the "stooges" supported by the dominant political parties of upper castes and classes would be elected.

The Dalit leadership specially of the B.S.P. has been very critical of the political ideology of the national leadership in general. This chapter discusses the manifest and latent aspects of the ideology of general leadership at national level as explained by our respondents. They have termed it as propagator of higher caste interests and helpful to the forces of *status quoism*. As far as ideology of the Dalit leadership is concerned, they have defined it as the one having "Ambedkarism" in its core. But we have also mentioned in this chapter that with the emergence of the various types of Dalit movements at different points of time, the Dalit leaders have added some of the specific programmes in their ideology because of the contextual necessity. For example, with the emergence of Dalit Panthers movement in 1972, its leaders denounced the democratic path of the Dalits' emancipation and took to the revolutionary ideology despite their belief in 'Ambedkarism'. They desecrated national flag and burnt the Constitution as well as Manusmriti (Omvedt 1994:325). Similarly, the BSP has added in its ideological plank the issues of cultural transformation, capturing political power, etc. This chapter also states that in the absence of a single ideology it is difficult to evolve a unified Dalit leadership, which in turn, retards the organisation of the Dalit movement for socio-economic uplift of the Dalit masses in the country as well as in the state of Uttar Pradesh.

Further, this chapter focuses on another factor which has retarded the emergent Dalit consciousness, and finds the lack of growth of a unified identity among Dalits at the all India level. Dalits are known by various names in different geographical areas which have been accorded on them at different points of time in the history. These are not only names but are their socio-religious, political and constitutional identities which have remained in usage at the wider level, though at the local level they have invariably been known by their stigmatised caste identity. Later in the chapter, we have identified a number of problems faced by the Dalit leadership in the state. One such problem is to find permanent allies in the social and political arenas. The causes outlined for this lacuna are, one, the graded inequality of Hindu social order as suggested by Ambedkar (Ambedkar 1989:115-116). Secondly, the Dalit leadership is not strong enough to check the nefarious designs of the general leadership. Therefore, whenever there has been any alliance between the Dalit leadership and the like - minded political party, or parties, the latter has co-opted the former in its fold. Thirdly, the language of the Dalit leadership is very critical which often angers the general masses, and if the latter are polite then the Dalits do not believe them unconditionally. Hence, our respondents - the Dalit leaders have opined that now onward they would directly go for social alliance with other social groups and not with the political parties. They have identified the most backward castes in the state for this type of alliance.

The last chapter analyses the process of mobilisation adopted by the Dalit leadership and its role-played in the overall empowerment of the Dalit masses. We have accepted the process of mobilisation as defined by Rudolph and Rudolph (1987) in their study of political development and the role of caste in Indian politics. As far as the process of the mobilisation of Dalit masses by the Dalit leadership is concerned, we have analysed it under two categories, i.e. horizontal and differential mobilisations. Finding the vertical mobilisation not much relevant for the Dalit leadership, we have bracketed the 'contemptuous mobilisation' under which Dalit masses have mobilised by the upper caste - dominated political parties either through intimidation or luring them with liquor, clothes, food material, etc. As mentioned above, we have discussed in details the strategy or the *modus operandi* of the mobilisation of the masses by the Dalit leadership. The Dalit leaders specially of the BSP have been using the provocative language and slogans against the upper castes and classes, and raising the issues of economic and social disabilities of the Dalits to mobilise their support for the electoral purpose. Unlike in the past, they organise the local, intra and inter-regional, and open meetings in which they inform the masses about their policies, programmes, etc. Our respondents specially from the BSP lamented, "earlier, we could not assemble and speak in open. The BAMCEF and DS4 cadres used to come in night and discuss our problems in small huts with us. But now, it all open. We can organise our own meetings". The BSP leadership uses pamphlets, posters, banners, loud speakers, stickers, cassettes (audio and video), cut-outs of leaders for mobilising the masses. As mentioned in the previous chapter, the BSP has very recently built up, during the Chief Ministership of Mayawati, physical and cultural symbols like "Parivartan Chok" (Revolution Square) and Ambedkar Park, and organised *melas* (fairs) on the birth and death anniversaries of the Dalit leaders to attract the masses.

It has also been revealed by our respondents that the shift in the strategy of the Dalit leadership specially of the BSP from social reform to capturing political power has definitely aroused the aspiration of the Dalit masses. Now, more and more Dalits are getting politicised. The different political parties are forced to accept the Dalits in their organisation. The elevation of some Dalit leaders to different posts like the President and Vice-Presidents of India, Speaker of the Lok Sabha, Governors, and General Secretaries of different political parties is because of the increased level of mobilisation of the Dalit masses by the Dalit leadership.

Globalisation and Empowerment of Dalits

We have discussed in chapter 7 the diverse impact of the processes like globalisation, privatisation, liberalisation and the information revolution on reservation provided for Dalits under Article 335 of the Indian Constitution. Most of our respondents - Dalit leaders see these as threat to the existing provision of reservation and have demanded that, instead, it should be extended even in the private sector. They have also argued for inclusion of atrocities in the purview of the 'Human Right Violations' and link it with the International Human Rights Commission. As far as lack of international support for the Dalit movements is concerned, the respondents are well aware of some Dalit organisations working separately in USA and England but they are also informed about the absence of national or international platform for the same. In this regard, they have opined that in their fight the countries with Buddhism as their first or second religion may support them. Once the Dalit leadership captures power at the centre, it may bring these forces together. Also, they can pressurise the international organisations for conceding their demands.

As far as empowerment of the Dalit masses is concerned, the Dalit leaders have exploited, to some extent, the existing opportunities. They have used their democratic, civic and political rights to capture the various institutions in the state and want to change their composition. The BSP has succeeded, during a brief period, in doing so specially when it captured the power in the state. The BSP leaders tried to enthuse a different feeling in the administration as has been brought out by Mendelsohn and Vicziany (1998:228). They state, "this is by no means to say that this was not a significant or a distinctive administration. Part of its significance resides in the intrusion of a different culture into the machinery of government of state. Mayawati demonstrated that the Bahujan Samaj's antipathy to 'Brahminwadi' culture was no more abstraction but was to serve as a guide to the identity of the actual bureaucrats who could be trusted to direct the administration". This process of empowerment of Dalits will increase day-by-day as more and more educated and conscious Dalits are becoming politicised because of their mobilisation as revealed by the respondents. At this juncture, one may call it utopia but any mobilisation of people for bringing social transformation has some utopian aspects. It is only through the perpetual implementation of the policies and programmes the apparent utopia may be translated into reality. It is widely known that the Dalit leadership in the state till now has got very little opportunity to occupy the highest level of office. But once it gets the opportunity to rule the state for longer period, one can see greater structural changes in the society empowering the Dalits and integrating them in the Indian society.

References

Aggarwal, P.C., 1983, *Halfway to Equality*, Manohar, New Delhi.

Ambedkar, B.R., 1989, Untouchables or the Children of India's Ghetto and Other Essay, in *Dr. Babasaheb Ambedkar: Writings and Speeches Vol.5*, Education Department, Government of Maharashtra, Bombay.

Ambedkar, B.R., 1991, What Congress and Gandhi have done to the Untouchables, Mr. Gandhi and the Emancipation of Untouchables, in *Dr. Babaseheb Ambedkar: Writings and Speeches, Vol.9*, Education Department, Government of Maharashtra, Bombay.

Beteille, Andre, 1997, *Society and Politics in India: Essays in a Comparative Perspective*, Oxford University Press, Delhi.

Ganaveer, Ratnakar, (ed.), 1985, *Dr. Babasaheb Ambedkar Bahishkrit Bharatateel Agralekh* (Marathi), Ratnamitra Prakashan, Nagpur. (First Edition, 1976)

Gore, M.S., 1993, *The Social Context of an Ideology: Ambedkar's Political and Social Thought*, Sage Publications, New Delhi.

Joshi, Barbara R., 1982, *Democracy in search of Equality: Untouchables' Politics and Indian Social change*, Hindustan Publishing Corporation, Delhi.

Lynch, O.M., 1974, *Politics of Untouchability: Social Mobility and Social Change in a City of India*, National Publishing House, New Delhi.

Mandelsohn, Oliver & Marika Vicziany, 1998, *The Untouchables: Subordination, Poverty and State in modern India*, Cambridge University Press, New Delhi.

Omvedt, Gail, 1994, *Dalit and Democratic Revolution: Dr. Ambedkar and the Dalit Movement in Colonial India*, Sage Publications, New Delhi.

Rudolph L.I. & Sussane H., Rudolph, 1987, *The Modernity of Tradition: Political Development in India*, Orient Longman Delhi.

Appendix

Questionnaire

1. Socio-Personal Background

1. Name :
2. Age :
3. Education :
4. Residence : Rural: Urban:
5. Income :
6. Number of Family Members :
7. Do you belong to any political party? Yes/ No

7.1. If yes, which of the following:

(a) Cong (I); (b) BJP; (c) BSP; (d) CPI; (e) CPM; (f) JD; (g) Any Other.

7.2. If yes in what capacity:

(a) Only a sympathizer.
(b) Only a Cadre.
(c) Full timer without any office.
(d) Full timer with office: Seating/ Former
(e) Elected member of:
  (i) Parliament (Lok Sabha)
  (ii) Parliament (Rajya Sabha)
  (iii) Assembly (Vidhan Sabha)
  (iv) Assembly (Vidhan Parishad)
(f) Both full timer with office and elected member of any House.

8. For how many years have you been in the above capacity:

9. Have you ever been member of a political party other than the present one: Yes/ No.

9.1. If yes, please specify name of the party:

9.2. If yes, please mention the nature of your affiliation:

(i) Only a sympathizer.
(ii) Only a Cadre.
(g) Full timer without any office.

(h) Full timer with office: Seating/ Former

(i) Elected member of:

(i) Parliament (Lok Sabha)

(ii) Parliament (Rajya Sabha)

(iii) Assembly (Vidhan Sabha)

(iv) Assembly (Vidhan Parishad)

(V) Both full timer with office and elected member of the House.

10. Why do you prefer this party.

10.1. Its leadership is dominated by Dalit leaders.

10.2. It raises Dalit issues more vocally.

10.3. Its objectives and programmes are distinctively pro- Dalits and poor.

10.4. It is more committed to social justice and equality.

10.5. It gives more consideration to the Dalit personnel in the party organization.

10.6. It makes all out efforts for realizing Dalit interests.

10.7. It is capable of providing stable government.

2. Nature of Dalit Leadership

11. To whom you recognize a leader:

11.1. Elected to state Legislature / Parliament.

11.2. Non- Elected but only working in a political party as an office bearer or a cadre.

11.3. An ordinary worker listening and helping to the masses to resolve public grievances.

11.4. Only 11.1& 11.2.

11.5. All the above.

12. To whom you recognize a Dalit leader:

12.1. A leader who takes up the Dalit issues readily.

12.2. The elected leader who is Dalit by caste yet does not speak exclusively about Dalit issues.

12.3. The elected leader who is Dalit by caste and speaks only about Dalit issues.

12.4. The elected leader who is Dalit by caste and speaks about both Dalit and non-Dalit issues.

12.5. A Dalit social activist who is working with Dalit masses but does not take part in active politics.

12.6. A Dalit person such as Bureaucrat, Intellectual, or Businessman who is in prestigious position and also speaks about Dalit issues.

12.7. Only 12.2 & 12.3
12.8. Only 12.3 & 12.4
12.9. Only 12.2, 12.3 & 12.4
12.10. Only 12.3, 12.4, 12.5 & 12.6

13. What has been the nature of Dalit leadership in the country with regard to the issues and periods mentioned bellow:

13.1. Before 1920s:
   (i) Issues taken up by the leadership.
   (ii) Composition of the leadership in terms of socio-economic and educational status.
   (iii) Castes(s) of the Dominant Dalit leaders in the movement.
   (iv) Style of functioning: assertive/ persuasive.
   (v) Style of mobilization.

13.2. During the 1920s to 1937:
   (i) Issues taken up by the leadership.
   (ii) Composition of the leadership in terms cf socio-economic and educational status.
   (iii) Castes(s) of the Dominant Dȧlit leaders in the movement.
   (iv) Style of functioning: assertive/ persuasive.
   (v) Style of mobilization.

13.3. During the 1937 to 1947:
   (i) Issues taken up by the leadership.
   (ii) Composition of the leadership in terms of socio-economic and educational status.
   (iii) Castes(s) of the Dominant Dalit leaders in the movement.
   (iv) Style of functioning: assertive/ persuasive.
   (v) Style of mobilization.

13.4. During the 1947 to 1969:
   (i) Issues taken up by the leadership.
   (ii) Composition of the leadership in terms of socio-economic and educational status.
   (iii) Castes(s) of the Dominant Dalit leaders in the movement.
   (iv) Style of functioning: assertive/ persuasive.
   (v) Style of mobilization.

13.5. During the 1969 to 1989:
  (i) Issues taken up by the leadership.
  (ii) Composition of the leadership in terms of socio-economic and educational status.
  (iii) Castes(s) of the Dominant Dalit leaders in the movement.
  (iv) Style of functioning: assertive/persuasive.
  (v) Style of mobilization.

13.6. During 1989 till date:
  (i) Issues taken up by the leadership.
  (ii) Composition of the leadership in terms of socio-economic and educational status.
  (iii) Castes(s) of the Dominant Dalit leaders in the movement.
  (iv) Style of functioning: assertive/ persuasive.
  (v) Style of mobilization.

14. Which of the following issues of Dalits have been taken up by the contemporary Dalit Leadership:

14.1. Pursuing independent livelihood.

14.2. Leaving caste customs.

14.3. Giving up traditional caste occupations.

14.4. Removal of inferiority complexes.

14.5. Leaving traditional caste habits like non- judicious expenditure etc.

14.6. Removal of superstitions, belief in god and fate, witch-craft etc.

15. Is the contemporary Dalit leadership, in your opinion political in nature in terms of raising issues of Dalit political rights, representation in various government organizational/Institutions/ Bodies / Committees etc.

16. Has it made any effort in mobilizing Dalits for the above purpose?
Yes/ No:

Please Explain

17. Do you think that the prime object of the contemporary Dalit leadership is social transformation?
Yes/ No:

Please Explain

18. It has been visualized that the contemporary Dalit leadership should strive to capture political power to bring

about social transformation. Do you endorse this view?
Yes/ No:

Please Explain

19. Has the Dalit leadership been pursuing the said issues on its own or has it aligned with other socio- political forces for the purpose?

19.1. Please specify the nature of these socio- political forces:

20. Should the present Dalit leadership pursue the above mentioned issues independently or should it align with other political forces for the purpose?

20.1. In case it should align with other socio- political forces for the purpose, should the command of leadership remain solely with Dalit leaders?
Yes/ No:

Please Explain

21. It has been found that the Dalit leadership during the recent years has aligned with some socio-political forces for achieving its goal of social transformation. Has such alliance(s) in your opinion, diluted the nature of the issues pertaining to Dalits pursued by the Dalit leadership?
Yes/ No:

Please Explain

22. What do you feel about the status of Dalit leaders in the different political parties?

Please Explain

23. Do you agree that the Dalit leaders in different political parties act like a pressure group for resolving the issues pertaining to the Dalit?
Yes/ No:

Please Explain

24. Have such leaders ever transcended their party affiliation on certain vital issues pertaining to Dalits?
Yes/No:

Please Explain

25 It has been said in recent years that the Dalit leadership has created greater caste consciousness and caste hatred among Dalits towards caste Hindus. Do you agree with this viewpoint?
Yes/No:

Please Explain

26. It has been said that such role of Dalit leader vis-à-vis so called caste consciousness and hatred of Dalits towards Non -Dalits has created the same among the latter against the former. Do you agree with this viewpoint?
Yes/ No:

Please Explain

27. It has been observed that the Dalit leadership has become fragmented on caste lines in pursuing their specific caste agenda/ interests. How far is this true?
28. Do you agree that the economic and educational background of the Dalits play an important role in promoting leadership among them?
Yes/ No:

If yes, then to what Extent, Please Explain

29. Do you agree that the economic and educational background of Dalit leaders helps them in performing their roles more effectively?
Yes/ No:

Please Explain

30. Uttar Pradesh being the largest state in the country has always been regarded a modal of political leadership for the whole of India. In this light do you agree that the Dalit leadership in UP has also provided a model for the Dalit leadership in the entire country?
Yes/No:

Please Explain

31. Perhaps you may agree that the Dalit leadership in UP pursues the various issues pertaining to the Dalits within

the overall framework of the legacy of Ambedkar's leadership, which had an All India, appeal. In the light of this would you agree that the Dalit leadership in UP is a part of the national Dalit leadership in terms of addressing the issues related to Dalits?

Yes/ No:

Please Explain

32. Whether the national Dalit leadership in having unity in diversity or is fragmented on the Basis of primordial loyalties like region, language, sub-castes etc. ?

3. Dynamics of Dalit Leadership

33. Which of the following main issues the Dalit leadership at the national level had raised more effectively in general and at the state level in particular before and after independence:

Main Issues-National Level State Level

Religious. Temple entry, Rights of reading religious text, Performing common rights and rituals, etc.

33.2. Social:

- (j) Atrocities or Physical violence of Dalits
- (ii) Practice of Untouchability in crude form
- (iii) Reservations
- (iv) Renaming of institutions, cities, Public places etc.
- (v) Entry into public places

33.3. Educational

- (i) Issues of admissions in Schools/ Colleges:
- (ii) Raising amount and number of the scholarships for the Dalit students:
- (iii) Construction of educational institutions for Dalits:
- (iv) Construction of more hostels for Dalit Students:
- (v) Formulation of an educational policy which nurtures the suppressed Potential of the Dalit Students:
- (vi) To make Dalit students educationally equipped to face the challenges of Globalization, Liberalization, Privatization, and Information Revolution:

33.4. Employment:

- (i) Fulfillment of the reservation quotas in universities and other educational Institutions:

(ii) Transfers and Postings of Dalits (Bureaucrats, Ministers, Professors etc.) in key positions where decisions are made:

(iii) Generation of more employment for educated and non-educated Dalits in Government, Public Sector enterprises, and Private Sector:

33.5. Economic:

(i) Grant-in-Aids distributed by different economic institutions of government in welfare schemes (Cottage Industries, Animal Husbandry etc.):

(ii) Simplification of rules, procedures, terms and conditions of granting loans:

(iii) The issues of land reform:

(iv) The issues of distribution of surplus land:

(v) Government's help for sustaining the land holding distributed by the Government to the Dalits:

(vi) Implementation of minimum wages act:

34. If the social, Educational and Economic issues have not been raised by the Dalit leadership among the masses and in the State Legislature or in the National Parliament then according to you what are the main reasons for that?

(a) Lack of awareness.

(b) Difficulties involved in pursuing them.

(c) It is difficult to mobilize and garner the support of the masses on these issues.

(d) Due to joint electorate.

(e) Because he is afraid of losing his position in the party and thereby his chance of getting a ticket to contest the election.

(f) Because he is influenced by the money/ muscle power of his constituency.

(g) Because they are afraid of their party leadership.

(h) Because they are self -centered.

35. Why have the Dalit leaders time and again raised the issues of reservations and renaming of places?

(a) Because these issues are emotional in nature and Dalits can easily be mobilized.

(b) Because the chances of getting these demands accepted are relatively high and Dalit masses can be appeased that some thing is being done for them.

(c) Because these issues provide psychological satisfaction and self-confidence to the Dalits and to Dalit leaders.

36. Why the Dalit leadership has shifted its focus from social reform to political power?
    (a) The Dalit leaders have concluded that only social reform cannot uplift the Dalit masses.
    (b) They have been engaged in social reforms since long and are tired of it now.
    (c) They have also become power hungry like general caste leaders of the country.
    (d) They have now developed self-confidence that they can also form their own government.
    (e) They know that there is a qualitative change in the mobilization pattern in the Indian polity where Dalits as Vote Bank cannot be taken for granted by other political parties.

37. A Dalit leader elected from the reserved constituency is supposed to exclusively represent the interests of the Dalit masses. Since both Dalits and non-Dalits of the constituency elect such leader, do you think that he/she faces any dilemma in performing his/her role?
    Yes/ No:

Please Explain

38. As he/she is elected from the reserved constituency, he/she is supposed to represent the interest of the Dalits only. Do you think that he/she should represent the issues related to Dalits only?
    Yes/ No:

Please Explain

39. How far a reserved constituency has been helpful in:
    (a) Getting the interests of the Dalit masses properly articulated and their problems efficiently resolved.
    (b) Getting the committed Dalit leadership elected.
    (c) Whether it has produced self-aggrandizing leadership for the Dalits.
    (d) Whether it has produced puppets safeguarding the interests of upper castes.

(e) Whether it has harped the growing consciousness among the Dalits.

40. Do you think that the arrangement of a reserved constituency with joint electorate may be replaced by separate electorate?
Yes/ No:

Please Explain

41. Do you think that National leadership in the country is organized around some Ideology?
Yes/ No:

Please Explain

42. Do you think that Dalit leadership in the country is organized around some Ideology?
Yes/No:

Please Explain

42.1. Do you think that Dalit leadership in Uttar Pradesh is organized around some Ideology?
Yes/ No:

Please Explain

43. Without a common identity, it if generally difficult to mobilize the masses. Is the Dalit leadership aspiring for one common identity so that all the Dalits in the state may be united under one common Identity?
Yes/ No:

Please Explain

44. What are in your opinion basic differences between pre-independence Dalit leadership and that of present time with regard to the following:
   (a) The function of Dalit leadership.
   (b) Allies/ Political parties in political discourse for achieving their demands.
   (c) The crises of Dalit leadership.

45. Has the Dalit leadership organized some movements in the state after in dependence?
Yes/No

45.1. If yes, please furnish the following:

(a) Issues around which the movements have been organized.

(b) What have been the problems faced by the Dlit leadership in organizing the Dalit movement in terms of:

(i) The nature of leadership.

(ii) Formulation and implementation of a common ideology.

(iii) Forging common socio- political identity of the Leaders and of the Dalit masses.

(iv) Having temporary/ permanent allies.

46. Since the country has gone for globalization, liberalization, privatization and information revolution. How and by when the reservations in the job education and other institutions, for the Dalits, in your opinion will become redundant? Please explain.

47. Do you think that atrocities and various types of exploitation and discrimination against Dalits should fall within the purview of the Human Rights?
Yes/ No:

Please Explain

48. Why the contemporary Dalit leadership has failed to garner the International support on this issue?

49. If at all they can get International support, which countries in your opinion can support the Dalit issues? Name some countries.

4. Mobilisation Strategy

50. Why has the contemporary Dalit leadership shifted its focus from social -reforms among the Dalits to attainment of political power for them?

51. What have in your opinion, been the main differences in regard to the following between the Dalit leadership of the pre- independence period and of the present time.

(a) Issues in the socio- political mobilization of people in general and the Dalis in particular.

(c) Modus Operandi of socio-political mobilization.

52. What is the style of mobilization has the contemporary Dalit leadership adopted for the purpose:

Persuasive/Assertive/Emotional/any other.

53. Which of the following the Leaders usually adopt to mobilize the masses in general and Dalit masses in particular:
    (a) Organize local/ inter -regional conferences for the purpose.
    (b) They raise the Economic, Social, Educational, and other issues related to Dlits in legislature and Parliament.
    (c) How far have such strategies been effective in mobilizing the Dalit masses? Please explain.
54. Is there a need, in your opinion to adopt different strategy (es)? By the Dalit leadership to effectively mobilize the Dalit masses for capturing political power and achieving social Transformation?
    Yes/ No:

Please Explain

56. If yes, please specify the nature of statigy(es).

Bibliography

Abbasayulu, Y.B., 1978, *Scheduled Caste Elite: A Study of Scheduled Caste Elite in Andhra Pradesh*, Hyderabad, Department of Sociology, Osmania University.

Agarwal, L.B. , 1934, *Harijans in Rebellion*, Taraporewala and Sons, Bombay.

Agarwal, P.C., 1983, *Halfway To Equality*, Manohar, New Delhi.

Agarwal, P.C. and Mohd. Siddiq Ashrat, 1976, *Equality Through Privilege: A Study of Special Privileges of Scheduled Castes in Haryana*, Sri Ram Center, Delhi.

Ahir D.C., 1973, *Dr. Ambedkar and the Indian Constitution*, Buddha Vihara. Lucknow,

Aiyappan, A., 1965, *Social Resolutions in Kerala Village*, Asia publishing House London.

Akhtar, Mohd. Zamil, 1999, *Iron Lady: Km. Mayawati*, (Hindi), Bahujan Sangathak, New Delhi.

Alladi, Vagiswari, 1972, *Income Earning Trends and Social Status of the Harijan Community in Tamil Nadu*, Sangam Publication, Madras.

Ambedkar. Dr. Babasaheb, 1979, 'Annihilation of Caste' in *Writings and Speeches, Vol. 1*, Education Department, Government of Maharashtra, Bombay.

_______, 1982 Dr. Ambedkar in the 'Bombay Legislature with Simon Commission at the Round Table Conference', *Writings and Speeches, Vol. 2*, Education Department, Govt. of Maharastra, Bombay.

________, 1987, Philosophy of Hinduism, Revolution and counter Revolution in Ancient India, *Writings and Speechs, Vol. 3*, Education Department Govt. of Maharashtra, Bombay.

________, 1989, 'Untouchables or the Children of India's Ghetto and other essays on untouchables and Untouchability -Social

- Political - Religious' Writings and Speeches, Vol.5, Education Department, Govt. of Maharastra Bombay.

________, 1990, Who were the Shudras? How they came to be the Fourth Varna in the Indo-Aryan Society' *Writings and Speeches, Vol. 7.* Education Department, Govt. of Maharashtra Bombay.

________, 1991, 'What Congress and Gandhi have done to the Untouchables', 'Mr. Gandhi and the Emancipation of Untouchables', *Writings and Speeches, Vol. 9,* Education Department, Govt. of Maharashtra, Bombay.

Amin, Shahid, 1999, Gandhi as Mahatma: Gorakpur District, Eastern UP, 1921-22 in Ranjit Guha (ed.) *Subaltern Studies-III, Writings on South Asian History and Society,* Oxford University Press, Delhi.

Anand, M.R., 1970, *Untouchables,* Hind Pocket Books, Delhi.

Atey, Manohar, 1997, *The Editorials of Kanshi Ram, Part - I,* Bahujan Publications, Hydrabad.

Ayrookuzhiel, A.M. Abraham 1990, Dalit Dsiyatra, The Kerala Experience in *Development and Class Struggle,* ISPK, Delhi.

Barry, Mclaughlin, 1969, *Studies in Social Movements: A Social Psychological Perspective,* The Free Press, New York.

Baxi, Upendra and Mendelsohn 1996: *The Right of the Subordinated peoples,* Oxford University Press, Delhi.

Beals, Alzn R. and Bernard J. Siegel, 1967, *Divisiveness and Social Conflict: An Anthropological Approach,* Oxford University Press, Bombay.

Benjamin, Joseph, 1989, *Scheduled Castes in Indian Politics and Society,* Ess Ess Publications, New Delhi.

Berreman, Gerald, 1979, *Caste and other Inequalitiesm-Essays in Inequality,* Manohar, Delhi.

Beteille, Andre, 1966, *Caste, Class and Power,* Oxford University Press, New Delhi.

________, 1992, *The Backward Classes in Contemporary India,* Oxford University Press, Delhi.

________, 1997, *Society And Politics In India: Essays in comparative perspective*. Oxford University Press, Delhi.

Bharadwaj, A.N., 1979, *The Problems of Scheduled Castes and Scheduled Tribes in India*, Light and Life Publishers, New Delhi.

Bose, Nirmal Kumar, 1967, *Problems of National Integration*, Indian Institute Advanced Study, Simla

Brass P., 1985, *Caste, faction and party in Indian Politics. Vol. II* Delhi: Chanakya Publications.

________, 1965, *Factional Politics in an Indian State: The Congress Party In Uttar Pradesh*, University of California press, Berkely.

________, 1990, *The Politics of India Since Independence*, Cambridge University Press, New Delhi.

Briggs, G. W., 1920, *The Chamars*, Low Price Publications, Delhi.

Chandal, M. P., 1990, *A Social Forces in Politic: Study of Scheduled Caste in U.P.*, Mittal Publications Delhi.

Chauhan, B. R., 1975, *Scheduled Castes and Education*, Anu Publications, Meerut.

Chitnis, Suma, 1974, *Literacy and Educational Enrollment among the Schduled Castes of Maharashtra*, TISS Bombay.

________, 1981, *A Long way to go*, Allied Publishers Pvt. Ltd., New Delhi.

Chowdhury, J.N., 1971, *A Comparative Study of Adi Religion*, North-East Frontier Agency, Shillong.

Cohen, B.S., 1992, *An Anthropologist among the Historians and other Essays*, Oxford University Press, Delhi.

Damle, Y.B., 1977, Protest, Dissent and Social Reform: A Conceptual Note in S.C. Malik (ed.) *Dissent, Protest and Social Reform in Indian Civilization*, IIAS, Shimla.

Dangle, Arjun (ed), 1992, *Poisoned Bread*: Translations From modern Marathi Dalit Literature, Orient Longman Limited, Bombay.

Das, Bhagwan, 1969, *Thus Spoke Ambedkar*, Vol. II, Bheem Patrika Publications, Jullundur.

________, 1979, *Thus Spoke Ambedkar*, Vol. III, Bheem Patrika Publications, Jullundhur.

Desai, I.P., 1976, *Untouchability in Rural Gujarat*, Popular Prakashan, Bombay.

Deutch, Karl 1970, Social Mobilization and Political Development in *American Political Science Review*, 55.

Dube, Siddhart, 1998, *Words Like Freedom: The Memoirs of An Impoverished Indian Family: 1947-97*, Harper Collins, New Delhi.

Dube, S. C., 1968, Caste Dominance and Factionalism, *Contributions to Indian Sociology, New Series, No. II.*

Dushkin, Lelah, 1998, Scheduled Caste Politics, in J. Michael Mahar (ed.) *The Untouchable in Contemporary India*, Rawat Publications, Jaipur and New Delhi.

Fanon, Frantz, 1965, *The Wreched of the Earth*, Penguin Books.

Faruihar J. N., 1970, *Modern Religious Movements in India*, Chicago Press, Chicago.

Ferandes, Walter, 1983, *Caste, Religion and Social Change in India: Christianity and Conversion Movement*: in Jose Kananaikil (ed.), *Scheduled Castes and the Struggle Against Inequality*, Indian Social Institute, New Delhi.

Fiske, Adele M., 1992, Scheduled Caste Buddhist Organization in J. M. Mahar (ed.), *Untouchables in Contemporary India.*

Forester, D. B., 1977, *Depressed Classes and Concession to Christianity*, Manohar, Delhi.

Freeman, James M, 1997, *Untouchable: An Indian Life History*, George Allen and Unwin, London.

Fuchs, Stephen, 1965, *Rebellious Prophets: A Study of Messianic Movements in India Religions*, Asia Publishing House, Bombay.

Ganaveer, Ratnakar (ed), 1985, Dr. *Babasaheb Ambedkaranche Bahiskrit Bharateel Agralekh* (Marathi), Ratnamitra Prakashan, Nagpur.

Gore, M.S. 1993, *The Social Context of an Ideology: Ambedkar's Political and Social Thought*, Sage Publications, New Delhi.

Gare G. and Limaye, 1973, *The Depressed in Maharshtra - Survey and Findings*, Sahadhayaya Prakashan, Bombay.

Geeta,V., and Rajadurai, S.V. 1999, *Towards A Non-Brahmin Millenium:From Iyothee Thass To Periyar*, Samya, Calcutta.

Ghosh, Ashish (ed), 1999, *Dalits And Peasants: The Emerging Caste-Calas Dynamics*, Gyan Sagar Publications, New Delhi.

Gokhale, Jayashree, 1993, *From Concessions to Confrontation: The Politics of an Indian Untouchable Community*, Popular Prakashan, Bombay.

Gooptu, Nandni, 1993, *Caste and Labour: Untouchable Social Movements in Urban Uttar Pradesh* in The Early Twentieth Century in Peter Robb (ed.), Dalit *Movements and the Meanings of Labour in India*, Oxford University Press, Delhi.

Gould, Harold, 1965, Traditionalism and Modernism in U.P. in Myron Weiner and Rajni Kothari (eds), *Indian Voting Behaviour*, (Calcutta: Firma K.L. Mukhopadhyaya).

Gusfield, Joseph R. (ed.), 1970, *Protest, Reform and Revolt: A Reader in Social Movements*, John Wiley, New York.

Hassan, Zoya, 1998, *Quest for Power, Oppositional Movements and Post-Congress Politics in Uttar Pradesh*, Oxford University Press, Delhi.

Hardgrave, M. L, 1965, *The Dravidian Movement*, Popular Prakashan, Bombay.

Hardgrave, Robert, 1969, *The Nadars of Tamil Nadu: The Political Culture of a Community in Change*, University of California Press, Berkely.

Hiro, Dilip, 1984, *The Untouchables of India*, Dalit Sahitya Aacademy.

Hobsbawm, E. J., 1958, *Primitive Rebels: Studies in Archaic Froms of Social Movements in the 19th and 20th Centuries*, Norton, New York.

Imtiaj Ahmad and N.C. Saxena, 1998, Caste, Land and Political Power in Uttar Pradesh in K.L. Sharma (ed) *Caste and Class in India*, Rawat Publications, Jaipur and New Delhi.

Isaacs, Harold R, 1965, *India's Ex-Untouchables*, Asia Publishing House, Bombay.

Jatav, D. R., 1965, *Social Philosophy of B.R. Ambedkar*, Phoenix Publishing Agency, Agra.

________, 1965, *Political Philosophy of B.R. Ambedkar*, Phoenix Publishing Agency, Agra,

Jigyasu, Chandrika Prasad, 1968, *Adi Hindu Andolan Ke Prabartak Sri Swami Achutanand* (Hindi), Bahujan Prakashan, Lucknow.

Jogdand, P.C., 1991, *Dalit Movement in Maharashtra*, Kanak Publications, New Delhi.

Joshi, Barbara R., 1986, *Untouchable: Voices of the Dalit Liberation Movement*, Select Book Service Syndicate, New Delhi.

1982, *Democracy in Search of Equality: Untouchables Politics and Indian Social Change*, Hindustan Publishing Corporation, Delhi.

Juergensmeyer, Mark, 1974, *Political Hope: The Quest for Political Identity and Strategy in the Social Movements of the North India's Untouchables.*

________, 1982, *Religion as Social Vision: The Movement Against Untouchability in 20th Century Punjab*, University of California Press, Barkeley.

Justice V. R. Krishna Iyer, 1984, *Justice in Words and Justice in Deeds for the Depressed Classes*, Indian Social Institute, Delhi.

K., George, 1982, *Caste in the Catholic Community in Kerala*, St - Francis De Saks Press, Cochin.

________, 1990, *Dr. Ambedkar and the Dalit Future*, B. R. Publication, Delhi.

Kadam, K.N. (ed.), 1993, *Dr. Ambedkar the Emancipator of the Oppressed*, Popular Prakashan, Bombay.

Kagzi, M.C.G., 1976, *Segregation and Untouchability Abolition*, Metropolitan Book Co., Delhi.

Kamble, N.D., 1979, *Poverty within Poverty, A Study of the Weaker Sections in a Deccan Village*, Sterling, Bombay.

Kannanikil, Jose, 1982, *Scheduled Castes in the Constituent Assembly*, Indian Social Institute, New Delhi,

________, 1983, (A) *Christians of Scheduled Caste Origin*, Indian Social Institute, Delhi.

________, 1983, (B) *Scheduled Castes and The Struggle Against Inequality*, Indian Social Institution, Delhi.

________, 1984, *Constitutional Provision for the Scheduled Castes*, Indian Social Institute, Delhi.

________, 1986, *Scheduled Castes in Search of Justice: The Verdict of the Supreme Court*, Indian Social Institute, Delhi.

Keer, Dhananjay, 1997, *Dr. Ambedkar, Life and Mission*, Popular Prakashan, Mumbai.

Khairmode, C.B., 1998, *Dr. Bhimrao Ramji Ambedkar Charitra* (Marath-Eng), Sugawa Prakashan, Puri.

Khare, R. S., 1984, *The untouchable as himself: Ideology. Identity, and Pragmatism among the Lucknow Chamars* - Cambridge University Press.

Kohli Atul (ed.), 1991, (ed.), *India's Democracy: An Analysis of Changing State-Society Relations*, Orient Longman, New Delhi.

Kothari, Rajni, (ed.) 1986, *Caste in Indian Politics*, Orient Longman, New Delhi.

Kotani, H. (ed.), 1997, *Caste System, Untouchablility and the Depressed*, Manohar, New Delhi.

Kshirsagar, R.K., 1994, *Dalit Movement in India and its leaders*, M. D., Publications, New Delhi.

Kuber W. N., 1973, *Critical Study of Social and Political thoughts of Dr. Ambedkar*, Peoples Publishing House, Delhi.

Kumar, Vijay, 1989, *Scheduled Caste Panchyat Pradhans in India, A Study of Western Uttar Pradesh*, Ajanta Publications, New Delhi.

Kumar, Vivek, 1999a, Nature and Crisis of Dalit Leasership: A Brief Socio-Historocal Profile, in Ashish Ghos (ed), *Dalit and Peasants The Emerging Caste-Class Daynamics*, Gyan Sagar Publication, Delhi.

________, 1999b, Deconstruction and Reconstruction of Identities in UP, in Ambrose Pinto (ed.) *Dalit Assertion for Identity*, Indian Social Institute New Delhi.

________, 2001, Dalit Rajnaitik Sanghars BSP ke Bad in Prem Kapadia and Prakash Luois (ed.) *Nai Sadi Bhi Tod Pai Uttar Pradesh Mein Acchutpan Ko* {HINDI}, Indian Social Institute, New Delhi.

Lal, A. K., 1997, *Dalit in Action: An Evaluation of Bihar Dalit Vikas Samiti*, Concept Publishing Company, New Delhi.

Lerch, Jens, 1999, Politics of the Poor: Agricultural Labourers and Political Transformation in Uttar Pradesh in Jens Lerch (et.al), *Rural Labour Relations in India,* Frank class, London.

Lokhande, G.S., 1977, *Bheemrao Ramji Ambedkar - A Study in Social Democracy,* Sterling Publications, Bombay.

Lynch, O.M., 1974, *The Politics of Untouchability: Social Mobility and Social Change in a City of India,* National Publishing House, New Delhi.

MacIver, R.M. and PAGE, 1986, *Society An Introductory Analysis*: Macmillan, Delhi.

Mahar, Michael, J. (ed.), 1998, *The Untouchables in Contemporary India,* Rawat Publications, Jaipur and New Delhi.

Marsh, Alan, 1977, *Protest and Political Consciousness,* Sage Publications, London.

Mathew, Joseph, 1986, *Ideology, Protest and Social Mobility: Case Study of Maharas and Pulayas,* Inter India Publications, New Delhi.

Malik, S.C. (ed.), 1977, *Dissent, Protest and Reform in Indian Civilization,* IIAS, Shimla.

Malik, Suneila, 1979, *Social Integration of Scheduled Castes,* Abhinav, New Delhi.

Michel, S.M., 1999, *Dalits in Modern India: Vision and Values,* Vistar Publication, New Delhi.

Michels, Robert (1911), 1959, *Political Parties: A Sociological Study of the Oligarchical Tendencies of Modern Democracy,* Dover, New York

Mitra, Subrata Kumar (ed.), 1990, *Politics of Positive Discrimination: A Cross-national Perspective,* Popular Prakashan, Bombay.

Moffatt, Michael, 1979, *An Untouchable Community in South India: Structure and Consensus,* Princiton University Press; Princeton, New Jersey.

Mukherjee, Prabhali, 1988, *Beyond the Four Varnas: The Untouchables in India,* Motilal Banarsidass, Delhi.

Murugkar, Lata. 1991, *Dalit Panthers Movement in Maharashtra: A Sociological Appraisal,* Popular Prakashan Bombay.

Neelen, John, P. (ed.), 1983, *Social Inequality and Political Structures,*

Studies an Interest articulation in an Indian Coalfied and its Rural hinterland, Manohar, New Delhi..

O' Hanlon, Rosalind, 1985, *Caste, Conflict, and Ideology: Mahatma Jotirao Phule And Low Caste Protest in Nineteenth - Century western India*, Orient Longman, Bombay.

Omvedt, Gail, 1998, Kanshi Ram and the Bahujan Samaj Party, in K.L. Sharma (ed) *Caste and Class in India*, Rawat Publications, Jaipur and New Delhi.

________, 1994, *Dalit and the Democratic Revolution, Dr. Ambedkaer and the Dalit Movement in Colonial India*, Sage Publications, New Delhi.

________, 1995, *Dalit Visions: The anti-caste movement and the construction of an Indian identity*, Orient Longman, Limited, Delhi.

________, 1994, Peasant Revolt and Indian Nationalism: The peasant Movement in Awadh, 1919-1922 in, Ranjit Guha (ed), *Subaltern Studies I, Writings on South Asian History and Society*, Oxford University Press, Delhi

Oommen, T. K., 1977, Sociological Issues in the Analysis of Social Movements in Independent India, *Sociological Bulletin*, 26(1).

________, 1990, *Protest and Change: Studies in Social Movements*, Sage Publications, New Delhi.

Pai, Sudha, 2000, *State Politics, New Dimensions*, Shipra Publications, New Delhi.

Pande, Gyan, 1993, Rallying Round the Cow : Sectrarian Strife in the Bhojpuri Region, c. 1888-1917, in Ranjit Guha (ed) *Subarrn Studies II, Writings on South Asian History and Society*, Oxford University Press, Delhi.

________, 1994, Peasant Revolt and Indian Nationalism: The Peasant Movement in Awadh, 1919-1922 in Ranajit Guha (ed.), *Subaltern Studies I, Writings on South Asian History and Society*, Oxford, University Press, India.

Pradhan, Atul Chandra, 1986, *The Emergence of the Depressed Classes*, Bookland International, Bhubaneshwar.

Pardhan, G.R., 1938, *Untouchable Workers of Bombay City*, Karnataka Publishing House.

________, 1976, *Cultural Revolt in a Colonial Society: The Non - Brahman Movement in Northern India (1873-1930)*, Scientific Socialist Education Trust, Bombay.

Patankar, Bharat Ovedt, and Gail, 1979, The Dalit Liberation Movement in Colonial Period: *Economic and Political Weekly*, (Annual Number), Vol. XIV, Nos. 7 and 8.

Pinto, Ambrose (ed.), 1999, *Dalits: Assertion for Identity*, Indian Social Institute, New Delhi.

Pantawane, Gangadher, 1986, *Evolving a New Identity: The Development of a Dalit Culture* in Barbera R. Joshi (ed.), *Untouchable: Voices of the Dalit Liberation Movement*, Select Book Service Syndicate, New Delhi.

Punalekar, S.P., 1985, *Caste Ideology and Class Interests: Reflections on Violence in Maratwada* Region in I. P. Desai, et. al. *Caste, Class Conflict and Reservation*, Ajanta Publications, Delhi.

Rajan, Ambeth, 1994, *My Bahujan Samaj Party*, ABCDE Publication, SQ-133, North Avenue, New Delhi.

Ram, Jagivan, 1980, *Caste Challenge in India*, Vision Books, New Delhi.

Ram Nandu, 1988, *From Atrocities to Protest Movement: an urge for Social Development* in S. K. Srivastava and A. L. Srivastava (eds.), *Social Movements for Development*, Chug Publications, Allahabad.

________, 1988, *The Mobile Scheduled Castes, Rise of a New Middle Class*, Hindustan Publishing Corporation, Delhi.

________, 1995, *Beyond Ambedkar: Essays on Dalits in India*, Har-Anand Publications, New Delhi.

Ramaswamy, Uma, 1978, *The Belief System of the Non-Brahmin Movement in India: The Andhra Caste*, Asian Survey, 18.

Ramteke, D. L., 1983, *Revival of Buddhism in Modern India*, Deep and Deep, Delhi.

Rao, M.S.A., 1977, *Themes in the Ideology of Protest Movements* in S.C. Malik (ed.), *Dissent, Protest and Reform in Indian Civilization*, II AS, Shimla.

________, 1978, Backward Classes Movement in S.C. Malik (ed.), *Indian Movements: Some Aspects of Disent, Protest and Reform*, IIAS, Shimla.

________, 1978, (ed.), *Social Movements in India, Vols. I and II*, Manohar, New Delhi.

________, 1984, (ed.), *Social Movement in India: Studies in Peasant, Backward Classes, Sectarian, Tribal and Women Movements*, Manohar, New Delhi.

________, 1987, *Social Movements and Social Transformation: A Study of Two Backward Classes Movements in India*, Manohar, New Delhi.

Robb Peter (ed), 1993, *Dalit Movements and the meanings of labour in India*, Oxford University Press, YMCA Library Building, Jaisingh Road, New Delhi.

Robbin, Jeanette, 1964, *Dr. Ambedkar and his Movement*, Dr. Ambedkar Publishing Society, Hyderabad.

Rudolph, Lloyd I. & Rudlph, Susanne Hoeber, 1987, *The Modernity of Tradition: Political Development in India*, Orient Longman, Delhi.

Saradmoni, K., 1980, *Emergence of a Slave Caste: Pulalyas of Kerela*, People's Publishing House, Delhi.

Sardar, G.B., 1978, *Saint-Poets of Maharashrtra:* Their Role in Social Transformation in S.C. Malik (ed.), *Indian Movements: Some Aspects of Dissent, Protest and Reform*, IIAS, Shimla.

Sarkar, Sumit, 1979, *Bibliographical Survery of Social Reform Movements in the 18th and 19th Centuries*, Institute of Historical Studies, Calcutta.

Searle, Hary Chatterjee, 1981, *Reversible Sex Roles: The Special Case of Benares Sweepers*, Pergamou Press, Oxford.

Sen, S.P., (ed.), 1979, *Social and Religious Reform Movements in the Nineteenth and Twentieth Centuries*, Institute of Historical Studies, Calcutta.

Seth, V. N., 1987, *Caste System and Status Change: A Study of Harijan Protest in Banda* in S. K. Sharma (ed.), *Reform, Protest and Social Transformation*, Ashish Publishing House, New Delhi.

Shah, Ghanshyam, 1977, *Protest Movements in Two Indian States*, Ajanta Publications, New Delhi.

________, 1990, *Social Movements in India: A Review of the Literature*, Sage Publications, New Delhi.

Shinde, J.R., 1985, *Dynamics of Cultural Revolution: the 19th Century Maharashtra*, Ajanta Publications, Delhi.

Singh, K.S., 1993, *The Scheduled Castes*, Oxford University Press, Delhi.

Singh, Rajendra, 2000, Peasant Movements in Uttar Pradesh, In M.S. Pao (ed.) *Social Movements In India*, Manohar, New Delhi.

Singh, R.K., 1994, *Kanshi Ram Aur B.S.P.*, (Hindi), Kushwaha Book Distributors, Allahabad.

Singh, Y 1994, *Modernization of Indian Tradition*, Rawat Publications, Jaipur.

________, 1996, *Social Change in India: Crisis and Resilience*, Har-Anand Publications, New Delhi.

________, 2000, The Changing Power Structure of Village Community- a Case Study of Six Villages in Eastern U.P., in A.R. Desai (ed.) *Rural Sociology in India*, Popular Prakashan, Mumbai.

Sundaram, S. and Singh S.S., 1987, *Emerging Harijan Elite: A Study of their Identity*, Uppal Publishing House, New Delhi- 1987

Viczany, Marika & Mendelsohn, 1998, *The Untouchables: Subordination, Poverty and the State in Modern India*, Cambridge University Press.

Webster, C.B. John, 1992, *The Dalit Christians; A History* I. S. C. K., Delhi.

Wilkinson, Paul, 1971, *Social Movement*, Macmillan Press, London.

Wilkinson, T. S. & M.M.Thomas, 1972, (ed.), *Ambedkar and Neo-Buddhist Movement, Christain* Literature Society, Madras.

Yadvendu, Ramnarayan, 1942, *Yaduvansh ka Itihas*, (Hindi), Navyug Sahitya Niketan, Agra.

Zelliot, Eleanor, 1966, Background of the Mahar Buddhist Conversion in R. K. Sakai (ed.) *Studies on Asia*, University of Nebraska Press, Lincon.

________, 1978, Buddhism and Politics in Maharshrta in Donald Smith (ed.), Politics *and Religion*, Princetion University Press, Princeton.

________, 1992, *From Untouchable to Dalit: Essays on Ambedkar Movement*, Manohar, Publications, New Delhi.

Periodicals and News Papers

Beteille, Andre, 1999, Empowerment, Economic and political Weekly March 6-13.

Fernandes, Walter, 1981, Caste and Conversion in India: Social Action 31(3).

Gajendran, A., 1998, Transforming Dalit Politics, Seminar, 417, New Delhi.

Gupta, Shiva K., 1980, Harijan Legislators: Their Alienation and Activism, Giri Institute of Development Studies, Lucknow.

Joshi, Barbara R., 1987, Recent Developments of Inter-Regional Mobilization of Dalit Protest in India, South Asian Bulletin, 7.

Kumar, Vivek, 1999, Emergence of Leadership Among Dalit Women, The Pioneer, 23rd September, Lucknow.

________, 2000 a, The Dalit Identity, The Pioneer, 26th January, New Delhi.

________, 2000 b, The OBC Assertion, The Pioneer, 18th Feb., New Delhi.

________, 2000 c, Desperately Seeking Dalits, The Pioneer, 7th March, New Delhi.

________, 2000 d, Relating to the Global World, The Pioneer, 15th April, New Delhi.

________, 2000 e, BSP Honeymooning with the Media, The Pioneer, 11th July, Lucknow.

________, 2000 f Convening Castes in the Cow Belt, The Pioneer, 15th August, New Delhi.

________, 2000 g, Any Answer to Dalit Question in UP? The Pioneer, 20th September, New Delhi.

________, 2000 h, Caste into Structural Gridlock of Poverty, The Pioneer, 4th October, New Delhi.

________, 2000 i, No Dalit Eqality in Sangh Parivar, The Pioneer, 6th November, New Delhi.

________, 2001 a, Political Utility of Dalits, The Pioneer, 15th Feburary, New Delhi.

________, 2001 b, The Empire Strikes Back in UP, The Pioneer, 22nd June, New Delhi.

________, 2001 c, A Blow for Dalit Digniy and Pride, The Pioneer, 25th September, New Delhi.

________, 2001 d, Untouchability in Uttaranchal, Economic and Politiacal Weekly, Vol. xxxvi, No. 49, December, Mumbai.

________, 2002 a, President, Dalits, and Bhopal Document, The Pioneer, 8th Feburary, New Delhi.

________, 2002 b, Caste Mobilizationin UP and its Impact on Assembly Elections 2002, Mainstream, Vol. xxx, No. 10, 23rd February, New Delhi.

________, 2002 c, Not Really a Case of 'Casteism', The Pioneer, 29th March, New Delhi.

Mukherjee, P.N., 1977, Social Movements and Social Change: Towards a Conceptual Clarification and Theoritical Framework., Socialogical Bultetion 26(1).

National Compaign Manifesto: 1998 Dalit Human Rights (10 Dec. 1998-15 Aug 199), Secanderabad, India.

Omvedt, Gail, 1999, Dalit elections, I & II, The Hindu, November 5th & 6th.

________, 2000, Reservation in the Private Sector, The Hindu, Jan.1.

Pai, Sudh., 1998, The BSP in Uttar Pradesh, Seminar, 417.

Praful Bidwai., 1994a, Relevance of Ambedkar: Modernity and Pseudo-Gandhians. Times of India, May 5.

Praful Bidwai., 1994b, An Unfinished Revolution The Meaning of Dalit Self-assertion, Frontline, May 20.

________, 1993, I don't Want Stable Government, Interview with Kanshi Ram. India Today, Dec. 31.

Radhika Ramaseshan, 1993, The Annihilator of Upper Caste, The Pioneer, Dec. 5, 1993.

________, 1993, Pressure from Below, The Pioneer, Dec. 12.

________, 1995, Dalit Politics in U.P., Seminar, 425-Annual, January.

Rajni Kothari., 1994, Dalits of Today: The Context and Content of Identity. Times of India, May 16.

Rudolph, Hoeber S. 1949, Observations on the Sociology of Social Movements, American Sociological Review 14 (3).

Seema Mustafa., 1994, Kanshi Ram cannot be Trusted,The Pioneer, Feb. 7.

Sehgal, Rashme, 1998, They Donit Dare Abouse us Any More, The Sunday Times of India, October 4.

Singh, Jaspal, 1998, Ambedkaristion and Assertion of Dalit Identity: Socio-Cultural Protest in Meerut District of Western Uttar Pradesh, Economic and Political Weekly, Vol. XXXIII, No. 40, October.

Social Action, 1993, A Quarterly Review of Social Trends, The Emerging Dalit Identity. Vol. 43, no. 4, Oct. Dec.

T.K. Oommen., 1994, Panchamas to Dalits: The Context and Content of Identity. Times of India, May.

________, 1999, Dalits and Production of knowledge, I & II, The Hindu, September 13th and 14th.

Ventkitesh Ramakrishnan, 1993, The Winning Duo: Mulayam Singh Yadav and Kanshi Ram, Frontline, Dec. 17.

Xaxa, Virginius, 2001, Protective Discrimination: Why Scheduled Tribe Lag Brhind Scheduled Castes, Economic and Political Weekly, Vol. XXXVI, No. 29, July 21-27.

The Administrator, Special Issue on Dalits, January-March 1997, Vol. XIII, No. Journal of the Lal Bahadur Shastri National Academy of Administration.

Uttar Pradesh Annual, 1996-97.

Index